Russian Constitutional Law

Russian Constitutional Law

By

Elena A. Kremyanskaya, Tamara O. Kuznetsova
and Inna A. Rakitskaya

CAMBRIDGE
SCHOLARS
PUBLISHING

Russian Constitutional Law,
by Elena A. Kremyanskaya, Tamara O. Kuznetsova and Inna A. Rakitskaya

This book first published 2014

Cambridge Scholars Publishing

12 Back Chapman Street, Newcastle upon Tyne, NE6 2XX, UK

British Library Cataloguing in Publication Data
A catalogue record for this book is available from the British Library

ISBN (10): 1-4438-6394-7, ISBN (13): 978-1-4438-6394-0

TABLE OF CONTENTS

Acknowledgements viii

Foreword ix
Dr. Vladimir Pligin

Chapter One 1
The Constitutional Law of Russia
1. The Subject, Method and System of Constitutional Law in Russia and its Place in the System of National Law
2. Constitutional Development of Russia

Chapter Two 13
The Constitution of Russia
1. General Description of the Constitution 1993
2. Structure of the Constitution
3. Amendments to the Constitution of the Russian Federation
4. Protection of the Constitution
5. Domestic Law and International Law
6. The Constitutional Order
7. Features of the Russian State

Chapter Three 36
The Legal Status of the Individual
1. The International Standards of Human Rights and Freedoms
2. Citizenship of the Russian Federation
3. Rights and Freedoms in the Russian Federation
4. Constitutional Duties of Man and Citizen
5. Constitutional Guarantees of Rights and Freedoms

Chapter Four 67
The Federation in Russia
1. History of the Federation in Russia
2. Basics and Principles of the Federation in Russia
3. Separation of Powers between Federation and Subjects of Federation
4. Structure of the Federation
5. System of the State Bodies of the Subject of the Russian Federation. Federal Intervention
6. Federal Districts and Plenipotentiary Representatives of the President in Federal Districts
7. Current Tendencies in the Development of Federalism in Russia

Chapter Five 83
The Electoral System in Russia
1. The Overview of the Electoral System in Russia and Principles of Electoral Law
2. The System of Electoral Bodies in the Russian Federation
3. The Stages of the Electoral Process
4. Financing the Elections
5. Electoral Disputes
6. Referendum

Chapter Six 103
The President of the Russian Federation
1. Separation of Powers in Russia
2. Elections of the President
3. Termination of the Presidential Authorities
4. Competence of the President
5. Acts of the President
6. State Institutions Connected with the President

Chapter Seven 121
The Legislative Power: The Federal Assembly Legislative Process
1. History of the Russian Parliament
2. Status of the Federal Assembly
3. The Federation Council
4. The State Duma
5. Parliamentary Control
6. Status of the Member of Parliament in Russia
7. Legislative Process
8. Accounts Chamber

Chapter Eight 151
The Executive Power in Russia
1. Federal Executive Bodies
2. Composition and Nomination of the Government of the Russian Federation. Structure of the Government
3. Structure of the Government of the Russian Federation
4. Responsibility of the Government of the Russian Federation
5. Competence of the Government of the Russian Federation
6. The Central Bank of the Russian Federation (Bank of Russia)

Chapter Nine 169
The Judicial Power and Prosecution Office in Russia
1. The Judicial System of the Russian Federation
2. The Constitutional Provisions on the Judicial Power in the Russian Federation
3. The Constitutional Court of the Russian Federation
4. Courts of General Jurisdiction in the Russian Federation
5. The System of the Arbitration (Commercial) Courts in Russia
6. The Prosecution Service

Chapter Ten 207
Local Self-Government and Municipal Service
1. The Legal Basis, Constitutional Principles and Duties of Local Self-Government in the Russian Federation
2. Forms of Direct Participation of People in Exercise of Local Self-Government
3. Structure of Bodies of Local Self-Government
4. Control Over Local Government Operations
5. Municipal Service and Municipal Employees

About the Authors 220

ACKNOWLEDGEMENTS

The authors are very grateful for the support provided to the team by MGIMO-University and namely to the Rector of MGIMO-University **Prof. Anatoly Torkunov**, the Vice Rector of MGIMO-University **Dr. Artem Malgin** and the Dean of the International Law Faculty, MGIMO-University **Prof. Gennady Tolstopyatenko**

FOREWORD

The book–"*Russian Constitutional Law*", prepared by Russian constitutionalists is one of the first works of this type, written in English. It is construed as a full course on Russian Constitutional Law, combining both Russian and western academic approaches.

It is indicative that this book was written in the year of the *20th Jubilee of the Russian Constitution.* The authors of this first edition provide a profound review of the main institutes of Russian Constitutional Law, giving the reader an understanding of the functioning of state power in Russia, and also providing the basics and main principles of the Russian Constitution, specifics of Human Rights regulations, characteristics of the three branches of state power: the legislative, the executive and the judiciary, and the performance of self-government in Russia. Legal rules and regulations are clarified by examples from Russian history.

Inevitably, the advantage of this book is that the authors are analyzing the latest changes in Russian Constitutional Law, making readers acquainted with innovations in the formation of the Russian Parliament, the new regulations on the Accounts Chamber, and updates in the legislation of the Government.

There is no doubt that this research will be useful for all readers interested in the Russian Constitution, Russian political studies, Russian legislation, the government and traditions, and especially those representing an academic environment or foreign state bodies and international organizations, who are willing to build stable and productive relations with the Russian Federation.

Chairman of the State Duma Committee
on Constitutional Legislation and State Development

Dr. Vladimir Pligin

CHAPTER ONE

THE CONSTITUTIONAL LAW OF RUSSIA

1. The Subject, Method and System of Constitutional Law in Russia and its Place in the System of National Law

The term "Constitutional Law" is generally used in three ways: as a branch of law, the corresponding branch of science and as an academic discipline.

As the *branch of law* Constitutional Law commonly refers to the legal regulations (sub-branches and institutions), subject to certain terms of public relations covered by the Constitutional law branch.

The *branch of science* is the whole complex of knowledge (doctrines, teachings, theories, beliefs, hypotheses, etc.) in relevant fields of law, history, prospects of relations within the branch, the improvement of legislation and other sources of legal regulation, etc.

The *academic discipline* is usually based on the existing branch of law and represents the aggregate of knowledge on the existing rules of regulations, and the state of science.

The main defining criteria for any branch of law are an independent *subject and a specific method of legal regulation.* The subjects of any branch of law are certain groups of public relations, governed by the rule of the industry. According to the dominant approach to understanding, the subject matter of constitutional law (sometimes named as the "*object of the constitutional and legal regulation*") in Russia, as in any country, governs *two main components of public relations:*

1) related to the *individual's legal status* and its relationship with the state and civil society;
2) related to the *organization of the state* and the *operation of public authorities.*

From the second half of the twentieth century there has been a tendency to expand the subject of constitutional and legal regulation. This regulation has spread to various institutions of civil society (associations, political parties, trade unions, churches, etc.) through which people integrate into society and which are often a kind of mediator in the relationship between the individual and the state. This trend is also visible in Russia, although there is no detailed regulation of the political, social, economic and cultural aspects of society at the level of the constitutional law.

Like any *branch of law*, constitutional law affects social relations by a variety of *legal methods* and means (order, permission, prohibition, etc.). The distinguishing feature of the method of constitutional law is *its imperative character.*

Thus, the constitutional law of Russia is the leading branch of the Russian law, the body of law that reinforces the foundations of the legal and regulatory status of individuals, and the economic, political, social and cultural life of the community, the organization and functioning of the state of public administration.

The constitutional law is at the heart of the entire legal system in Russia, based on the norms of the constitutional branch operating the Russian state and society; the constitutional norms underlie the development of sectoral branches.

The system of any branch of law constitutes the components of the branches' rule of law, combined in institutions, sub-institutes and sub-sectors.

Describing the system of constitutional law in Russia, it should be noted, *first,* that in contrast to the *"binary"* sectors (civil–civil procedure, criminal law–criminal procedure, administrative law–the administrative process, etc.) in constitutional law it is difficult to distinguish purely substantive constitutional law and constitutional process, although of course, there are the procedural rules in constitutional law. These regulations govern the dynamics of the legislative process, the electoral process, the referendum procedure, etc.

Secondly, the system of constitutional law, in contrast to other sectors of the national legal systems (civil, administrative, criminal, labour, land, etc.), is difficult to divide into the general and particular (special). Usually the system of constitutional rights directly includes its constituent sub-sectors and institutions. In this case, there is no clear boundary between the sub-sectors and institutions (sub-institutions): in particular, it is difficult to relate to the scope and content of government institutions, on the one hand, and sub-parliamentary law and electoral law–the institution of the head of state–on the other.

The system of any branch is expressed in its internal structure, caused by the connections that exist between its norms, determine the basis for differentiation and integration in certain legal education, possessing the features and elements of the system and the structure of the regulations.

The following elements are contributing to the system of constitutional law:

- The foundations of the Constitutional system;
- The basis of the legal status of a person and citizen;
- The federal structure of the state;
- The system of government and a system of local government.

2. Constitutional Development of Russia

Constitutionalism in Russia appeared later than in other countries. It was quite a long period of development, characterized by contradictions, stages of formation, and the full revival of basic ideas and principles.

The constitutional development of the country should not only be associated with the adoption and change of formal constitutions. It must be analyzed, and the formation of (approval) constitutional ideas and principles, the adoption of acts of constitutional supreme bodies of state power, etc., should be taken into account.

For this reason, the history of Russian constitutionalism can be divided into three periods:

1*) Pre-Soviet* (to October 1917);

2) *Soviet* (from October 1917 until the second half of the 1980s); and

3) *Post-Soviet* (current).

There was no Constitution in Russia before the October revolution. But there was a range of acts that can be described as constitutional.

If we proceed from the position that the constitution is the act of the State in which are fixed the political system, the system of state bodies, their powers and the way of forming, territorial division and the organization of relations between the centre and the regions, and the foundations of the legal status of citizens, then in the Russian Empire in the early twentieth century acts were adopted that without exaggeration can be called the first, although unwritten, constitution of Russia.

The Imperial manifesto of October 17, 1905 *"On improvement of public order*", designed by Witte first proclaimed "unshakeable foundations on the basis of a valid civil integrity, freedom of conscience, expressions, assembly and association". Second, it made the rules, according to which "no law could not take effect without the approval of the State Duma". Thus, the monarch limited his power in favour of the State Duma, which gave legislative functions and transformed it into the highest legislative body of the state.

The decree of December 11, 1905, "to amend the provisions of the State Duma elections", was in contrast to the provisions of the State Duma elections in 1905, increasing the number from three curiae (landowning, urban and peasant) to four (working) and enlarging the number of voters in the urban curia. At the same time, the elections to the Duma were not universal, for the number of voters excluded women, soldiers on active duty, a number of ethnic minorities and young people up to 25 years, as well as nomads. The elections were two-staged, and for the workers and peasants three- and four-staged. In total the new system elected 524 deputies from 53 provinces of the European part of Russia–488 deputies and 36–from national regions in accordance with local conditions and customs.

At the beginning of 1906 the Manifesto "*About change the establishment of the State Council, and reviewing the founding of the State Duma*" was adopted. This document defined the procedure for the establishing and election of members of the State Council, as well as the internal structure and competence of the State Duma. The result was a new Russian parliament, consisting of two equal chambers: the State Duma and the Council of State. The State Council consisted of 98 members, with 50 members elected from the provincial zemstvo, six from the Orthodox Church and the Academy of Sciences and universities, and twelve from the exchange committee of Commerce and Manufactures.

One more decree was issued in March 1906 which was called "*On the provisional rules of associations and unions*". The ideas of the Manifesto of October 17, 1905 were developed in this document, and it was the first act in the history of the Russian Empire which admitted various activities of political entities, including the opposition.

In 1906 the State Duma accepted the basic laws of the Russian empire, perceived by the scientific community not as the Constitution, but, as the acts of differing legal force as compared to ordinary law. At least, until the revolution of 1917 a number of scientists, state and public men in Russia regarded these basic laws as the constitution in whole or in part. In the 1920s the famous Russian scientist V. N. Durdenevsky, called them the "very moderate constitution of an individualistic type with elements of imitation of the texts of Prussia and Japan".

After the February Revolution of 1917 a special committee was formed to draft the basic laws of the Provisional Government. The purpose of the committee was not only the development of the Constitution, but also its judicial protection. At the first meeting of the Committee on October 11, 1917 the estimated program was issued. Number 16 of the program was called the "Revision of the Constitution. Guarantees of the Constitution". At the next meeting, on October 14, 1917, the second part of this issue was clarified, and was called the "*Legal guarantee of the Constitution*".

The October Revolution of 1917 did not allow the realization of these intentions, and the first Russian constitution was adopted in Soviet times.

From the first day of its existence, the Soviet state issued a series of acts of a constitutional nature. These were: the Decree on Peace, the Decree on Land, the Decree on Court and others, the Appeal of the Petrograd Military Revolutionary Committee "to the Citizens of Russia" and the Appeal of the II Congress of Soviets "To workers, soldiers and peasants". An important legal act, which was almost entirely included into the first Soviet Constitution, was the Declaration of the Rights of Working and Exploited People, adopted by the III All-Russian Congress of Soviets on January 25, 1918.

On July 10, 1918 the all-Russian Congress of Soviets as the supreme body of the new government approved the Basic Law, which laid down the principles of the organization of the Soviet government, the form of government, the territorial structure and the relations of power and the people, and state symbols. This was essentially the first formal constitution in the history of Russia, presented in a single legal act.

The Constitution of the Russian Federation was adopted by the V all-Russian Congress of Soviets, which opened on July 4, 1918 at the Bolshoi Theatre in Moscow. 1164 delegates came to the Congress. At the final meeting the Congress heard a report on the draft of the Constitution and the draft was approved.

The first Constitution included six sections, 17 chapters and 90 articles.

From the point of view of formal constitutionalism, the Constitution of 1918 certainly had all the features of the Basic Act: it was approved by an elective authority, the proclaimed republican form of government, i.e. the federal government (Clause 1 of Chapter 1 of Section I); it established a procedure for the formation of representative bodies through the electoral system (Section IV). For the first time, workers were assigned some of the political and socio-economic rights (Chapter 5): equal rights regardless of race and nationality.

In 1919, during the Civil War, the Central Executive Committee of the RSFSR with the participation of representatives of the Soviet Republic issued a Decree "On the Unification of the Soviet republics: Russia, Ukraine, Latvia, Lithuania and Belarus to fight with global imperialism".

In January 1923, the Presidium of the Central Executive Committee of the USSR formed six committees to prepare the future Constitution. In the summer of 1923 the session of the CEC approved and enacted the Constitution. Final approval was given at the II Congress of Soviets in

January 1924. The Supreme authority was proclaimed the Congress of Soviets.

On January 31, 1924 the II Congress of Soviets of the USSR ratified the Constitution.

Analysis of the main parts of the Constitution shows that the main meaning of the Constitution of the USSR in 1924 was the constitutional recognition of the USSR and the division of the authority of the Union and Republics of the Union. The Constitution of the USSR in 1924 consisted of two sections: the Declaration on the Establishment of the USSR and the Treaty establishing the USSR.

The Declaration reflected the principles of voluntariness and equality in the Union Republics of the USSR. Each Union Republic reserved the right to withdraw from the USSR.

The second part of the Constitution was an agreement on the formation of the Soviet Union and included the *following chapters*:

Chapter 1: The jurisdiction of the supreme authorities of the Union of Soviet Socialist Republics;

Chapter 2: The sovereignty of the Union Republics and the federal citizenship;

Chapter 3: The Congress of Soviets of the Union of Soviet Socialist Republics;

Chapter 4: On the Central Executive Committee of the Union of Soviet Socialist Republics;

Chapter 5: The Presidium of the Central Executive Committee of the Union of Soviet Socialist Republics;

Chapter 6: The Council of People's Commissars of the Union of Soviet Socialist Republics;

Chapter 7: On the Supreme Court of the Union of Soviet Socialist Republics;

Chapter 8: About People's Commissariat of the Union of Soviet Socialist Republics;

Chapter 9: On the Joint State Political Administration;

Chapter 10: On the Republics of the Union

Chapter 11**:** On the state emblem, the flag and the capital of the Union of Soviet Socialist Republics.

The content analysis shows the basic law–the Constitution of the Soviet Union in 1924 is unlike any other Soviet constitution. It has no characteristics of the social order; there is no chapter on the rights and responsibilities of citizens, suffrage, local authorities and government. All this is reflected in the Republics' constitutions, which were adopted some time later, and included in the new Constitution of the RSFSR in 1925.

The Constitution of the Russian Federation was approved on May 11, 1925. The Constitution of the USSR in 1924 and the Republicans' constitutions, including the Constitution of the Russian Federation in 1925, as a complement to each other, formed a single Soviet Constitution.

On February 6, 1935 the Constitutional Commission was formed to draft a new Constitution of the USSR. The Resolution reads: to amend the Constitution of the Union of Soviet Socialist Republics in the direction of:

a) the further democratization of the electoral system by replacing not quite equal elections to equal, multistage to direct, open to closed; and

b) to clarify the social and economic fabric of the Constitution in the sense of the Constitution in line with the present relation of class forces in the USSR (the creation of a new socialist industry, the defeat of the kulaks, the victory of the collective farm system, the adoption of socialist property as the foundation of the Soviet society, etc.).

In the autumn of 1935, the CEC of the USSR created a Constitutional Commission, chaired by I. V. Stalin and twelve sub-committees. Those who participated included (among others) Andrey Vyshinsky, Andrey Zdanov, Maksim Litvinov, Kliment Voroshilov, Vyacheslav Molotov, Lasar Kaganovich and Nikolai Bukharin.

On June 12, 1936 the draft of the Constitution was published and discussed in six months at all levels–from the assembly of workers in enterprises to the Republican Congress. The discussion was attended by more than half of the adult population, and the Commission received 154 thousand suggestions, corrections and additions.

In the final version *the Constitution of 1936* was composed of 13 chapters and 146 articles. They are:

Chapter I: Social Order;

Chapter II: State Order;

Chapter III: Highest Governmental Authorities of the USSR;

Chapter IV: Higher Bodies of State of the Republics;

Chapter V: Bodies of Government of the Union of Soviet Socialist Republics;

Chapter VI: Bodies of the Republics;

Chapter VII: Highest Governmental Bodies of the Autonomous Soviet Socialist Republics;

Chapter VIII: Local Authorities;

Chapter IX: Courts and Prosecutors;

Chapter X: Fundamental Rights and Duties of Citizens;

Chapter XI: The Electoral System;

Chapter XII: The State Emblem, the Flag and the Capital;
Chapter XIII: The Order of the Amending to the Constitution.

The Constitution repealed restrictions on voting and added universal direct suffrage and the right to work to rights guaranteed by the previous constitution. In addition, the Constitution recognized collective social and economic rights including the rights to work, rest and leisure, health protection, care in old age and sickness, housing, education, and cultural benefits. The Constitution also provided for the direct election of all Government bodies and their reorganization into a single, uniform system.

The 1936 Constitution replaced the Congress of Soviets of the Soviet Union and its Central Executive Committee by the Supreme Soviet of the Union of Soviet Socialist Republics. Like its predecessor, the Supreme Soviet contained two chambers: the Soviet of the Union and the Soviet of Nationalities. The Constitution empowered the Supreme Soviet to elect commissions, which performed most of the Supreme Soviet's work. As under the former Constitution, the Presidium of the Supreme Soviet exercised the full powers of the Supreme Soviet between sessions and had the right to interpret laws. The Chairman of the Presidium of the Supreme Soviet became the titular head of state. The Sovnarkom (after 1946 known as the Council of Ministers) continued to act as the executive arm of the Government.

For the first time, the role of the Communist Party was clearly defined. Article 126 stated that the party was "a vanguard of the working people in their struggle to strengthen and develop the socialist system and is the leading core of all organizations of the working people, both public and state". This provision was used to justify banning all other parties from functioning in the Soviet Union.

Of the three Soviet constitutions, the 1936 Constitution survived for the longest period. It was amended regularly, but replaced in 1977.

As the researchers note, for the time the USSR Constitution of 1936 formally was *one the most democratic constitution in Europe*. How far its provisions have been implemented in political practice, however, is another question.

During 1937 the Constitutions of the Union Republics were adopted, based on the Constitution of the Soviet Union of 1936. The Constitution of the Russian Federation was approved at the XVII All-Russian Congress of Soviets on January 21, 1937.

At the Seventh (Special) Session of the Supreme Soviet of the Union of Soviet Socialist Republics' Ninth Convocation on October 7, 1977, the third and last Soviet Constitution was unanimously adopted.

The preamble stated that "the aims of the dictatorship of the proletariat having been fulfilled, the Soviet state has become the state of the whole people". Compared with previous constitutions, the Constitution of 1977 extended the bounds of the constitutional regulation of society. The first chapter defined the leading role of the Communist Party of the Soviet Union.

The 1977 Constitution was long and detailed. It included 9 sections, 21 chapters and 174 articles.

The structure of the Constitution at the time of adoption (7 October 1977) was:

Preamble
Section 1: Foundations of the Social Structure and Policy of the USSR;
Chapter 1: The Political System;
Chapter 2: The Economic System;
Chapter 3: Social Development and Culture;
Chapter 4: Foreign Policy;
Chapter 5: Defence of the Socialist Fatherland.
Section 2: The State and Identity;
Chapter 6: Soviet Citizenship. Equality of Citizens;
Chapter 7: Fundamental Rights, Freedoms and Responsibilities of Citizens of the USSR.
Section 3: National and State Structure of the USSR;
Chapter 8: The USSR–Union State;
Chapter 9: Federal Soviet Socialist Republic;
Chapter 10: Autonomous Soviet Socialist Republic;
Chapter 11: Autonomous Region and Autonomous Territory.
Section 4: Soviets and the Order of their Election;
Chapter 12: System and Principles of the Soviets;
Chapter 13: The Electoral System;
Chapter 14: People's Deputy.
Section 5: Supreme Bodies of State Power and Administration of the USSR;
Chapter 15: The Supreme Soviet of the USSR;
Chapter 16: The Council of Ministers.
Section 6: Base for the Construction of State Power and Administration in Union Republics;
Chapter 17: Supreme Bodies of State Power and of the Federal Republic;
Chapter 18: Supreme Bodies of State Power and the Administration of the Autonomous Republic;
Chapter 19: Local Authorities and Management.

Section 7: Justice, Arbitration, and the Prosecutor's Supervision;
Chapter 20: Court and Arbitration;
Chapter 21: Prosecutors.
Section 8: Coat of Arms, Flag, Anthem and the Soviet Capital.
Section 9: The Constitution of the USSR and the Procedure for Amendments.

The Soviet Constitution included a series of civil and political rights. Among these were the rights to freedom of speech, freedom of press, and freedom of assembly and the right to religious belief and worship. In addition, the Constitution provided for freedom of artistic work, protection of the family, inviolability of the person and home, and the right to privacy. Among these were the rights to work, rest and leisure, health protection, care in old age and sickness, housing, education, and cultural benefits.

The Soviet Constitution outlined limitations on political rights. Article 6 effectively eliminated partisan opposition and division within Government by granting to the Communist Party of the Soviet Union the power to lead and guide society. Article 39 enabled the Government to prohibit any activities it considered detrimental by stating that "Enjoyment of the rights and freedoms of citizens must not be to the detriment of the interests of society or the state". The constitution provided a "freedom of conscience, that is, the right to profess or not to profess any religion, and to conduct religious worship or atheistic propaganda". It prohibited the incitement of hatred or hostility on religious grounds.

The Constitution also failed to provide political and judicial mechanisms for the protection of rights. Thus, the Constitution lacked explicit guarantees protecting the rights of the people. The Supreme Court had no power to ensure that constitutional rights were observed by legislation or respected by the rest of the Government.

At its Extraordinary Session of April 12, 1978, the Supreme Soviet of the Russian SFSR adopted a new republican Constitution, to replace the previous Russian Constitution of 1937. The new Constitution initially consisted of a Preamble and 185 articles, and was prepared as part of the whole project of adjusting all 15 republican Constitutions to the new Constitution of the Soviet Union of October 1977. It was the fourth Constitution of the Russian SFSR. The Constitution was amended several times. It lost its legal force by the referendum of December 12, 1993.

Until 1989 amendments were made to the Constitution of the Russian Federation (RSFSR). The need to amend the Constitution of the Russian Federation only arose for the first time in 1988-1989 due to the need to bring Russia's Basic Law in accordance with the Constitution of the USSR.

On June 16, 1990, an amendment establishing a multi-party system in the Russian Federation was adopted. Unlike federal law the new version of Article 6 of the Constitution of the Russian Federation did not mention the Communist Party of the Soviet Union. On December 15, 1990 the Declaration of State Sovereignty of the Russian Federation was included in the Constitution Preamble and Article 1.

On December 9, 1992, further revisions were made to the Constitution. The reference to the Soviet Union was removed from the Preamble.

In 1991-1993 there was a political crisis in the Russian Federation.

At the I Congress of People's Deputies (June 22, 1990) the Constitutional Commission was formed, chaired by B. N. Yeltsin to prepare the text of the new Constitution. The Commission included representatives of all Republics, territories, regions, and the national autonomy of the Russian Federation.

In May 1993 a draft Constitution approved by the Supreme Council was published. Putting forward the idea of parliamentarianism, the authors of the Constitution insisted on the leading role of Parliament in the system of higher government authorities.

At the same time on May 12, 1993 the Russian President issued Decree № 660 "On measures to finalize the new Constitution of the Russian Federation", convened in order to complete the drafting of the Constitution in Moscow. The Constitutional Council was intended as a broad forum, combining the highest representation of all public authorities, and the public. The Constitutional Council thus actually received, although a number of invited members of the Constitutional Commission of People's Deputies, as well as political parties participating in its work were not accepted. On June 24, 1993 the Supreme Council refused to cooperate with the Constitutional Conference.

Since the autumn of 1993 a constitutional crisis entered into a new phase. The legislative and the executive had its own draft constitution and its own view of the process of its adoption. The agreement was not possible.

The constitutional crisis reached a tipping point on September 21, 1993, when President Boris Yeltsin purported to dissolve the country's legislature (the Congress of People's Deputies and its Supreme Soviet) by Decree 1400, although the President did not have the power to dissolve the parliament according to the current Constitution.

A temporary Decree, until the adoption of the Constitution, was introduced in the Regulations of the federal government for a transitional period, prepared on the basis of the draft constitution, and approved by the Constitutional Conference on July 12, 1993. The provisions on the elections of deputies of the State Duma deputes was legally enforced

The State Duma elections were scheduled for December 11-12. The activities of the Constitutional Court were suspended.

The constitutional crisis immediately escalated into a constitutional war. On the same day, the Supreme Soviet Presidium, referring to Article 1216 of the Constitution, announced the immediate termination of the powers of President Boris Yeltsin, and the President's powers were transferred to the Vice-president A. V. Rutskoi. The Supreme Council praised the actions of the President as a coup. The Constitutional Court, recognizing the presidential decree as unconstitutional, called for the resignation of the President from office.

Attempts to reach agreement were unsuccessful, and the crisis was to generate social unrest and military actions. Supporters of the President organized a blockade of the Council House, and supporters of the Supreme Council attempted to seize the Moscow City Hall building, one of the military headquarters, and the TV centre "Ostankino". This led to bloodshed (mostly on 2 and 3 October) and the intervention of the army, when a few tanks shelled the Council House building. There was a state of emergency in Moscow.

The 1993 Constitution was adopted by referendum.

A national vote on the draft of the new Constitution was attended by 58 million 187 thousand and 755 registered voters, or 54.8%. A total of 32 million 937 thousand and 630 voters, or 58.4% of the voters who took part, voted for the adoption of the Constitution. This meant that the Constitution was adopted. The Constitution entered into force on December 25, 1993.

CHAPTER TWO

THE CONSTITUTION OF RUSSIA

1. General Description of the Constitution 1993

The term "constitution" is derived from the Latin word «constitutio», which means the establishment or institution. That was the name of one of the decrees of the Roman emperors. In the modern world the constitution is the basic law, which has the highest legal force.

The Constitution of the Russian Federation–is a legal act, which has the highest legal force, fixing the basis of the constitutional system, the basis of the legal status of man and citizen, the federal structure, the system of bodies of state power and the principles of the organization of local self-government.

Legal features of the Constitution are signs that distinguish it from the acts of the current legislation.

The legal features of the Constitution include the constituent nature, legitimacy, highest legal force, stability, direct action, the base of the current legislation, and the reality.

The constituent character of the Constitution shows that its rules consolidate the foundations of the state and the social order and establish an institute, which is implemented through state power, and the principles of their establishment and functioning. In addition, the constitutional provisions govern the creation of all operating in the state of law in the hierarchy of the legal system.

The legitimacy of the Constitution is that it takes people (by referendum), or it is on behalf of the people (the representative body of the state–parliament or the same body, specially created for the adoption of the constitution–the constituent assembly), which belongs to the fullness of state power. The Russian Constitution, adopted by popular vote on December 12, 1993 can be called legitimate because it was approved by 58.4% of voters who participated in the voting.

The supremacy of the Constitution means its priority position in the system of laws and regulations in force in the territory of Russia. "*The laws and other legal acts adopted in the Russian Federation shall not contradict the Constitution of the Russian Federation*"–proclaims part 1 of Article 15 of the Constitution. The supremacy of the Constitution is shown not only in relation to the legislation to be adopted in the future, but also to the legislation adopted before the entry into force of the Constitution. Thus, in paragraph 2 of Section II of the Constitution of the Russian Federation it is stated that "the laws and other legal acts in force in the territory of the Russian Federation to the entry into force of this Constitution shall apply to the extent not contrary to the Constitution of the Russian Federation". The *supremacy of the Constitution* takes on added significance in a federal state system of Russia, when the subjects of the Federation have their own constitution and its laws. Constitutions of the republics of the Russian Federation and other subjects' regulations must not contradict the Federal Constitution (Part 1 of Art. 15 of the Constitution). The supremacy of the Constitution provides a special procedure of its adoption and change, giving the constitutional norms of higher force; enhanced legal protection of constitutional provisions.

The stability of the Constitution–the most important condition for regime legitimacy, stability of the legal system and the organization of the government, determines the relationship between the individual and the state. The stability of the Constitution depends on many factors (on the arrangement of social and political forces on the political arena of the country, the level of the political and legal culture of citizens from perfection provisions of the Constitution itself, etc.). Guarantee of the stability of the Constitution is a rigid procedure for review and constitutional amendments.

The Constitution of the Russian Federation has a direct action (Part 2 of Art. 15 of the Constitution). This means that the provisions of the Constitution of the Russian Federation shall have direct effect, that is, their implementation is not required as a condition of additional, specifying laws. However, many provisions of the Constitution of the Russian Federation, by the high level of generality of legal regulation, require additional regulation by the adoption of acts of the current legislation.

The problem of providing a direct effect of the Constitution of the Russian Federation in the administration of justice was allowed in the Resolution of the Plenum of the Supreme Court of October 31, 1995 "On some issues of application of the Constitution by the courts in the exercise of justice", which states that the court decided the case, applying directly to the Russian Constitution, *in particular*:

a) when a fixed rate of the Constitution provisions on the basis of its meaning, does not require further regulations and does not indicate the possibility of its application, subject to a federal law regulating the rights, freedoms, rights and duties of citizens and other provisions;

b) when the Court concludes that the federal law in force in the territory of the Russian Federation is contrary to that enforced by the Constitution

c) when the court comes to the conclusion that a federal law passed after the entry into force of the Constitution, is in contradiction to relevant provisions of the Constitution;

d) when the law or other normative legal act adopted by the subject of the Russian Federation on the joint jurisdiction of the Russian Federation and the subjects of the Russian Federation, is contrary to the Constitution and federal law, which shall regulate the relationship before a court, is absent.

The reality of the Constitution means the relevant constitutional provisions (constitutional law) which consist in reality of social relations (actual Constitution). In other words, the Constitution should reflect the level of development reached by the social relations in the political, economic and social spheres, otherwise it would be a sham.

The reality of the Constitution demonstrates its feasibility and warranty provisions. For example, the ability of citizens, guided by the Constitution, and referring to it, to seek judicial protection of the rights and freedoms is an indicator of the reality of constitutional rules on the legal status of the individual.

The Constitution is the legal basis of the current legislation. This provision appears in the Constitution that the constitutional provisions serve as the starting point for all branches of Russian law. Thus, on the basis of the constitutional provisions, there is provision for freedom of economic activity, the equality of all forms of ownership and the development of civil law in Russia.

2. Structure of the Constitution

The structure of the Constitution is adopted in its order, which establishes a certain system of homogeneous grouping of constitutional provisions in sections, chapters and the sequence of their location. On the basis of summarizing the constitutional norms in general sections, at the head is the unity of the subject matter, i.e., their connectedness and unity of social relations, which affect those rules.

In its structure, the *1993 Constitution* consists of a preamble and two sections. The *first section* consists of nine chapters and 137 articles:

1. The Fundamentals of the Constitutional System;
2. Rights and Freedoms of Man and Citizen;
3. The Federal Structure;
4. The President;
5. The Federal Assembly;
6. The Government of the Russian Federation;
7. Judicial Power and Prosecutuion Office;
8. Local Self-government;
9. Constitutional Amendments and Revision of the Constitution.

The second section is called “Final and Transitional Provisions”.

The Russian Constitution opens with the preamble, i.e. the prodrome preceding the text of the Constitution. The preamble has no legal status, but it is essential for understanding the meaning of the Constitution as a whole and its individual articles, as the introduction indicates the grounds and circumstances that triggered the publication of the Constitution and determines its content.

The *Preamble* states, first of all, that the Constitution was adopted by the multinational people of the Russian Federation, united by a common fate in our land, and emphasizes the particular importance of this act for the further development of the state and society.

The *Preamble to the Constitution* contains the six core objectives, the implementation of which is the main task of the state. They reflect the essence of whole constitutional reform in Russia.

They are as follows:

- ➢ The statement of rights and freedoms;
- ➢ The approval of civil peace and accord in the Russian Federation;
- ➢ To preserve the historically established state unity;
- ➢ The revival of the sovereign state of Russia;
- ➢ The approval of the inviolability of the democratic foundations of the Russian state;
- ➢ The well-being and prosperity of Russia.

These goals are the basis of all constitutional norms impregnating the content of the Constitution.

Section II of the Constitution, “the final and transitional provisions” is fixing the position on issues related to the introduction of a new Constitution, the fixed termination of the Constitution, and the Federal Treaty, the order of the application of laws and other legal acts in force before the entry into force of this Constitution, the grounds which continue to apply to the earlier formed bodies.

3. Amendments to the Constitution of the Russian Federation

Chapter nine of the Constitution of Russia establishes a special procedure for making changes to the text and revising its provisions.

More detailed procedural aspects are described in the Federal Law № 33-FZ "*On the procedure of adoption and entry into force of amendments to the Constitution of the Russian Federation*", dated March 4, 1998. As explained by the decision of the Constitutional Court on October 31, 1995 № 12-P "On the Interpretation of Article 136 of the Constitution of the Russian Federation", the change is to enact a special legal act–the Russian Federation Law on the amendment of the Constitution, and this same federal constitutional law was adopted by Parliament, but to enter into force it also required ratification by regional legislatures.

The Russian Constitution establishes *three procedures to change its text*:

- Amendments (chapters 3-8);
- The revision of the Constitution (chapters 1, 2 and 9); and
- A change in the text (Article 65).

According to Article 134 of the Constitution of Russia, suggestions for amendments and revision of the Constitution of the Russian Federation may be made by the President of the Russian Federation, the Federation Council, the State Duma of the Russian Federation, the legislative (representative) bodies of the subjects of the Russian Federation, as well as by a group of at least one-fifth of the members of the Federation Council and deputies of the State Duma.

In accordance with Article 136, the amendments to chapters 3-8 of the Constitution (the federal structure of the state (Articles 65-79), the President (Articles 80-93), the Parliament (Articles 94-109), the Government (Articles 110-117) the Judiciary Power (Articles 118-129) and local self-government (Articles 130-133)) are taken in the manner provided for the adoption of federal constitutional law, and shall take effect upon approval by the legislature–at least two-thirds of the subjects of the Russian Federation.

So they must be approved by a two-thirds majority of the Duma and a three-fourths vote of the members of the Federation Council (Paragraph 2 of Article 108). After this, the proposal for constitutional amendments is forwarded by the legislative (representative) bodies of subjects of the Russian Federation. Within the year, the proposal must be approved by the legislative (representative) bodies of at least two-thirds of the subjects of the Russian Federation. After the establishment of the review, within seven days the Federation Council sends the law on the amendment of the Constitution to the President who, within fourteen days, signs and publishes it.

Article 135 of the Constitution states that the provisions of Chapters 1, 2 and 9 of the Constitution (the constitutional order (Articles 1-16), the rights and freedoms of man and citizen (Articles 17-64), as well as constitutional amendments and revision of the Constitution (Article 134-137)) cannot be reviewed by the Federal Assembly. However, if a proposal to revise the provisions of the Constitution of the chapters is supported by three-fifths of the members of the Federation Council and the State Duma, in accordance with federal constitutional law it shall be convened by the *Constitutional Assembly*.

According to the third part of Article 135, the Constitutional Assembly shall either confirm the immutability of the Constitution, or draft a new Constitution of Russia. The new draft Constitution of Russia can be adopted either by a two-thirds vote of the members of the Constitutional Assembly, or the popular vote. In the case of a referendum a new Constitution of Russia is considered adopted if more than half of the voters participating in the vote actually voted for it, providing that it was attended by more than half the voters.. Thus, a change to the fundamental provisions (of the constitutional system of Russia, as well as the rights and freedoms of man and citizen) cannot take place until the new Constitutionis in force.

According to Article 137 of the Constitution, changes to Article 65 of the Constitution of the Russian Federation, which determines the structure of the Russian Federation, shall be made on the basis of Federal Constitutional Law on admission to the Russian Federation and the creation of new subjects of the Russian Federation, and on changes in the constitutional and legal status of the Russian Federation. That is, on the occasion of the appearance of new subjects (as a result of any new territory to Russia and the elimination, consolidation or separation of the existing entities of the Russian Federation), or a change in its status (for example, the area of the Republic) to be adopted by the federal constitutional law that applies for a change in Article 65 of the Constitution.

For example, in the case of the entry into force of this law on the merger of regions, Article 65 ought to include the name of the newly-formed entity and delete names of suppressed subjects. The second part of Article 137 provides that in the case of a simple change of the name of the republic, territory, region, federal cities or autonomous regions, the new name of the Russian Federation shall be included in Article 65 of the Constitution of the Russian Federation. This action (the new name of inclusion and exclusion of the former) is the Decree of the President of Russia without the participation of the Federal Assembly.

From 1993 to 2008, there were no serious amendments in the Constitution (Article 65 changed only in connection with the change of the name of several subjects of the Russian Federation).

The amendments of 2008, which were proposed in November 2008 and came into force on December 31, 2008, have become the first substantial amendments to the Constitution of Russia of 1993, have extended the terms of the President of Russia and the State Duma from four to six and five years respectively, and have also introduced a mandatory report of the Government in the State Duma.

4. Protection of the Constitution

The legal protection of the Constitution is a set of legal tools which ensures the implementation of all the established rules of the Constitution and adherence to constitutional legality.

In a broader sense, the legal protection of the Constitution is the creation of the necessary conditions for the development of appropriate safeguards, and the improvement of state-legal means and methods for the operation of the constitutional norms. The special value involves the use of specific constitutional and legal means to ensure the supremacy of the Constitution in the legal system.

The need for the legal protection of the Constitution is determined by its specific role in society. The Constitution defines the overriding principles of the society and the state. It applies to the whole system of social relations. In all the activities of the state bodies and public associations, each citizen must clearly meet the letter of the Constitution. The practical reality is equally important. It shows that there are cases of the violation of the Constitution, the adoption of acts inconsistent with it and the debate on its use. The rule of the Constitution as the highest attribute of a democratic state based on the principle of the separation of powers is the effective legal protection of the Constitution.

The legal protection of the Basic Law is carried by the relevant institutions. Together they represent a mechanism for the legal protection of the Constitution. First of all, such an institution is a special procedure for the preparation, adoption and amendment of the Constitution. It must meet two basic, interrelated requirements: first, the stability of the Constitution, and, second, the possibility to change it. This approach is designed to ensure the stability of the constitutional system and at the same time, the dynamics of its development, taking into account possible changes in the society.

The next institute of legal protection of the Constitution–is its interpretation. It is a special kind of legal action. Constitutional interpretation–is the part of a common interpretation of the law. However, the interpretation of the Constitution is different: *first,* constitutional interpretation is a special kind of legal work of the highest judicial authority to evaluate the legislation and the protection of the Constitution, to ensure the implementation of all the norms of law, and to prevent all types of offences. *Secondly*, constitutional interpretation is a kind of legal activity with high legal rank. *Thirdly*, it is a kind of legal activity constitutional interpretation is of importance not only for law-making, but for all the right forms, including compliance, enforcement and the implementation of the legal provisions.

Institution of constitutional control plays central role in the legal protection of the Constitution. This is the most powerful and effective tool.

Constitutional control is verification, as well as constant monitoring to check the regulations in force in the Russian Federation for their compliance with the Constitution.

The method of protection is an act or system used by public authorities in the exercise of the legal protection of the Constitution. State protection is defined as one of the functions of public authorities. This function is not the exclusive jurisdiction of only one government agency. Its implementation involves all state agencies whose performance of their immediate tasks in any way exercises state protection. As the scope of a separate activity, state protection is a set of activities, functions and tasks of state bodies in the security of state protection. According to the text definition *state protection* is based on the totality of legal, organizational, security, technical and other measures.

According to Part 2 of Article 15 of the Constitution, public authorities, local governments, officials, citizens and their associations must comply with the Constitution and laws of the Russian Federation.

In the protection of the Constitution the entire system of state authorities responsible for this protection in various forms is involved. The main subjects of the legal protection of the Constitution are the President of the Russian Federation, the Constitutional Court of the Russian Federation, the Federal Assembly of the Russian Federation, the Government of the Russian Federation, the federal courts and the Prosecutor's Office. The President of the Russian Federation, who is the guarantor of the Constitution must observe and protect the right to suspend acts of the executive authorities of the Federation, contradicting the federal

Constitution. At the same time, the protection of the Constitution of the Russian Federation according to the procedure of constitutional control is exercised by the Constitutional Court of the Russian Federation, and in the order of constitutional supervision, carried out by a number of bodies such as the Office of the Public Prosecutor of the Russian Federation.

An important component of the protection of the Constitution is judicial control. *The Constitutional Court of the Russian Federation*–the judicial body of constitutional control, independently exercises judicial power through constitutional proceedings. It was established in order to ensure the supremacy and direct effect of the Constitution of the Russian Federation on the entire territory of the Russian Federation (Articles 1 and 3 of the Federal Constitutional Law *"On the Constitutional Court of the Russian Federation"*).

In accordance with paragraph 2 of the Decree of the Plenum of the Supreme Court of the Russian Federation N 8 of October 31, 1995 "*On some issues of application of the Constitution by the courts in the exercise of justice*", the courts of general jurisdiction and arbitration courts do not have the right to apply the law in the following cases:

- When the court concludes that the federal law in force in the territory of the Russian Federation to the entry into force of the Constitution is contrary to it;
- When the court comes to the conclusion that a federal law passed after the entry into force of the Constitution is in contradiction to the relevant provisions of the Constitution;
- When a law or other legal act adopted by the subject of the Russian Federation on the joint jurisdiction of the Russian Federation and the subjects of the Russian Federation, with the Constitution of the Russian Federation, as a federal law that is supposed to regulate legal relations before a court is absent.

The Constitutional Court of the Russian Federation acts as a kind of point of reference performing in the imperative form of corrective function. Its decisions on the constitutionality or unconstitutionality of legislation or constitutional dispute are final and without appeal. The legal position of the Constitutional Court can be considered by other courts as a "sample" to ensure constitutionality.

5. Domestic Law and International Law

According to the Constitution of the Russian Federation, the generally recognized principles and norms of international law and the international treaties of the Russian Federation are a component part of its legal system.

If an international treaty of the Russian Federation stipulates other rules than those stipulated by law, the rules of the international agreement are applied (Clause 4 of Article 15).

The adoption of an international treaty is a long process, consisting of a series of successive stages. The Law on International Treaties of the Russian Federation 1995 clearly and comprehensively defines the entire process. The most important stage is the acceptance of the contract signing by an authorized person, usually the head of state. The next step - is the ratification of an international treaty of the Russian Federation by Federal Assembly.

Russian Federation international treaties which come into force are published in the *Bulletin of International Treaties*, published by the Executive Office of the President. The publication is accompanied by information on the date of entry into force, if it does not enter into force on the date of signing. The termination of international treaties of Russia is included in the same published information.

6. The Constitutional Order

The Constitutional order is the system of legal relations that fixes the organization of the state, which recognizes and guarantees the rights and freedoms of man and citizen, and that the state is subject to law and, above all, a democratic constitution.

The concept of the constitutional order has two main features:

1) This is a way of organizing the state–a set of features by which one state can be distinguished from the other (the form of government, political system, etc.);
2) This is a method of organization of the state, which puts it (the state) in subordination to the interests of people, their natural rights and freedoms through the regulation of activity of the state legal restrictions and limits, beyond which the state should not go.

A crucial role in this restriction is the Constitution.

The constitutional order is fixed throughout the system of legal norms, the various branches of the Russian law. The constitutional right of the statutory framework of the constitutional order–the fundamental principles of the state and its relationship to the individual and society, it (the state) has essential characteristics, which together form an orderly and relatively complete system, and are projected to all other regulations' established rules. In this case, all the further regulation of public relations is a reflection, specification and development of these fundamental principles.

These basic principles are so important that they are contained in the fundamental law of the state–the Constitution.

The Russian Constitution dedicates the first chapter to the constitutional order, which has the same name. The provisions of the Constitution define the fundamentals of the constitutional system of the highest legal authority of all the rules of the Russian legal system. Article 16 of the Constitution stipulates that no other provision of the Constitution (and, consequently, other instruments) can contradict the principles of the constitutional order. Foundations of the constitutional system are designed to be the core of regulation and therefore need to have an increased stability of its content.

Constitutional basics are particular characteristic of the constitutional order, which means the kind of political and social system based on the principles of democracy, the separation of powers, the recognition of human rights and freedoms highest value of society, the subordination of the state's priorities and interests of civil society. Standards, the principles included in the chapter "Principles of the constitutional order" constitute a system and can be divided into four main groups:

- Humanistic Fundamentals of the Constitutional Order;
- Features of the Russian State;
- The Basis of the Organization of State Power;
- Economic and Political Fundamentals of the Constitutional System.

Humanistic Fundamentals of the Constitutional Order

Humanistic fundamentals of the constitutional order are those fundamental principles that reinforce the key role of citizens in the building of the state.

The state regulates human behaviour only to a certain extent, so as not to affect freedom and to ensure the public interest. Such an understanding of the relation of man, society and the state emphasizes the humanistic essence of the constitutional order.

The basic principle in this group is the recognition of human rights and freedoms in his primary relationship with the state. Article 2 of the Constitution stipulates that "a person's rights and freedoms are the supreme value. Recognition, respect and protection of the rights and freedoms of man and citizen are the state's duty".

In the Constitution and the laws, recognition means the scope of the rights and freedoms under the generally recognized rules of international law, as well as the inalienable rights and freedoms flowing from the natural law.

Compliance requires the government not only to refrain from any actions that violate or infringe the rights and freedoms, but also to create the conditions for people to implement them.

Recognition of human rights and freedoms' highest value does not mean that the state, in all cases, may not limit the actions of people. This is to ensure that the exercise of the rights and freedoms of one person does not infringe the rights and freedoms of others, not to the detriment of society.

Another important principle is the principle of peoples' sovereignty, enshrined in Article 3 of the Constitution. Peoples' sovereignty is the primary source of power. The will of the people expressed in a legally relevant form, is genuine and the only basis of the state, it comes from the mandate of the device and any changes to the form of government.

The implementation of the power of the people is done in two ways:

1) Directly;
2) Through the bodies of state power and local self-government.

The basic institutions of direct democracy are *elections* and *referendum.*

An election–is the participation of citizens in the formation of state and local self-governments. Legal rules governing the election form election law which is an integral part (institution) of the Constitutional law. In the Constitution there is no separate chapter about the elections, it only secures rules on Presidential elections.

The main principles of the election law (the electoral system) are universality, equality, direct suffrage by secret ballot and free elections.

A referendum is carried out by secret ballot approval (or disapproval) of the citizens of any document or project solutions or agreement (or disagreement) with various acts of parliament or the president or the government–along with national referenda, a possible referendum on the level of the subjects of the Federation and local authorities.

The order of holding a referendum in the Russian Federation is established by the Federal Constitutional Law "*On the Referendum of the Russian Federation*" dated 2004.

The law prohibits the submission of a number of issues to a referendum: changing the status of the subjects of the Russian Federation, the early termination or extension of the term of office of the President of the Russian Federation, the Federation Council or the State Duma, as well as their early election. It is also not possible to submit issues to referendum related to the adoption and amendment of the federal budget, the change and cancellation of federal taxation, issues of amnesty and pardon, and emergency and urgent measures to ensure the health and safety of the public.

Referendum is used to achieve the highest legitimacy in some critical cases (for example, the adoption of the Constitution or amendments), which is specifically provided for in the Constitutions. Another common reason for holding a referendum is to obtain the approval of any act, when the government has decided not to take on the responsibility. In Russia a referendum was held for the adoption of the Constitution in December 1993.

The functioning of the bodies of state power and local self-government is the mediated form of the power of the people. These bodies are formed with the participation of citizens, i.e. based on eligibility or subordination elected bodies. It is an opportunity for Russian citizens to express their will in the process, as the formation of the bodies of the state, and their work enshrined in the Constitution in Article 32.

7. Features of the Russian State

The fundamentals of the Constitutional order include state features. Article 1 of the Russian Constitution stipulates that the Russian Federation is a democratic, federal, law-bound state with a republican form of government. Article 7 describes the Russian Federation as social and Article 14 as secular.

A democratic state is a state which aims to recognize and ensure the sovereignty of the people and the rights and freedoms of man and citizen. The Russian Constitution does not limit the insured (in Art. 1) Russian democracy. The democratic character of the state is enshrined in a number of constitutional provisions. It is, for example, the responsibility of the State, its agencies and officials to recognize, respect and protect the rights and freedoms of man and citizen (Article 2), the recognition of the multinational people of the bearer of sovereignty and the only source of power in the Russian Federation (Part 1 of Art. 3), the consolidation of the people's right to exercise its authority (to implement sovereignty), both directly and through bodies of state power and local self-government (Part 2 of Art. 3) recognition of the referendum and free elections' supreme direct expression of the people (Part 3.3), the constitutional ban on usurp power in the Russian Federation (part 4.3), of the principle of separation of powers (Article 10); ideological and political diversity (Article 13); the constitutional ability of citizens to participate in public affairs (Part 1 of Art. 32), etc.

The most important features of a democratic state are:

- ✓ a real representative democracy;
- ✓ a real guarantee of the rights and freedoms of man and citizen.

Federal Form of State Territorial Organization

A federation is a form of territorial structuring of the State. The form of state territorial organization is a territorial organization of state power, the ratio of the state as a whole with its parts. A federal state is a form of territorial structuring in which the constituent parts of the state (subjects) have the autonomy and authority in the division of competence between the Federation and its subjects.

The fundamentals of the constitutional system of territorial structuring are formulated in *Article 5 of the Constitution.*

a) The Russian Federation consists of republics, territories (oblast), regions (kray), cities of federal importance, autonomous regions and autonomous territories;
b) The Republics have their own constitution and laws, and other subjects–charter and legislation;
c) The federal structure of the Russian Federation is based on its state integrity, the unity of the system of state authority, the division of subjects of authority and powers between the bodies of state power of the Russian Federation and bodies of state power of the subjects of the Russian Federation, the equality and self-determination of peoples in the Russian Federation;
d) In relations with federal bodies of state authority all the subjects of the Russian Federation shall be equal among themselves.

The essence of Russian federalism constitutes: state integrity, unity of power, separation of powers between the federal authorities and the authorities of the Federation, equality and self-determination of peoples.

The subjects that are part of the Russian Federation can be divided into nation-states (the Republics), administrative areas (territories, regions and federal cities) and national-territorial (autonomous regions and autonomous territories). Article 65 of the Constitution contains a specific list of subjects of the Federation. The article begins with a list of the republics of the Russian Federation (22 republics). The name of each of them is provided in the Constitution in the form specified by the republic, which is free to decide on its name. Following on from this are listed all the republics within the Russian Federation.

At the time of the adoption of the Constitution the number of subjects was 89. The consequence of union was that the number of subjects had fallen to 83 by 2008 and two more subjects were added as a result of accession of Crimea and Sevastopol in March 2014. Now there are 85 subjects.

Law-governed State

A law-governed State is a state in which the organization and activities of the government in its relations with individuals and their associations are based on law and correspond to it.

The idea of the rule-of-law seeks to limit the power of the state law, to establish a government of laws and not of men, and on human security in its interactions with the state.

The main features of the law-governed State:

1. The exercise of public power in accordance with the principle of the separation of legislative, executive and judicial order to prevent the concentration of entire state power in the hands of one person, excluding its monopoly, usurpation of a face, body, social stratum;
2. The presence of the Constitutional Court–the guarantor of stability of the constitutional order–the body that provides the constitutional law and supremacy of the Constitution, the corresponding laws and other acts of the legislative and executive branches;
3. The law-governed State means that nobody except the supreme representative (legislative) state body may not revoke or modify the law. All other regulations should not be contrary to the law;
4. The law-governed State is equal for states through their agencies, officials, and citizens and their associations.
5. The mutual responsibility of the state and the individual–an individual responsibility to the state, but the state is not free from liability to a person for non-commitments and for the violation of providing individual rights;
6. Reality enshrined in law the basic human rights and the rights and freedoms of the individual, which ensure the existence of a legal framework for their implementation and the ability to protect in the most effective way–in court;
7. Reality, the effectiveness of monitoring and supervision of the implementation of laws and other regulations, which result in people's trust in state institutions, the appeal for the resolution of legal disputes exclusively to them, and not, for example, in newspapers, on radio and television;
8. Legal culture of citizens–the knowledge of their responsibilities and rights, the ability to use them and respect for the law.

Republican Form of Government

The Russian Federation is declared as a *republic*.

The supreme bodies of the state power in the Republic are elected and shall serve for the particular time. World constitutional practice knows three types of republics: *parliamentary, presidential and mixed.*

In a *presidential republic* the President is elected by the people and forms a government that is accountable only to him. Parliament has no right to pass a vote of no confidence in the government. The President has the right to dissolve parliament. The principle of separation of powers is firmly and consistently implemented.

In a *parliamentary republic* the President is elected by the Parliament or with the participation of parliament and the head of Government is the leader of the party which won the election. The Parliament exercises control over the the Government. The Parliament and the Government are working closely and the principle of separation of powers is applied more flexibly than in a presidential republic.

In a classic example of *mixed republic* (France) the President is elected by the people and has a broad range of powers. The Government is formed jointly by the President and the Parliament, taking into account the balance of forces in Parliament and has a dual responsibility. The Parliament has the right to express confidence in the government, but the question of resignation is taken by the President. The President has the right to dissolve the Parliament.

The Russian Constitution does not determine the type of republican form of the government. It only talks about "*a state with a republican form of government*" (Article 1), but on the analysis of articles of the Constitution dealing with the formation of the government and its responsibilities, it can be concluded that, despite a number of features, particularly the lack of connection of the government with the balance of power in Parliament, the republican form of government in Russia has the features of a mixed republic.

Social (Welfare) State

The welfare state is a principle involving the constitutional guarantee of economic and social rights and freedoms of man and citizen, and the respective responsibilities of the state. Meaning that the state serves the society and aims to eliminate or minimize the social differences. The Russian Constitution (Article 7) states: "*Russia–social state whose policy is aimed at creating the conditions for a dignified life and free development of the individual*". This general situation leads to the following constitutional duties of the Russian state:

a) The labour and health of people;
b) To establish a minimum guaranteed wage;
c) To provide state support for the family, motherhood, fatherhood and childhood, the disabled and senior citizens;
d) To develop human services;
e) To establish government pensions, benefits and other social security guarantees.

Features of the welfare state are:

1. The democratic organization of state power;
2. The high level of legal culture of citizens;
3. The strong economic capacity to implement measures to redistribute income without compromising the substantive provisions of owners;
4. A socially-oriented economic structure, which is manifested in the existence of different forms of property with significant state ownership in the right areas of the economy;
5. The legal development of the state and the presence of its qualities of law;
6. The existence of civil society, in whose hands the state is an instrument of social-oriented policies;
7. A pronounced social orientation of policy, which is manifested in the development of a variety of social programs and a prioritization of their implementation;
8. The presence of state goals such as the establishment of the common good, the statement in the society of social justice, ensuring every citizen:
   a) a decent existence;
   b) social security;
   c) equal opportunities for personal fulfillment.
9. A well-developed social legislation;
10. Fixing the formula of "social state" in the constitution.

The most important task of the welfare state is holding a social policy that would ensure the adequate standard of living of every member of society, including cases of unemployment which are due to circumstances beyond an individual's control. The condition of its realization is an effective social security system, which includes a set of measures taken by the state to provide and care for citizens in old age, invalidity, survivors, in the period of unemployment, sickness, pregnancy, and in other situations where there is a lack of a systematic income or wages. Grounds for granting social assistance are determined by the state according to its socio-economic development, so their list cannot be exhaustive.

The main types of social services are pensions, benefits and various social services. Social security is provided in cash (pension benefits) and in kind (social services), including a set of social services (care, meals, assistance in obtaining medical, legal, social, psychological and natural forms of aid, assistance in vocational training, job placement, recreation, etc.).

According to Article 5 of the Federal Law № 122-FZ *"On the social care of elderly and disabled people*", dated August 2, 1995 citizens of pension age (*women over 55 and men over 60*) and disabled persons in need of permanent or temporary outside assistance in connection with the loss of opportunities to meet their own basic needs due to limited capacity for self-care and mobility, have a right to social services.

Social benefits are cash payments provided to compensate for lost wages and other lawful income persons (families) to social support at elevated costs associated, as a rule, with the birth and upbringing of children. Various types of benefits are introduced by the law:

- ✓ Temporary disability (in the case of illness, care for a sick family member, quarantine, etc.);
- ✓ Maternity, a monthly allowance for the care of children up to the age of eighteen years;
- ✓ A lump sum at the birth of the child;
- ✓ Benefits to citizens with children;
- ✓ Unemployment benefits;
- ✓ Funeral benefit, etc.

Currently, the regulation of social benefits is not codified and consists of a set of laws and other legal acts. Legislative practice suggests the possibility of codifying the rules that make up an institution of social protection as a benefit. In 1995, rules were codified governing the provision of benefits for pregnant women and women with young children, through the adoption of the Federal Law № 81-FZ "On state benefits to citizens with children", dated May 19, 1995.

Secular State

The concept of a *"secular state*" reflects the approach of the state towards religion. A *secular state* is a state in which the church and religious associations are separated from and do not interfere in the activities of government agencies, having their own sphere of activity, which does not interfere with the state.

Secular state recognizes the church and religious organizations other than government institutions but civil society, non-governmental. In such a state the following is fixed:

The equality of different faiths, the freedom of organization and activities of the religious (and atheist) associations within the limits set by law, the non-interference of the state in relation to the church and citizens in the internal affairs of religious organizations, and the non-interference of the church and religious associations affairs of the state, politics, local government, etc.

The secular state in its pure form, cannot and should not build on any religion as a State (official), understand it mandatorily or otherwise emphasize it or protect it. But in real life, many democratic countries often officially recognize the special role of a religion based on its real place in the real life of the society and the state. They also recognize that they do not cease to be a secular state, and furthermore this recognition occurs on the background of democratic institutions on the equality of all before the law, regardless of religion, freedom of religion, state interference in church affairs, neutrality, education and respect for the religious beliefs of minorities.

The Russian Federation is characterized by the fact that its religious associations are separated from the state and that no religion, according to the Constitution (Article 14) "can be established as state or obligatory". The content of this situation reveals Article 4 of the Federal Law N 125-FZ "*On Freedom of Conscience and Religious Associations*" dated by September 26, 1997 which states that religious groups are equal in the face of the law.

The state protects the lawful activity of religious associations. It regulates the provision of religious organizations in terms of tax and other benefits, provides financial, material and other religious organizations to help in the restoration, maintenance and protection of buildings and facilities, which are monuments of history and culture, and to ensure the teaching of general subjects in educational institutions established by religious organizations in accordance with the legislation of the Russian Federation on education.

The separation of religious associations from the state does not lead to restrictions on the rights of members of these associations to take part on an equal basis with other citizens in public affairs, in the elections to the bodies of state power and local self-government, political parties, political movements and other public associations.

The Basis of the Organization of the State Power

The principles of the organization and operation of state bodies are the fundamental principles and ideas that define the character of the functioning and development of the apparatus of the state in general. The modern state and the state apparatus are built on principles which have the following requirements:

- ✓ Established in the law (directly or indirectly) and bound to create public authorities;
- ✓ Consistency, i.e., there cannot be multiple conflicting principles;
- ✓ Completeness, in accordance with it there is pre-set the most important conditions for the formation and implementation of public authorities.

The state as the official representative of the people expresses the will of its citizens, ensuring their character and interests. The state should have sovereignty in order to perform these tasks. Under the sovereignty of the state means the rule of the government in its independence of the country and in relations with other states.

The rule of the government–is, above all, that it is unbounded by anything except the Constitution, natural law and the law. It is also reflected in the fact that in the state there is no other, competing authorities issuing laws and regulations and freedoms, i.e., dual power is excluded and is recognized as the only legitimate and higher legal force of laws issued by the supreme bodies of state power.

The independence of the government means that only the state has the right to enact legislation and ensure the constitutional order. No political or other forces can intervene into the exclusive right of every public authority to act within their constitutional competence. This independence of the government is necessary to ensure the absence of dependence (political, financial, etc.) of the government on anyone inside and outside the state.

Constitutional principles apply throughout the state mechanism and are divided politically and organizationally. The political principles include:

1. *Separation of powers*. There are three branches of government: legislative, executive and judicial;
2. *Democracy*. According to the guidelines, all citizens have the same opportunity to influence policy and exercise control over the actions of government agencies;
3. *Openness (information).* The contents include the need for sufficient awareness, which provides consistent and systematic coverage of the bodies of state power of the media, and the right of everyone to

receive information that is directly related to his legitimate rights and interests;

4. *Legality (rule-of-law)*–stern and strict observance by all state bodies of legal regulations and laws;
5. *Professionalism and competence.* This principle provides for the mandatory availability of knowledge and skills, the scientific approach to management which is very complex and specific;
6. *Humanism*–a principle which is designed to ensure the priority of the rights and interests of the individual person and the citizen in the implementation of the state apparatus;
7. *Equal access to public service* in accordance with which any person, regardless of nationality, race, religion, etc., has the opportunity to replace their public office, with the same conditions;
8. *Federalism*–a principle which establishes the relationship of government entities in the subjects with federal government agencies;
9. *Local self-government*. The Constitution of the Russian Federation considers local self-government as a form of realization of the people's power, and recognizes and guarantees it. Article 12 of the Constitution provides that "*Local authorities are not included in the system of state power*". Local self-government is a type of power, but the power of the people, not the state. Local self-government, though it is not included in the system of state power, by its nature is still a public authority. Acts of local self-government should be in line with the Constitution and federal laws, and, therefore, it is derived from the state.

The organizational principles of local self-government include:

1. Hierarchy;
2. Differentiation and legislative consolidation of functions and powers;
3. The responsibility of public authorities for their actions and for the non-performance or improper performance of official duties in prescribed authority;
4. The combination of collegiality and unity of command in decision-making;
5. The ratio of sectoral and territorial control.

Economic and Political Fundamentals of the Constitutional System

The Constitution in Article 8 defines the basis of the economic system in Russia.

Constitutional guarantees that define the principles of market economy are as follows:

✓ Unity of economic space;
✓ Free movement of goods, services and financial resources;
✓ Support for the competition.

Another fundamental principle of the market economy is the freedom of economic activity. The freedom of economic activity means that people are free to create and transform enterprise and dispose of the products of their activities in order to profit. They are free to trade and open banks, thus creating economic associations.

Two major provisions concerning property issues are secured in the foundations of the constitutional order of the Russian Federation (Part 2 of Art. 8 of the Constitution):

1) To recognize private property, state property and other forms of property;
2) That all forms of property are protected equally.

An innovation for the constitutional law of Russia is part 2 of Article 9, which establishes that "land and other natural resources may be private, state, municipal and other forms of property". Here is a common approach for property rights in relation to natural resources used as articulated in Article 8 above, i.e. the recognition and protection of all forms of ownership. But the most important and principle is a direct and unconditional binding like privacy and ownership of land.

The recognition of ideological diversity means the right of each man, political party and public organization to promote ideas and theories about the economic, social and political structure of human society, to protect their views and opinions.

Ideological diversity includes:

1) The freedom of ideas and beliefs of the citizens;
2) Political pluralism and the freedom of political organizations;
3) Religious liberty.

The freedom of ideas and views are expressed by the citizens of the Russian Federation in the universal right to determine their own worldview and not set any limits based on these ideas and views.

The political system is a set of interacting norms and ideas based on their political institutions of society, its institutions, organizing political power and the interaction of the state and the individual.

The elements of the political system in Russia:

1) Political parties and associations;
2) The political system of the state, etc.

The Russian political system is based on the principles of multi-party and ideological diversity. The State Duma of the Russian Federation is represented by a large number of political parties that defend the interests of a diverse population, which provides an implementation of the principle of the multi-party system in Russia.

Political diversity (pluralism)–the presence of various destinations in the practice of politics in the country, is expressed as a campaign for or against certain trends, programs, laws, etc., in political life, for or against certain candidates in the election or for a given solution to issues submitted to referendum, etc.

Currently, the aggregate of political parties in Russia is a significant number of political parties and political associations that pursue different goals. Political diversity implies the freedom of citizens to choose the form of participation in the political life of the country. All citizens of the Russian Federation have the right to:

1) Create a voluntary political party in accordance with their beliefs;
2) Join a political party or to refrain from joining a political party;
3) Participate in the activities of political parties in accordance with their charters;
4) Leave political parties.

Religious freedom includes the right of citizens to practice any religion or no religion at all, to freely choose, possess and disseminate religious and other beliefs and to act in accordance with them.

CHAPTER THREE

THE LEGAL STATUS OF THE INDIVIDUAL

The legal status of the individual–is the legally enforceable individual's position in society; it is a complex category which reflects the relationship of the individual and the state.

1. The International Standards of Human Rights and Freedoms

The Institute of Human Rights and Freedoms and the citizen is largely standardized and has regulated many international treaties, covenants and conventions.

The first major international act was the Universal Declaration of Human Rights, adopted by the UN General Assembly on December 10, 1948.

In 1966, the UN General Assembly adopted two more important acts– the *International Covenant on Economic, Social and Cultural Rights* and the *International Covenant on Civil and Political Rights*. These acts provide a more detailed list of human and civil rights, and in addition, the Covenant on Civil and Political Rights provides for the establishment of the Committee for Human Rights.

One of the main instruments of the Council of Europe is the Convention for the Protection of Human Rights and Fundamental Freedoms. This international treaty was signed in 1950 and entered into force on September 3, 1953. The Convention establishes the inalienable rights and freedoms for everyone and requires States to guarantee these rights to each person who is under their jurisdiction. The Convention establishes a mechanism for the protection of the declared rights; this is the *European Court of Human Rights*, which considers individual complaints on violations of the Convention. Any citizen or resident of a country of the Council of Europe, who believes that his or her rights and freedoms set forth in any of the articles of the Convention have been violated, has the opportunity to appeal to the *European Court of Human Rights*.

The Institution of the legal status of the individual occupies an important place in the constitutional law. Constitutional embodiment of the institution was in chapter 2 of the Constitution of the Russian Federation, "The rights and freedoms of man and citizen". The rules of this chapter concretized one of the fundamentals of the constitutional order of Russia, as enshrined in Art. 2 of the Constitution, and in which it is established that a person's rights and freedoms are the supreme value, and the recognition, respect and protection of the rights and freedoms of man and citizen, the obligation of the state. The rules of the institution are also found in the general system of laws, disclosed in detail in the content and order of implementation of the constitutional rights and freedoms of man and citizen. These acts include the laws of the Russian Federation: "On Citizenship of the Russian Federation" (2002), "The Right of Citizens of the Russian Federation to the freedom of movement and choice of residence within the Russian Federation" (1993), the federal constitutional law "On the referendum in the Russian Federation" (2004), "On the Commissioner for Human Rights in the Russian Federation" (1997), and many others.

The constitutional law is a binding framework for personal rights. This is explicitly expressed in Article 64 of the Constitution. It states that the provisions of this chapter are the basis of personal rights in the Russian Federation.

The concept of this basis "reflects, above all, a system of relations between the state and the individual". It includes the *following elements:*

1. *The legal condition* is associated with belonging to the citizenship of regulation of relations over nationality. Citizenship is one of the main elements of the legal status of a person that determines his/her relationship with the state, generally, the main thing you need to spread on the person of all of the rights, freedoms and duties recognized as well as for the protection of his country, wherever that person is located. The possession of citizenship is a universal condition of universal full legal status;
2. *Fundamental rights and freedoms*, which are inseparable from the person, belong to any person as a subject of rights, regardless of their implementation and their capacity Fundamental rights and freedoms are at the core of the legal status of the individual, as a defined set of norms of all branches of Russian law;
3. *Fundamental responsibilities*. The legal status of the individual is characterized not only by the rights and freedoms but by responsibilities as well. These duties involve multiple areas of relationship. Responsibilities are different in their nature. Some of them stem from the fact that the

person is the citizenship of the state, others–are not associated with this status, and are assigned to each;
4. *Guarantees of the rights and freedoms of man and citizen*–a combination of constitutional and legal norms, institutions, tools, techniques, mechanisms and procedures for the implementation, safety and protection of constitutional rights and freedoms of man and citizen.

2. Citizenship of the Russian Federation

Citizenship is a stable legal relationship between a person and the state, as expressed in their mutual rights and obligations. Citizenship of the Russian Federation is one of the institutions of constitutional law in Russia and is regulated by the Constitution and other legal acts of the Russian Federation.

Citizenship Certified Passport

In the Russian Federation, the fundamental principles of citizenship are among the foundations of the constitutional order (Article 6 of the Constitution), nationality is one and equal, regardless of the basis of purchase. A citizen cannot be deprived of his citizenship or the right to change it.

The chapter "*The rights and freedoms of man and citizen*" contains guarantees of citizenship. Thus, a Russian citizen cannot be deported from Russia or extradited to another state. The Russian Federation shall guarantee its citizens protection and patronage abroad.

Federal law governing citizenship in the Russian Federation is *the Federal Law on Citizenship, dated by May 31, 2002.*

Citizenship law governs a wide range of issues related to citizenship, and first of all conditions for the acquisition and termination of citizenship of the Russian Federation. The law regulates the authority of state bodies in charge of the affairs of citizenship and determines the order of proceedings in matters of citizenship.

Article 4 of the Law on Citizenship of the Russian Federation establishes the *principles of citizenship.* Principles of citizenship of the Russian Federation and the rules governing the citizenship of the Russian Federation should not contain provisions that limit the rights of citizens on social, racial, national, linguistic or religious identity;

- ➢ Citizenship of the Russian Federation is uniform and equal regardless of how it was acquired;

- ➢ Residence of a citizen of the Russian Federation outside the Russian Federation does not terminate his Russian citizenship;
- ➢ A Russian citizen cannot be deprived of Russian citizenship or the right to change it;
- ➢ A citizen of the Russian Federation should not be deported from Russia or extradited to a foreign state;
- ➢ Russia promotes the acquisition of Russian citizenship by stateless persons residing in the territory of the Russian Federation;
- ➢ The existence of the citizenship of the Russian Federation or the fact that a person had Soviet citizenship in the past is determined by the laws of the Russian Federation, the Soviet Union or the Russian Federation, international treaties of the Russian Federation or the USSR.

The Russian Constitution allows citizens to hold dual citizenship under federal law or an international treaty of the Russian Federation (Article 62). A foreign citizen may simultaneously have Russian citizenship on the basis of an international agreement (between the State and the Russian Federation). But if there is no international treaty with the State in the Russian Federation then the acquisition of Russian citizenship is possible only if the person renounces previous citizenship. The Constitution clearly states that in the acquisition of a Russian national, second citizenship does not change its legal status as a citizen of Russia. A person retains all rights and freedoms, and it is not released from the obligations arising from Russian citizenship.

Acquisition of Russian Citizenship

Citizenship law establishes *four grounds for the acquisition of citizenship* of the Russian Federation.

Russian citizenship is acquired on the following grounds:

✓ By birth;

✓ As a result of admission to citizenship of the Russian Federation;

✓ As a result of restoration of the citizenship of the Russian Federation;

✓ On other grounds provided for by this Federal law or an international treaty of the Russian Federation.

1. By Birth

By birth ("*filiation*") is not associated with the will of the person and does not require any activity indicating his desire to acquire the nationality of that State. It is performed automatically based on current legislation. At the same time the basic principles "*right of blood*" and the "*right of soil*" apply. The so-called principle of "*blood*" is applied to a child of any person born of citizens of the State. The territory of a State on which a person was born does not matter. The principle of the "*right of soil*" is applied when a child of any person is born on the territory of the State, regardless of the nationality of their parents. Russia is characterized by a combination of the two as for most modern states, but the priority is the "*right of blood*".

A child, whose parents were citizens of the Russian Federation at the time of his birth, also becomes a citizen, regardless of the place of birth. The child is also a citizen of Russia, when one of the parents has Russian citizenship, and the other is a stateless person (the place of birth is not important). If the other parent is a foreign citizen, the situation changes; the child's citizenship is determined by written agreement between the parents, (the place of birth does not matter), and if there is no agreement, then the child acquires Russian citizenship on the condition that he was born in Russia, otherwise he remains stateless. The citizenship of a child born in the territory of Russia, whose parents are foreigners, is defined in such way that the child becomes a citizen of the Russian Federation, if the States do not grant him his citizenship.

The Russian Federation provides a full possibility of acquiring Russian citizenship by birth.

Admission to the citizenship of the Russian Federation (Article 13 Part 1)

1. Foreign citizens and stateless persons who have attained the age of eighteen years and have legal capacity, may apply for citizenship of the Russian Federation, on the condition, that these citizens and persons:

a) *Reside* in the territory of the Russian Federation from the residence permit and up to the date of application for admission to the citizenship of the Russian Federation *for five consecutive years*, except in cases specified in the law. The period of residence in the territory of the Russian Federation shall be considered continuous if the person left the Russian Federation for not more than three months in one year. The period of residence in the territory of the Russian Federation for persons who arrived in the Russian Federation before July 1, 2002 and do not have a residence permit, is calculated from the date of registration of residence and they must;

b) *Undertake to abide by the* Constitution and laws of the Russian Federation;

c) *Have a legitimate source of income*;

d) *Apply to the authority of a foreign country*, with statements renouncing their other existing nationality. Waiver of any other citizenship is not required if there is an international treaty of the Russian Federation or present Federal law or if the failure of the other citizenship is impossible and failed due to reasons beyond the person's control;

e) *Have knowledge of Russian*: the procedure for determining the level of knowledge of the Russian language was established in the regulation of the order of consideration of issues of citizenship of the Russian Federation.

The period of residence in the territory of the Russian Federation is *reduced to one year* if at least one of the following grounds is fulfilled:

a) *The presence of high achievement* in science, technology and culture or if a person in a skilled profession is useful to the Russian Federation;

b) The provision of *individual political asylum* in the Russian Federation;

c) The recognition of *refugee status* in accordance with the federal law.

Persons having special merits to the Russian Federation and the citizens of the states that constituted the Soviet Union, passing at least *three years of military service* under contract in the Armed Forces of the Russian Federation, other troops and military formations, may apply for citizenship of the Russian Federation without complying with the above-mentioned conditions.

Simplified procedure for granting citizenship

Simplified procedure means that a person is not subject to such conditions as provided in paragraph a) of part 1 of Article 13.

Simplified procedure may be applied to persons who:

a) Have at least one parent who is a citizen of the Russian Federation and a resident of the Russian Federation;

b) Had the citizenship of the USSR, lived and currently live in states that were part of the Soviet Union and did not receive citizenship of these countries, and as a result are stateless;

c) Are citizens of the states that constituted the Soviet Union, have received *vocational* or *higher education* in the educational institutions of the Russian Federation since July 1, 2002.

Special simplified procedure applies to individuals who were born on the territory of the Russian Federation, have had citizenship of the former Soviet Union, have been married to a citizen of the Russian Federation for at least three years, who are unable to work and havea capable son or daughter under the age of eighteen years and who are citizens of the

Russian Federation; World War II veterans who had citizenship of the former Soviet Union and were residing in the territory of the Russian Federation and some other category of persons.

Restoration of Citizenship of the Russian Federation

Restoration of Citizenship can be applied to foreign citizens and persons without citizenship, previously having citizenship of the Russian Federation, and the duration of their stay in the Russian Federation *is reduced to three years*.

By "*other reasons*" the law considers the choice of citizenship when there is a change of the state border of the Russian Federation. So, when the state border of the Russian Federation in accordance with the international treaties of the Russian Federation is changed, persons residing in the territory which has changed are entitled to choose their citizenship (*option*) in the manner and timeframe relevant to an international treaty of the Russian Federation.

Grounds for termination of citizenship of the Russian Federation (Article 18)

Citizenship of the Russian Federation shall be terminated:

a) Due to loss of citizenship of the Russian Federation;

b) On other grounds provided by Federal law or an international treaty of the Russian Federation.

The renunciation of citizenship of the Russian Federation is available in three cases:

1. The renunciation of citizenship of the Russian Federation of a person residing in the territory of the Russian Federation shall be based on the free will of the person in a general way;
2. The renunciation of citizenship of the Russian Federation of a person residing in a foreign country pursuant to the voluntary will of the person in a simplified manner;
3. The renunciation of citizenship of the Russian Federation of a child, one of whose parents is a citizen of the Russian Federation and the other parent is a foreign national or a single parent who is a foreign national, is a simplified procedure at the request of both parents, or a single parent, on the application.

Article 20 of the federal law provides *three reasons for the refusal of withdrawal from the citizenship of the Russian Federation*, in cases where a person:

a) Has not performed to the Russian Federation liability established by federal law;

b) Is held by the competent authorities of the Russian Federation as a defendant in a criminal case or in relation to it has come into force and executory judgment of conviction;
c) Has no other citizenship and guarantee of obtaining one.

Acquisition and termination of citizenship are solved only by well-defined public authorities, whose powers are established by law. These bodies are: the President, the Commission on Citizenship under the President of the Russian Federation, the Ministry of Internal Affairs, the Ministry of Foreign Affairs, the diplomatic missions and consular offices of the Russian Federation abroad.

3. Rights and Freedoms in the Russian Federation

Human rights can be classified according to the following reasons:

✓ On the basis of the time period that they were created (generation of human rights);

✓ Areas of activity (private (civil), political, economic, social and cultural rights and freedoms);

✓ The degree of warranty (absolute and those that may be limited);

✓ To individual and collective.

There *are three generations of human rights*.

The first generation includes the traditional values of classical liberalism and the first conquest of the bourgeois revolutions–personal and political rights.

The second generation of human rights is based on the idea of a social reform society where the State guarantees to all people a decent life. A significant role in the second generation of rights is played by social, economic and cultural rights. This is reflected in the *Universal Declaration of Human Nature and the International Covenant on Economic, Social and Cultural Rights* of December 16, 1966.

The third generation of human rights is represented by collective rights (solidarity)–on the world, unpolluted environment, general safety, etc., and does not expand the range of the new character of the individual. Third-generation rights include the protection of the personal status of a person included in the integrity of the social community. There is interaction between individual rights and collective rights based on the principle that collective rights should not restrain individual rights.

The rights and freedoms of man and citizen are divided into *three groups*:

- Personal (civil);
- Political;

➢ Social, economic and cultural.

Scholars have identified the absolute rights and freedoms (those rights and freedoms that cannot be limited under any circumstances), and the rights and freedoms that may be restricted by law. The former include the right to life, human dignity, the right to housing, to judicial protection, freedom of conscience, freedom of entrepreneurship, privacy, etc. The second group includes the freedom of the press, freedom of movement, property, correspondence, etc.

Rights and freedoms are divided into *individual* and *collective*. The majority of individual rights and freedoms of man and citizen may be in groups, while the collective rights and individual freedom cannot be implemented. By collective, in particular, are the right of association (*Article 30 of the Constitution*), the freedom of meetings, rallies, demonstrations, marches (*Article 31),* the right to strike (*Part 4 of Art. 37*), the rights of indigenous peoples and national minorities (Article 69 of the Constitution, the Federal Law № 82-FZ "*On Guarantees of the Rights of Indigenous Peoples of the Russian Federation*", dated April 30, 1999), the right of petition, the right to civil disobedience, etc.

The most common is a division by personal, political and economic, social and cultural rights and freedoms. This classification is arbitrary, because the particular right of nature can be assigned to different groups by its nature. For example, freedom of speech is equally attributed to both the personal and the political rights and the right of private property can be classified as personal and economic as well.

The Constitution introduces the institute restrictions on rights and freedoms for the protection of the constitutional order, morality, health, rights and lawful interests of persons, the defence and security of the State.

There are two important conditions:

➢ The rights may be limited by federal law only;

➢ Only to the extent that this is necessary.

Article 19 of the Constitution fixes the principles of equity and equality. First of all, it is established that "*all are equal in face of the law*." The sense of formal equality is to provide equal opportunities to all, the implementation of which has been dependent on the abilities of each person. Equally important is the equality of persons before the court. The legal status of a person does not matter–every person, citizens and non-citizens as well as foreigners are tried in equal status receiving equal protection of their legal rights.

The Constitution prohibits any form of discrimination. The State shall guarantee the equality of rights and freedoms of man and citizen, regardless of sex, race, nationality, language, origin, property and official status, place of residence, religion, convictions, membership of public associations, and also of other circumstances. All forms of limitations of human rights on social, racial, national, linguistic or religious grounds shall be banned. Man and woman shall enjoy equal rights and freedoms and have equal possibilities to exercise them.

Personal rights and freedoms

Personal (civil) rights and freedoms–those rights and freedoms that constitute the basis of the constitutional and legal status of the individual, providing constitutional protection of the privacy of a person from undue interference by the state and other entities. Most of these rights and freedoms are natural and absolute, and available to all members of society in Russia, regardless of whether they have citizenship of the Russian Federation or not.

Personal rights and freedoms enshrined in the Constitution in Articles from 20 to 29.

Article 20 recognizes the right to life.

1. *Everyone shall have the right to life.*
2. *Capital punishment until its complete elimination may be envisaged by a federal law as an exclusive penalty for especially grave crimes against life, and the accused shall be granted the right to have his case examined by jury trial.*

The right to life is at the maximum legal protection. This is the way it is enshrined in the international instruments which are very clearly defined cases limiting this right. The Russian Constitution recognizes that the right to life cannot be limited by the state of emergency (Article 56).

The death penalty in Russia has been indefinitely suspended although it is legally allowed. There exists both an implicit *moratorium* established by the President and an explicit one, established by the nation's highest court. Russia has not executed anyone since 1996, and the regulations of the Council of Europe prohibit it from doing so at any time in the future. However, the death penalty still remains codified. In November 2009, the Constitutional Court of Russia extended the ban. The Constitutional Court of the Russian Federation recognized the impossibility of the death penalty, even after the introduction of *jury trials* throughout Russia, explaining it by the fact that after a long moratorium on the death penalty there have developed consistent guaranteed human rights not to be subjected to the death penalty.

Article 21 says:

1. *Human dignity shall be protected by the State. Nothing may serve as a basis for its derogation;*

2. *No one shall be subject to torture, violence or other severe or humiliating treatment or punishment. No one may be subject to medical, scientific and other experiments without voluntary consent.*

The Russian Constitution protects the dignity of the individual, establishing an absolute principle: "*Nothing can be the basis for its derogation*". There are many other provisions of the Constitution which aim to protect dignity: the right to live in dignity, privacy, the protection of man's honour and good name, the prohibition of collecting information about private life, the prohibition of forced entry into the home, etc. This principle is revealed in criminal law and criminal procedure. Thus, in the Criminal Code there are offences such as libel and slander. The Code of Criminal Procedure requires that the investigator must take steps during the search to ensure that it does not announce and identify the intimate circumstances of the life of a person.

The Civil Code of Russia classifies the life, health, dignity, personal integrity, honour and good name, reputation, privacy, personal and family privacy, the right to a name and credit of authorship and other constitutional rights and personal freedom as intangible benefits (Article 150).

Article 22 says:

1. *Everyone shall have the right to freedom and personal immunity.*
2. *Arrest, detention and remanding in custody shall be allowed only by court decision. Without the court's decision a person may not be detained for a term more than 48 hours.*

The right to freedom is the ability to take any legitimate action. No one has the right to force or threaten to compel a person to any action, expose him to search or be harmful. The man has self-determination. Restrictions of this freedom may only be based on the law and legal forms, all coercive measures should be under judicial control. The Constitution sets such an important guarantee of freedom and personal integrity as a judicial procedure for arrest, detention and custody.

Articles 23 and 24 of the Constitution provide *the right to privacy.* They say that everyone shall have the right to the inviolability of private life, personal and family secrets, the protection of honour and good name. One more important statement is that everyone shall have the right to privacy of correspondence, of telephone conversations, postal, telegraph and other messages. Limitations of this right shall be allowed only by court decision. The collection, keeping, use and dissemination of information about the private life of a person shall not be allowed without his or her consent. The bodies of state authority and local self-government and their officials shall ensure the possibility of acquainting everyone with the documents and materials directly affecting his or her rights and freedoms, unless otherwise provided for by law.

Civil society is based on the fact that the invasion of privacy in order to identify the illegal actions of a person should only be made on the basis of the law if there are legitimate grounds for suspicion or accusation of the person of a crime, that is, in a criminal case. Outside of that privacy is inviolable. The institute of privacy includes a lot of different safeguards that are contained in various articles of the Constitution.

Article 25 establishes the right of privacy of the home. The home shall be inviolable. No one shall have the right to get into a house against the will of those living there, except for the cases established by a federal law or by court decision.

The right to protection of homes belongs to persons who are their owners, tenants or legal residents. The place of temporary stay is recognized as housing as well (hotel, hostel and pension). Inviolability applies to personal items and papers, which eliminates the illegal search and seizure of documents.

In certain circumstances it is necessary to penetrate a home against the will of its inhabitants. This is possible only by law or court order. Laws in this case are the Criminal Procedure Code, the Police Act and so on. The Court must immediately consider the material on entry into a home in search operations.

Besides the individual rights and freedoms which are traditionally found in democratic constitutions the Constitution of the Russian Federation provides norms, which are rather rare in the other constitutions, such as the right to determine nationality and the right to use the native language.

> *Everyone shall have the right to determine and indicate his nationality. No one may be forced to determine and indicate his or her nationality. Everyone shall have the right to use his or her native language, to a free choice of the language of communication, upbringing, education and creative work.* (Article 26)

The right to determine nationality does not entail any legal consequences since under Russian law no one can enjoy the privileges or be discriminated based on nationality.

Thus, the state considers ethnicity as a purely private matter of man and as the question of his self-identification. The language of communication is established by the people themselves, without any regulation. The person has all the constitutional rights and freedoms, regardless of knowledge of a language. Russian citizens have the right to appeal to the authorities in their native language or any other language of the peoples of Russia that they know. These constitutional provisions are implemented through the Law on Languages of the Peoples of the Russian Federation 1991.

Article 28 recognizes the *right to free travel and choice of place of residence.* Everyone who legally stays in the territory of the Russian Federation shall have the right to free travel and choice of place of stay or residence. Everyone may freely leave the Russian Federation. Citizens of the Russian Federation shall have the right to freely return to the Russian Federation.

The right to choice of place of residence is realized in a certain order. The law establishes the obligation of the citizen who is coming to a new place of residence to register with the police within seven days. The registration and removal of citizens of the Russian Federation with the register at the place of stay or residence within Russia by the rules were approved by the Government of the Russian Federation of July 17, 1995. These Rules regulate in detail the rights and responsibilities of citizens, the freedom of movement and the seat of the person and residence.

Also, these questions are regulated by the *Law on the Right of Citizens of the Russian Federation to the freedom of movement and choice of residence within the Russian Federation* on June 25, 1993. The law restricts the freedom of movement in certain areas (in the frontier zone, closed military bases in areas with emergency or martial law, etc.). Therefore, outside of such areas no other restrictions are allowed.

The constitutional *right to leave the Russian Federation and return freely* is also very important. The procedure for the exercise of this right is set by the Law on the Procedure for Exit and Entry from and into the Russian Federation. The exit of citizens having access to state secrets is separately regulated.

Article 28 says that:

> *everyone shall be guaranteed the freedom of conscience, the freedom of religion, including the right to profess individually or together with other any religion or to profess no religion at all, to freely choose, possess and disseminate religious and other views and act according to them.*

The freedom of conscience and religion deals with *a Federal Law: "On Freedom of Conscience and Religious Associations" of 1997.*

The Russian Constitution in Article 29 *guarantees freedom of thought and speech*, but it quickly finds that the propaganda or agitation instigating social, racial, national or religious hatred and strife shall not be allowed. The propaganda of social, racial, national, religious or linguistic supremacy shall be banned. Also no one may be forced to express his views and convictions or to reject them.

Manifold manifestations of freedom of speech give reason to take it in equal measure to the personal and to the political rights. So the first three parts of Article 29 interpreted this freedom as personal, and the other two– as political terms.

In contrast to the personal rights that belong to everyone, many political rights and freedoms belong only to citizens of the state. This situation is explained by the above-mentioned specificity of this group of rights and freedoms. But all political rights and freedoms that belong to both man and citizen shall enjoy equal legal protection, guaranteed by the state, although the content of many of them involve criticism, dissent, opposition to the government, and direct action against the government.

The first political rights in the Constitution mention the freedom of the press and the prohibition of censorship.

> *Everyone shall have the right to freely look for, receive, transmit, produce and distribute information by any legal way. The list of data comprising state secrets shall be determined by a federal law. The freedom of mass communication shall be guaranteed. Censorship shall be banned.* (Article 29 pp. 4, 5)

In the development of these provisions of the Constitution were adopted such laws as the Federal Law of 1991 "*On mass media*", the Federal Law of 1995 "*On Information, Informatization and Protection of Information*" and the Federal Law of 1993 "*On State Secrets*".

Article 30 declares that everyone shall have *the right to association, including the right to create trade unions for the protection of his or her interests.* The freedom of activity of public association shall be guaranteed and no one may be compelled to join any association and remain in it.

Associations are formed without the prior permission of government agencies, and their articles are accepted by themselves and only registered with the Ministry of Justice and its agencies. The Ministry supervises the legality of the goals and objectives of an association and the financial authorities supervise the source of their income. Public associations can only be dissolved in two cases (and only by a court decision): 1) the violation of Part 5, Art. 13 of the Constitution, and other criminal acts, 2) recommit during one year of action beyond the statutory goals and objectives, or violations of law.

On July 11, 2001 a *Federal Law on Political Parties* was passed. Prior to that, the creation and activity of political parties were governed by the Law on Associations of 1995.

The creation of party organizations in government–the military, the police, the prosecution service, the higher education institutions–is prohibited. Political parties and movements are not entitled to create their structures on the production principle.

Article 31 says that the citizens of the Russian Federation shall have the right to assemble peacefully without weapons, hold rallies, meetings and demonstrations, marches and pickets. In the Russian Federation the right only belongs to its citizens while the International Covenant on Civil and Political Rights provides for it without the restriction.

Public events are regulated by Federal Law of the Russian Federation "*on the meetings, marches, demonstrations and pickets*" in 2004, which requires for a notification procedure to hold public events. Notice (a written statement) is served on the local administration. The notification shall specify the objectives, timing and location of the event. The local administration is obliged to consider it and give an answer about the decision. It may propose to change the time and place of the event, but the decision may be appealed to a higher executive and administrative body.

The right to participate in managing the affairs of a state belongs only to the citizens of the Russian Federation as it is stated in Article 32 of the Constitution. It could be done in two ways–*directly* and *through the representatives*. This right is regulated by Article 3 and specifically establishes the right of citizens to participate in referendums and free elections, and to be elected to bodies of state power and bodies of local self-government, and to have access to public service and justice, access to state and local governments.

Unlike many foreign constitutions, the Russian Constitution does not contain a chapter about the election. The most common standards are included in Parts 2 and 3 of Article 32. Specific rules are associated with the election of the President and the Federal Assembly. However the Constitution provides that the procedure for the election to these bodies of state power must be determined by federal law. General principles of electoral law were provided for by the Constitution of the Russian Federation and the Federal Law on Basic Guarantees of Electoral Rights of Citizens of the Russian Federation in 2005. Russian legislation provides for the following basic principles of electoral rights–universality, equality, freedom of expression and direct suffrage by secret ballot. The Russian Constitution provides for active and passive suffrage.

Right of choice means that a citizen cannot be refused inclusion in the voting lists, to be issued ballot papers, or the possibility of nominating candidates for certain positions in accordance with the law. This right includes the full range of rights related to the influence on the formation of national government.

The right to vote (active suffrage) is available to citizens from the age of 18 years.

Passive suffrage is the ability to raise himself as a candidate for any elected office. Passive suffrage occurs at different ages–depending on the nature of a public authority or a local government. So, for the election of the President of Russia a person should be 35 years old, and for the election as the deputy of the State Duma–21 years old.

Suffrage realized by citizens of the Russian Federation is completely voluntary. Russia does not establish *compulsory voting*.

The Constitution specifically provides for the deprivation of electoral rights of citizens: it is about two categories of citizens: recognized as incapable and sentenced to imprisonment by a court, and in both cases it requires judgement.

Citizens of the Russian Federation shall enjoy equal access to the state service.

Equal access to public service means the right of citizens to engage in any public office without discrimination and equal opportunity for every citizen to join the public service in the presence of vacancies and professional correspondence. You cannot deny a citizen because of his race, sex, nationality, language, social origin, property, place of residence, attitude to religion, convictions, membership of public associations, etc.

Questions of the civil service are regulated by the *Federal Law on Civil Service* on July 31 1995. The right to enter the service is possessed by citizens aged at least 18 years, and the age limit for public office is 60 years. The replacement must be done by appointment or by tender.

The right to participate in the administration of justice is to ensure the formation of a democratic order of the judiciary. It provides an opportunity for every citizen, without discrimination, to take the position of a judge, or to be a juror or lawyer.

Citizens of the Russian Federation shall have the right to personally address, as well as to *submit individual and collective appeals,* to state bodies and local self-government bodies. This right includes the possibility to put in a request, complaint or suggestion to any body and any officer, up to the President of Russia, and the duty of the officer is to respond to this appeal. Appeal can keep personal issues as well as public.

Article 34 ofthe Constitution regulates the *economic, social and cultural rights and freedoms*. The economic, social and cultural rights reveal the meaning of the social state. One of the obligations of the social state is to provide to the citizens the opportunity of a decent life.

The legal process of these rights is not the same. Some certain rights are the rights of direct action, others are subjective rights, the specific content of which flows from sector-specific legislation, others rise to the state only as the general duty to assist in policy implementation.

The right to economic activities includes the freedom of use of a person's abilities and property for entrepreneurialism and not forbidden by the law of economic activities (Article 34 of the Constitution).

Entrepreneurship is an independent activity at a person's own risk aiming for systematic profit from the use of property, sale of goods, works or services by persons registered as such in accordance with the law (Article 2 of the Civil Code).

The state prohibits certain kinds of economic activity but allows some activities with special permits (licences). Public authorities may require entrepreneur financial statements, without affecting trade secrets.

The right to private property is often seen as an economic right and as private. It belongs to everyone and is one of the cornerstones of freedom of the individual, as well–one of the fundamentals of the constitutional system, as established by Articles 8 and 9 of the Constitution. The right to private property has a broad concept. The owner has the right to perform any action with property, if it is not contrary to the laws and does not violate the rights and lawful interests of other persons.

The Constitution of the Russian Federation establishes an important legal guarantee of the *right for private property*. *Firstly*, no one can be deprived of his property except by court order. *Secondly*, expropriation of property for public use can be made only with prior and fair compensation. Guarantee of the right of private property is the right of inheritance. After his death an owner's property passes to the heirs at law or by will. Inheritance law will ensure the implementation of ownership over the property and at the same time ensure fairness, especially when it comes to protecting the interests of the disabled or young relatives.

The Constitution enshrines the right to private ownership of the land (Article 36). It belongs only to the citizens of the Russian Federation, as well as their associations.

The Constitution stipulates that the possession, use and disposal of land and other natural resources are managed by the owners freely, if this does not harm the environment and does not violate the rights and lawful interests of other persons. There are only two constitutional limitations on the right of private ownership of land, under which the owner is left free in their actions. But this freedom is very relative, because in the same article of the Constitution it stipulates that the conditions and procedure for the possession of the land shall be determined on the basis of federal law–the *Land Code* of 2001.

Article 37 regulates the right to work.

1. *Labour is free. Everyone shall have the right to freely use his labour capabilities, to choose the type of activity and profession;*
2. *Forced labour shall be banned;*
3. *Everyone shall have the right to labour conditions meeting the safety and hygienic requirements, for labour remuneration without any discrimination whatsoever and not lower than minimum wages and salaries established by the federal law, as well as the right to protection against unemployment;*
4. *Recognition shall be given to the right to individual and collective labour disputes with the use of methods of their adjustment fixed by the federal law, including the right to strike;*
5. *Everyone shall have the right to rest and licence. Those working by labour contracts shall be guaranteed the fixed duration of the working time, days off and holidays, and the annual paid leave established by the federal law.*

The Russian Constitution provides the freedom of labour. A person has the right to work as well as to stay away from work. There is no such constitutional duty to work. The labour rights are regulated in detail by the *Labour Code* 2001.

The state helps unemployed citizens with employment. The Labour Code protects employees against unlawful dismissal. In the absence of work there is the possibility for its citizens to get unemployment benefits.

The Constitution provides the right to strike as the solution of labour disputes with the use specified by federal law for their resolution.

Everyone has the right to rest but for those who work under an employment contract the Constitution has guaranteed the statutory working hours, weekends and holidays, and paid annual leave. The current Labour Code sets the maximum working time of 40 hours a week.

Article 38 says:

1. Maternity and childhood and the family shall be protected by the State;

2. Care for children and their upbringing shall be equally the right and obligation of parents;

3. Able-bodied children over 18 years of age shall take care of disabled parents.

The State contributes to the strengthening of the family, prohibits discrimination in marriage, and establishes the equality of men and women.

Motherhood and childhood are protected and other legal branches. Most full marital and family relations are governed by the *Family Code* 1995.

Care for children and their education is the right and duty of parents and they have no right to transfer to the function of the state. Parents have equal rights and responsibilities for the upbringing of children, ensuring their health, education and economic status. All the issues of child rearing, both in marriage and at its dissolution, are decided by the parents together.

Article 39 establishes the right to social security as follows:

1. *Everyone shall be guaranteed social security at the expense of the State in old age, in case of an illness, disability, loss of the bread-winner, for upbringing of children and in other cases established by law;*
2. *State pensions and social allowances shall be established by law;*
3. *Promotion shall be given to voluntary social insurance and the creation of additional forms of social security and charity.*

The principle of a democratic society is that everyone must ensure their existence themselves. But in any society there are people who are not able to do this.

Each of these cases is characterized by loss of earnings or insufficiencies for the sustenance of man and disabled family members.

The law sets the retirement age for men at 60 years and for women from 55 years, linking pensions with work experience. In detail the grounds for a disability pension are the loss of capacity for the long term or on a permanent basis, as well as the loss of a breadwinner. The main act governing state pensions is a Federal Law on Retirement Pensions 2001.

Article 40 is dedicated to the right to a home.

1. *Everyone shall have the right to a home. No one may be arbitrarily deprived of his or her home;*
2. *The bodies of state authority and local self-government shall encourage housing construction and create conditions for exercising the right to a home;*
3. *Low-income people and other persons mentioned in law and in need of a home shall receive it gratis or for reasonable payment from the state, municipal and other housing stocks according to the norms fixed by law.*

The Constitution stipulates that the State and local governments encourage housing construction and create conditions for the realization of the right to a home. This is the material guarantee of the right. But the centre of gravity moves from state provision to the actual provision of people–from their own funds, loans, etc. But there is a category of people that stands by the Constitution as eligible for priority and the preferential provision of housing. We are talking about the poor and others specified in the law as requiring citizens' homes, which the government agrees to provide out of state, municipal and other funds for free or for a reasonable fee.

The next right in the Russian Constitution is *the right to health protection and medical aid (Article 41).*

1. *Everyone shall have the right to health protection and medical aid. Medical aid in state and municipal health establishments shall be rendered to individuals gratis, at the expense of the corresponding budget, insurance contributions, and other proceeds;*
2. *In the Russian Federation federal programmes of protecting and strengthening the health of the population shall be financed by the State; measures shall be adopted to develop state, municipal and private health services; activities shall be promoted which facilitate the strengthening of health, the development of physical culture and sport, ecological and sanitary-epidemiological well-being;*
3. *The concealment by officials of the facts and circumstances posing a threat to the life and health of people shall entail responsibility according to the federal law.*

Health protection is a comprehensive institution which includes the training of medical personnel, numerous social, organizational, economic, scientific, medical, sanitary and epidemiological and preventive measures that must carry the State in the interests of their citizens. The right to health protection means the combination of these duties, with the assistance of state agencies of public organizations to create a national health care system.

Right to medical aid is a subjective human right to be treated in clinics, hospitals and special hospitals. Medical aid in the state and municipal health care centres is provided to citizens free of charge at the expense of the budget, insurance premiums and other revenues. This assistance is provided to all citizens without any discrimination. The right to health and medical aid is regulated by the Federal Law on Health Care 2011.

The following policies are for the environmental rights (Article 42) of the next generation. Everyone shall have the right to a favourable environment, reliable information about its state and for a restitution of damage inflicted on his health and property by ecological transgressions. It is important that information about the state of the environment should not be a state secret. Information on the state of the environment is possessed by competent state bodies and they are required to provide it even without any requirements.

The Russian Constitution provides for the *right to education* (Article 43) and establishes different approaches to obtain basic types of education. Pre-school, basic secondary (high school of 9 classes) and vocational (technical and vocational schools) education in state and municipal educational institutions and enterprises is public and free. The Constitution also guarantees free higher education. However, the Constitution does not provide for full accessibility of this level of education, and provides citizens with the right to receive it on a competitive basis.

Basic general education is free of charge. And there are parents or guardians who shall enable their children to receive a basic general education.

Also, the Russian Federation establishes federal state educational standards and supports various forms of education and self-education.

Article 44 establishes the *freedom of creative activity and the right to participate in cultural life* as follows:

1. *Everyone shall be guaranteed the freedom of literary, artistic, scientific, technical and other types of creative activity, and teaching. Intellectual property shall be protected by law.*
2. *Everyone shall have the right to participate in cultural life and use cultural establishments and to have access to cultural values.*
3. *Everyone shall be obliged to care for the preservation of cultural and historical heritage and protect monuments of history and culture.*

The constitutional provision on the protection of intellectual property is very important. Intellectual property refers to the exclusive rights to the results of creative activity. Intellectual property is very diverse. Copyright on the results of an author's work is recognized for the author during his lifetime and for his heirs for 50 years after the author's death. The patent is valid for 20 years. Violation of the rights of authors leads to compensation of damages and lost profits.

The right to participate in cultural life extends to the use of cultural institutions and access to culture. The state is obliged to ensure the availability of theatres, art exhibitions and museums for all citizens.

4. Constitutional Duties of Man and Citizen

Responsibilities are an integral part of the legal status of the individual. They are closely related to the rights and freedoms of man and citizen, and this should be explained by the fact that most of the duties are assigned in chapter two of the Constitution of Russia, although some responsibilities are written in chapter one.

Most of the duties are addressed to the citizens of Russia but there are also those that apply to foreigners and stateless persons.

The main responsibility lies with all persons in the territory of the Russian Federation–this is the *observance of the Constitution and the laws described* in Part 2 of Article 15 of the Constitution of Russia. The upholding of the Constitution and laws is the universal rule that knows no exceptions.

The next duty is *respect for the rights and freedoms of others*. This is an essential condition of freedom; it has necessary limitations and the fundamental principle of the rule of law. Part 3 of Article 17 of the Constitution provides that the rights and freedoms of man and citizen shall not violate the rights and freedoms of others. The implementation of this obligation is based on a developed sense of justice of the majority of society.

The care of children and disabled parents is contained in Parts 2 and 3 of Article 38 of the Constitution. Thus are secured two constitutional duties of citizens. First, parents should take care of children and their upbringing. Second, able-bodied children over 18 years should take care of disabled parents. These charges express the personal responsibility of the individual for the fate of their parents and children, when they are not in a position to provide for their own subsistence needs.

The duty to receive basic general education is entrusted to every citizen, and the parents or parents-in-law must ensure that their children receive an education (Part 4 of Article 43). Naturally, the children cannot be held liable for a breach of this duty. The only consequence for an uneducated person is the inability to receive revenue without matriculation to university classes and a number of posts.

The duty of parents to ensure children get an education is more specific, but the breach of duty does not imply any liability as well.

The care of monuments of history and culture is addressed to all. Everyone must take care to preserve the historical and cultural heritage and protect monuments of history and culture (Part 3 of Article 44 of the Constitution). The relationship in this area regulates framework legislation of the Russian Federation on culture in 1992, *the Law "On the Protection and Use of Historical and Cultural Monuments"* of 1978. The Presidential Decree of 1995 approved a list of historical and cultural heritage of federal (national) value, including such facilities throughout the country.

Everyone is obliged to *pay the legally established taxes and fees* (Article 57 of the Constitution). This is a requirement for a person and citizen who lives in the community and enjoys the benefits of government activities.

Taxes are divided into federal, federation members and local. They are paid in a certain size and in a pre-specified time. For evasion and violation of the order of payment of taxes the taxpayers bear the administrative costs and in some cases face criminal prosecution.

The preservation of the environment is not only the duty of every person, but also one of the global problems for which a solution is of paramount importance. The Russian Constitution states: "*Everyone shall be obliged to preserve nature and the environment, and care for the natural resources* (Article 58)".

Constitutional duty is concretized in a number of legislative acts. Thus, *the Law "On Environmental Protection", dated by 2002* establishes an obligation of citizens to comply with environmental laws and established standards of environmental quality. There are also the *Air Code 1997*, the *Water Code 2006,* the *Land Code 2001*, the *Forest Code 2006*, the *Law on Mineral Resources 1992,* and other acts.

The Russian Constitution declares the *protection of the Fatherland "duty and obligation of the citizen of the Russian Federation*" (Article 59).

Citizens of Russia perform military service in accordance with Federal law.

Federal law "*On Military Duty and Military Service"* 1998 regulates that military service is urged for all male citizens between the ages of 18 and 27 who are not eligible for exemption or deferment of army call.

There are many people whose beliefs or religious beliefs contradict military service. In these and in other cases provided by law citizens have the right to replace military service by alternative civil service. *Alternative service* can be done in health centres and other institutions as stated in the Federal law on Alternative Civil Service 2002.

5. Constitutional Guarantees of Rights and Freedoms

Guarantees are legal means to ensure the implementation of human and civil rights. Constitutional guarantees of rights and freedoms are the duty of the State. The Constitution of the Russian Federation contains special provisions which guarantee the rights and freedoms of citizens.

These guarantees can be divided into two groups:

- *General guarantees*;
- *Guarantees' justice.*

The protection of rights and freedoms is the duty of the State. The Constitution guarantees that the State protects the rights and freedoms of man and citizen in Part 1 of Article 45. This general rule establishes the obligation of the state by various legal means to ensure the protection of rights and freedoms. A large role in this regard is given to the President who is the guarantor of the rights and freedoms.

The Constitution provides the right of men to protect their rights and freedoms by all means not prohibited by law (Part 2 of Article 45). Such a guarantee is called self-defence. The methods of self-defence are manifold such as the appeal of actions of officials, handling to the media, the use of human rights organizations and non-government organizations, etc. Citizens have the right to defend their rights by weapons as set out in the *Weapons Act of 1993*. This act provides the right to purchase and use firearms for the protection of life, health and property.

The Russian Constitution guarantees everyone the *judicial protection of his rights and freedoms* (Article 46). Such protection is the most effective and is accessible to everyone, because courts allow appeals to the decisions and actions (or inaction) of state authorities, local self-government, public associations and officials. The object of the appeal may be laws, acts and decrees of the President, the decision of the Government, etc. The Courts supervise legality in the country and give priority to the rights and freedoms of citizens before any shares in the state.

The Russian Constitution gives everyone the *right to make a complaint to international bodies for the protection of human rights and freedoms* (Part 3 of Article 46). This right is due to the presence of the relevant international treaties of the Russian Federation and is used when all available domestic remedies have been exhausted. This means that a complaint may be filed after consideration in the three courts of the Russian Federation. Complaints must not be anonymous and do not represent an abuse of the right of appeal and they should not be given to several international bodies.

At present the Russian Federation is a party to two international treaties: the International Covenant on Civil and Political Rights and the European Convention for the Protection of Human Rights and Fundamental Freedoms, according to which persons under the jurisdiction of the Russian Federation may appeal to international bodies for the protection of their rights. Russian citizens may apply for international protection in two instances–the *UN Committee on Human Rights* and the *European Court of Human Rights*. If a person applies for protection to the United Nations, the appeal is submitted to the Committee on Human Rights, established in accordance with the *International Covenant on Civil and Political Rights 1966*. Russia's accession to the Optional Protocol of the Covenant creates the conditions for the realization of the constitutional right of access to that authority. The complaint is brought to the attention of the proper State and within six months it shall submit to the Committee written explanations or statements clarifying the matter and notify the measures taken. The Committee is not empowered to make binding decisions but publishes an annual report on complaints which entails negative political consequences for the state in which human rights are violated.

The European Convention on Human Rights was adopted in 1950. The Convention adopted a number of inherent civil and political rights for the Member States of the Council of Europe. The European Court of Human Rights was set up in 1959 to deal with individual complaints and appeals of citizens for the violation of the rights and freedoms provided for by the Convention. The main function of the Court is to verify the compliance of States Parties' obligations under the European Convention, and to make decisions about whether the state has violated any of the provisions of the Convention. Violation of the European Convention can take place at three different levels:

- ✓ When the public authorities themselves violate the Convention;
- ✓ When the authorities have failed to conduct a proper investigation of violation and cannot provide adequate reparation to the victims of violations;
- ✓ When the state does not protect citizens from violation of their rights.

The procedure of the European Court of Human Rights was largely simplified in 1998. The trial, which operated until 1998 as a bicameral body, consisting of the European Commission of Human Rights and the European Court of Human Rights, has been converted into a single body, and began to act only as the European Court of Human Rights, which has worked on a permanent basis.

Violation of rights and freedoms is often accompanied by an injury to the person. The constitutional guarantee in such cases is not only to restore the right violated and provide its implementation, but also relates to the compensation of the human material and moral damages caused. According to Article 53 of the Constitution, "*everyone has the right to state compensation for damages caused by unlawful actions (or inaction) of state bodies and their officials*". Compensation is subject to the harm caused to a person, such as illegal criminal charges, unlawful conviction and unlawful detention or house arrest or the illegal imposition of an administrative penalty in the form of arrest or community service. The amount of compensation of damages is determined by the court which also has the right to determine the compensation (compensation) for moral damages caused to a person.

The Russian Constitution in Part 2 of Article 55 sets the irrevocability of the rights and freedoms–"*in the Russian Federation no laws shall be adopted cancelling or derogating human rights and freedoms*". The Constitution allows for the possibility of restricting the rights and freedoms of man and citizen. But the restrictions are not identical to the cancellation or diminution of rights and freedoms and are implemented only to the extent that it is strictly necessary in as established by the Constitution.

An important constitutional guarantee of personal rights is the establishment in Russia of the *Commissioner for Human Rights* (Part 1 ofArticle 103). The establishment of the Commissioner for Human Rights in the Russian Federation as a state agency is one of the most important achievements of democratic reform in Russia. The Commissioner for Human Rights in the Russian Federation was established in order to guarantee the protection of public rights and freedoms of citizens, their observance of and respect for government agencies, local authorities, officials and public servants. His activity complements the existing means of protecting the rights and freedoms of citizens, which do not change and do not involve a review of the competence of state bodies ensuring the protection and restoration of violated rights and freedoms. The Federal Constitutional Law "*On the Commissioner for Human Rights in the Russian Federation*" entered into force in 1997. It defined the status of the Commissioner, his competence, appointment and dismissal. Federal constitutional law established that the Commissioner for Human Rights is independent and accountable to any government agencies and officials.

The main activities of the Commissioner for Human Rights in the Russian Federation are the following:

- ✓ Complaints and appeals on violations of the rights and freedoms of man and citizen and the adoption of measures for their rehabilitation;
- ✓ Analysis of the legislation of the Russian Federation in the field of human and civil rights and to make recommendations for its improvement and alignment with the generally recognized principles and norms of international law;
- ✓ Development of international cooperation in the field of human rights;
- ✓ Legal education on human rights and freedoms, forms and methods of their protection;
- ✓ Preparing an annual report on its activities and the direction of the President of the Russian Federation, the Federation Council and the State Duma, the Government of the Russian Federation, the

Constitutional Court of the Russian Federation, the Supreme Court of the Russian Federation and the Prosecutor General of the Russian Federation;

- ✓ Making presentations at meetings of the State Duma in cases of gross or mass violations of human rights and freedoms;
- ✓ The direction of the State Duma of special reports on specific issues of rights and freedoms of citizens in the Russian Federation;
- ✓ Appeal to the State Duma with a proposal to create a parliamentary commission to investigate violations of the rights and freedoms of citizens, and to hold parliamentary hearings, participation in the work of these committees and conducted hearings;
- ✓ Recourse to the courts of general jurisdiction and the Constitutional Court of the Russian Federation for the protection of the rights and freedoms of citizens;
- ✓ Action on its own initiative, appropriate measures within their competence when there is information about mass and gross violations of human rights and freedoms of citizens, or in cases of particular public importance or the need to protect the interests of persons not able to use their own legal remedies;
- ✓ Analysis of legal practice in the field of human and civil rights and proposals for its improvement;
- ✓ Informing the public authorities and the public on the status of the rights and freedoms of citizens in the Russian Federation;
- ✓ Direction of state authorities, local self-government and officials of the comments and suggestions of a general nature relating to the rights and freedoms of man and citizen, to improve administrative procedures.

The Constitution of the Russian Federation establishes that a Russian citizen may exercise fully their rights and obligations at the age of 18 (Article 60). The key words in this rule are the words "self" and "in full" because citizens have the constitutional right and at an earlier age, selling them through their legal representatives.

The Russian Constitution enshrines the conventional warranties that are also the principles of democratic justice. These guarantees lay the basis of the criminal procedure law and seek to avoid arbitrariness in the proceedings.

It is important that the case is heard in court and by the judge who should consider it in accordance with the law. The definition of the law of that court and the judge is called jurisdiction. Jurisdiction is a set of symptoms of the case according to which the court is competent to hear the case as a court of first instance is determined by the procedural law.

This rule applies to any judicial process. The Constitution says: "No one may be deprived of the right to the consideration of his or her case in that court and by that judge in whose cognizance the given case is according to law" (Part 1 of Article 47).

An important guarantee of democratic justice is *the jury* (Part 2 of Article 20 and Part 2 of Article 47). A jury is recognized as the most reliable system of judicial protection of the rights and legitimate interests of the individual against arbitrariness and judicial error. The Constitution guarantees the accused of a crime the right to have his case tried by jury in cases provided for by federal law. Jurors in their judgement act independently of the professional courts. The doubtless advantage of a jury lies in the fact that it is provided with the use of the law as it is understood by the public. It should be convinced of the fact that a person brought before the court understands or could understand the law, and a violation of which he was convicted. A jury composed of citizens of the Russian Federation is responsible for only one question about the guilt or innocence of the defendant. The jurors are chosen by lot from among voters aged from 25 to 70 years.

The natural and inalienable right of every human being is *the right to legal aid*. The right to legal assistance is universal, since it acts as a constitutional guarantee of the effective implementation of all other rights and freedoms. The right to legal assistance is a subjective ability of individuals to use the services of a specialist lawyer in violation or threatened violation of their real rights and interests protected by law.

The right to legal assistance has its inherent principles. The main ones are: the freedom of every person to choose a person who is able to provide legal assistance, the freedom of human communication with a person providing him legal assistance and the principle of confidentiality of communication with the provider of legal aid. The minimum standards for competent legal assistance are mandatory requirements to its quality which include: the availability of legal education in the person providing legal assistance; presentation for a person providing certain types of legal aid and special requirements (membership in the bar association, etc.), the activity and constructiveness of legal aid. The assistance of counsel is payable. But not every person is able to pay for this care. Therefore the Constitution provides that in cases provided by law legal assistance is provided free of charge. This constitutional provision has an important meaning, which sets out that each person detained, arrested or accused of a crime has the right to legal counsel (a lawyer) from the moment of arrest, detention or indictment (Article 48 of the Constitution).

In the Constitution of the Russian Federation, the definition of the principle of the presumption of innocence is given in Part 1 of Article 49: "*Everyone accused of committing a crime shall be considered innocent until his guilt is proved according to the rules fixed by the federal law and confirmed by the sentence of a court which has come into legal force*". This principle is enunciated in Article 11 of the Universal Declaration of Human Rights, adopted by the General Assembly of the United Nations, as well as in Article 14 of the International Covenant on Civil and Political Rights. The presumption of innocence does not express the personal attitude of a particular person to the accused. State and civil society believe in good faith and the bona fide of a person until his objective legal position is proven otherwise. Only a court may determine a person guilty of an offence. Without such recognition no one should be subject to criminal penalties. The accused is not obliged to prove his innocence. The burden of proof is on the prosecutor, the investigator and the person conducting the inquiry. Failure to comply with these requirements of the law leads to the termination of the case and the defendant's acquittal. The presumption of innocence has another important dimension: irremovable doubts about the guilt of a person shall be interpreted in favour of the accused. Consequently, any fact or the evidence, the doubt that cannot dispel, is recognized as non-existent.

Article 50 of the Constitution of the Russian Federation contains an important warranty, which states that no person shall be tried twice for the same crime. This means that the criminal case against a citizen cannot be initiated and the case instituted shall be terminated if that person was already tried on the same charges, and the court sentenced or dismissed the case.

Nobody should use evidence obtained in violation of the law (Part 2 of Article 50 of the Constitution). Evidence cannot be used in the preparation which allows the humiliation of human dignity, torture and violence, unlawful entry into a dwelling, etc. There are not recognized any proof of information which is obtained in the violation of the rights and freedoms of man and citizen.

Everyone convicted of a crime shall have the right to review the judgement of a superior court, as well as to seek a pardon or commutation of sentence. The review of the sentence is a necessary safeguard against miscarriages of justice and it is provided by the Criminal Procedure Code. Higher courts should prevent the entry into force and implementation of an illegal sentence and thus serve for a citizen of the state of society as a guarantee against the unlawful and unjustified condemnation of man, or vice versa, leaving the impunity of the perpetrators. Part 3 of Article 50 of the Constitution reads: "*Everyone convicted of a crime shall have the right to review the judgement of a superior court in the manner prescribed by federal law*".

A pardon is an exemption from punishment or a replacement with another, more lenient punishment. *A pardon* as well as an *amnesty* is an extrajudicial act. In accordance with the Constitution of the Russian Federation a pardon is the prerogative of the President of the Russian Federation who can use any form of release at any stage of the criminal process and in any criminal case.

The Constitution establishes a *guarantee against self-incrimination* (Article 51). No one shall be compelled to testify against himself or to confess guilt. No one can also give evidence against her spouse and close relatives as defined by federal law. A person has the right to refuse to testify if the testimony convicts him and his close relatives in an offence that could be used against their interests.

The Constitution also protects *the rights of victims*. If as a result of a crime or abuse of power a man suffered moral, physical or property damage, that damage is refundable. The State shall provide access to justice and compensation for damages. Until recently the rights of the victims have not been resolved in legislation. They were considered "applicants" and the court system treated them only as carriers of information, witnesses for the prosecution, etc. *The Law "On the Rights of victims of crime" 2001* corrected the original position and granted the rights to victims of crime. The victim has the right to defend himself, to a feasible and appropriate extent, against him or against his closest criminal acts. When he is to testify in court he should be able to be protected from possible threats and acts of violence against him by the defendant or his friends. A victim may at any time apply to the investigating body or to the judge and ask him to report on the progress of the investigation or review and may claim a variety of applications. The victim and his counsel have the right to read the indictment against the accused and to receive a copy. If the victim has died as a result of acts of violence against him, his right to protection goes to the next of kin, such as his spouse, children, parents or brothers.

The victim's rights are guaranteed by the Constitution (Article 52) also on the "*abuse of power*" which means the possibility of judicial review of official actions that violate the law.

An important guarantee of justice in the Constitution is the principle of non-retroactivity of the law enshrined in Article 54. This legal act does not apply to matters arising prior to its entry into force. Only a few cases by the regulations fall within the relationship established before the effective date. If the opposite effect of the law specifically states in the Act or in the act of putting it into action.

If the criminal law eliminates or mitigates punishment:

a) a law establishing or increasing liability shall not have retroactive effect, and b) no one can be held liable for an act which at the time of its commission is not recognized as an offence.

This means that if, after the commission of the offence responsible for that is eliminated or reduced, the new law is applied.

CHAPTER FOUR

THE FEDERATION IN RUSSIA

The Constitution of the Russian Federation in Article 1 proclaims that "*The Russian Federation–Russia is a democratic federal law-governed State with a republican form of government. The names 'Russian Federation' and 'Russia' are equal*". From these provisions of the Constitution we may conclude that the basis of the constitutional order in Russia is a *federal state*, based on democracy and law.

Among the legal acts regulating the status of the Federation in Russia, we may mention the following important ones:

- *Constitution of the Russian Federation;*
- *Federation Agreement, dated by March 31, 1992;*
- *Federal Constitutional Law No. 6-FKZ "On the Order of Acceptance to the Russian Federation and creation of the New Subject of the Russian Federation", dated by December 17, 2001;*
- *Federal Law No. 184-FKZ "On the General Principles of Organization of the Legislative (Representative) and Executive Bodies of the State Power of the Subjects of the Russian Federation", dated by October 6, 1999.*

1. History of the Federation in Russia

Modern legal Russian doctrine separates three stages in the development of federalism in Russia, making the starting point the year of 1918, when officially the first Constitution of Russia was adopted.

These stages are:

1) 1st Stage. Creation and implementation of the basics of federalism during 1918-1936;

2) 2nd Stage. Factual unitary state with formal federation in Constitution during 1937-1985;

3) 3rd Stage. Reformation of the form of state during the years of 1985-1993;

4) 4th Stage. Development of federalism 1993-current time.

The 1st Stage started with the proclamation of the Russian Federation as an independent state in January 1918. The new territorial structure of Russia was adopted. A lot of new autonomies were created, both based on national or territorial principles. There were different types of subjects: republics, autonomies, regions and others and there were no clear criteria for the separation between them. At the end of the year 1922 there were 11 autonomic republics, 14 autonomic regions and 63 provinces. In 1922 new state appeared on the map–the USSR, which united equal participants of the federation with the Russian Federation (RSFSR) being one part of it. All subjects of the USSR were empowered with the right to freely leave the federation. When the RSFSR became part of the USSR the point of attention transferred from the RSFSR to the USSR and the federal development of the RSFSR stopped.

The 2nd Stage is characterized as a formal period of federalization, however in fact the RSFSR was purely a unitary state. Illustrating this point we may mention, that constitutions of autonomic republics were mandatorily agreed with the Supreme Soviet of the RSFSR–the main legislative body. There was not any sign of independence and special status of the subjects, and most of the decisions were taken on the level of the RSFSR state bodies.

The 3rd Stage is characterized by serious changes in the formal state system and finally in 1991 the disintegration of the Soviet Union and the formalization of the Russian Federation as the independent state with its own system of state bodies, and the horizontal and vertical separation of power. The period at the beginning of 90th is characterized by the "sovereignty parades" when autonomic republics started to proclaim themselves as independent states. This period is known by the Federative Agreement, signed on March 31, 1992, which became part of the existing constitution. It is interesting that republics were named as sovereign states, being part of the Russian Federation, thus constitutionally confirming a contradictory situation, with one sovereign state being part of another sovereign state.

The 4th Stage started from December 12, 1993 when the new Constitution of Russian was adopted. This Constitution included Chapter 3, devoted to the federal system of state. The Federative Agreement of 1992 stayed in force only in part, which was not contradictory to the Constitution of 1993. The Constitution consolidated the status of the subjects of the federation, the vertical separation of power system and the list of subjects of the Russian Federation. There were 89 subjects of six different types when the Constitution was adopted. In the year of 2013 there were 83 subjects, due to the process of restructuring the subjects, which we further describe in this book. In the year 2014 two more subjects entered the Russian Federation: the Republic of Crimea and the City of Sevastopol, thus the number of subjects rose to 85.

The subject of the Federation does not possess a secession right. The Federation is still in the process of transformation which may lead to subsequent changes in the legislation both on federal and subjects of federation levels.

2. Basics and Principles of the Federation in Russia

The Federation in Russia is based on the separation of powers between the State Federal Bodies and State bodies of the Subjects of the Russian Federation. This separation is named as the vertical separation of powers, which is of high importance for warranty of the independence and full power of the state bodies and the mitigation of arbitrariness of the state power.

One of the important issues of the Federation in Russia is whether the federation is grounded on the Constitution (the constitutional federation) or on the contract (the contractual federation). The Federation Agreement was adopted on March 31, 1992 regulating the relations between the Federation and its subjects. Until the adoption of the Constitution of Russia Federation in Russia it was regulating relations in the sphere of federation.

In accordance with Article 15 of the Constitution, it is applicable to the whole territory of the Russian Federation and is the act of the highest legal force.

The Constitution guarantees state integrity, the unity of the legal system and the equality of the subjects in relation with the State Federal Bodies. Thus, from the December 12, 1993 Russia became the constitutional federation.

In accordance with Article 67 of the Constitution of the Russian Federation:

> *The territory of the Russian Federation includes the territories of its subjects, inland waters and territorial sea, and the air space over them. The Russian Federation possesses sovereign rights and exercises the jurisdiction on the continental shelf and in the exclusive economic zone of the Russian Federation according to the rules fixed by the federal law and the norms of international law.*

Since the territory of the Russian Federation consists of the territory of the subjects of the Russian Federation the procedure of agreeing territorial changes should be done by mutual consent between the subjects. Such a process of agreeing borders provides a guarantee of the territorial integrity of the whole country.

The vertical separation of powers between the Federation and its subjects is regulated by Articles 71-73 of the Constitution as well as by the Federative Agreement and other agreements on the separation of powers, which are or may be signed between the Federation and its subjects.

Another specific character of the Federation is that Russia *combines both national and territorial principles*. Some of the subjects of Russia (for example, the republics and autonomic regions) are created based on national principle, when the core population of the subject belongs to the same nationality and another subjects, they are created based on pure territorial principle.

Russia is an *asymmetric federation*, when the status of the subjects is not equal. This statement is widely discussed by lawyers, scientists and practitioners, since from the formal constitutional point of view, as it is stated in Article 5 of the Constitution: "*In relations with federal bodies of state authority all the subjects of the Russian Federation shall be equal among themselves*". However from the practical perspective, and based on the other provisions of the Constitution, the subjects of the federation–republics historically and currently have another status, they are proclaimed as the State, which is specific comparing with other subjects of the Russian Federation. The status of the Republic is regulated by the *Constitution of the Republic*; however the status of the other subjects of the Russian Federation is regulated by *the Charter*. There are six different types of subjects, however only the Republic is proclaimed as the State. Only Republics may establish their state languages at the same time as the national state language, i.e. the Russian language. Another confirmation of the asymmetrical nature of the Russian Federation is the existence of the so-called "complex subject", when the territory of one subject is included in with the territory of another subject. Moscow, St. Petersburg and Sevastopol are separate subjects of the Federation having a special status and mixing with municipal regions.

The principles of the Russian Federation are established by the Constitution and are as follows:

1. Territorial integrity of the Federation

The subjects of the Russian Federation have no secession right; it is directly prohibited by the Constitution.

2. Unified economic and political space, free movement of individuals, goods and services

This principle includes the performance of the state bodies on federal and subjects of federation levels; the existence of the unified federal citizenship, which is equal despite the procedure of its acceptance. Unified economic space means that the government supports and establishes unified rules and regulations for civil relations, unified accounting rules and the equality of economic activity of all subjects. There are no custom borders inside the Federation; goods and services are moving freely. There is a single monetary system, one currency and emission system. The principles of taxation are regulated by federal power.

3. State sovereignty

This is one of the core principles of the Federation in Russia. State sovereignty is independence of the state power in internal and external relations. The sovereignty includes the leadership of the federal Constitution and federal laws in the territory of the Russian Federation. One of the issues of the Federation is whether subjects of the Russian Federation possess their own sovereignty.

Some historical trends in the development of the Federation in Russia during the 1990s led to the situation, when several subjects of the Russian Federation, mostly Republics declared themselves as sovereign states, however in accordance with Article 4 of the Constitution of the Russian Federation state sovereignty covers the whole territory of Russia and is non dividable. This "parade of sovereignty", which declared some subjects of the Russian Federation and fixed such provisions in their own constitutions was reviewed by the Constitutional Court of the Russian Federation, which finalized that sovereignty belongs only to the Federal power and it excludes the existence of two levels of sovereign powers on the territory of one federal state.

4. Free development of nationalities

The right of nations to self-determination is the cardinal principle in international law. In Russia this principle is included as an internal constitutional principle and realized within the Federation.

5. Inadmissibility of the actions directed on the unilateral change of status of territorial subjects of the Russian Federation

In accordance with Article 66 of the Constitution of the Russian Federation the status of the subject is regulated by the Federal Constitution, Constitution or other basic law of the subject of the Federation. The status of the subject of the Federation can be reviewed and changed only based on mutual agreement between the Federation and the subject of the Federation. All subjects possess constituent power and are empowered to adopt its constitution and other laws, being part of the legal system of the Federation; however they cannot be contradictory to the

Constitution and constitutional and other federal laws. No subject is empowered to change its constitutional status unilaterally.

6. Unity of the principles of the organization of the government in the subjects of the Russian Federation

The principles of the organization of the state power on the level of subjects of federation are regulated by federal Constitution and federal laws.

7. Rule of the federal legislation within the separation of powers between federation and subjects.

This principle is regulated by the Constitution. In accordance with Article 71 of the Constitution issues of adoption and amendment of the Constitution is pure federal power. Only the Federation is authorized to adopt the Constitution, federal constitutional laws and federal laws, having legal force on the whole territory of the Russian Federation.

3. Separation of Powers between Federation and Subjects of Federation

One of the most important issues of any federation is how the separation of powers between the federation and its substantial parts is implemented by legislation and in practice. The Russian Federation solves this issue by the constitutional separation of competence by three groups:

1) *Exclusive competence of the Federal State Bodies* (competence of the Federation);
2) *Joint competence* of the state bodies of the Federation and state bodies of the subjects of the Federation (joint competence);
3) *Exclusive competence of subjects* of the Federation (competence of subjects).

Initially such a split of competence was established by the Federation Agreement; later on in the year 1993 this principle was accommodated by the Constitution.

The Constitution of Russia in Articles 71-73 includes the split of competence. Article 71 is devoted to the list of the *exclusive competence of the Federation*; Article 72 describes *the joint competence* and Article 73 leaves all non-listed issues to the *exclusive competence of subjects.* Thus, the lists of federal exclusive competence and joint competence are closed and competence of subjects means an open list.

The Constitution of Russia regulates that the Federation and subjects may sign separate agreements, clarifying and detailing the competence already listed in the Constitution, however any changes to the Constitution are possible only by changing the constitutional text.

Realizing exclusive competence, regulated by Article 71 of the Constitution, the federative legislative body–the Parliament of Russia may issue federal constitutional laws and federal laws. The subject has no power for any legislative acts in this sphere. In the area of joint competence, the Federation and subjects are empowered for joint legislation, so that the Federation may issue federal laws and subjects may also issue their own laws; however the regional legislation should not contradict the Constitution and federal legislation. When federal law is not adopted, the subjects may introduce their own regulation, however after the Federation has adopted laws in this sphere, the subjects of the Federation should bring their own legislation in line with federal legislation.

As for the exclusive competence of subjects, the Federation has no right to adopt laws and subjects are free to solve issues independently, however with several conditions, that regional legislation should not contradict the Constitution and any regional act in force since it falls under the exclusive competence of the subject, not listed by Articles 71 and 72 of the Constitution.

The Constitution of Russia describes exclusive competence of the state bodies of the Federation in the following ways (Article 71 of the Constitution):

a) Adoption and amending of the Constitution of the Russian Federation and federal laws, and control over their observance;
b) Federal structure and the territory of the Russian Federation;
c) Regulation and protection of the rights and freedoms of man and citizen; citizenship in the Russian Federation, regulation and protection of the rights of national minorities;
d) Establishment of the system of the federal legislative, executive and judicial bodies, the rules for their organization and activities, the formation of federal bodies of state authority;
e) Federal state property and its management;
f) Establishment of the principles of federal policy and federal programs in the sphere of state, economic, ecological, social, cultural and national development of the Russian Federation;
g) Establishment of the legal basis for a single market; financial, currency, credit, and customs regulation, money issue, the principles of pricing policy; federal economic services, including federal banks;
h) Federal budget, federal taxes and dues, federal regional development funds;

i) Federal power systems, nuclear power-engineering, fissionable materials, federal transport, railways, information and communication, outer space activities;
j) Foreign policy and international relations of the Russian Federation, international treaties and agreements of the Russian Federation, issues of war and peace;
k) Foreign economic relations of the Russian Federation;
l) Defence and security; military production; determination of the rules of selling and purchasing weapons, ammunition, military equipment and other military property; production of poisonous substances, narcotic substances and rules for their use;
m) Determination of the status and protection of the state border, territorial sea, air space, exclusive economic zone and continental shelf of the Russian Federation;
n) Judicial system, procurator's office, criminal, criminal procedural and penal legislation, amnesty and pardoning, civil, civil procedural and arbitration procedural legislation, legal regulation of intellectual property;
o) Federal law of conflict of laws;
p) Meteorological service, standards, metric system, horometry, geodesy and cartography, names of geographical units, official statistics and accounting;
q) State awards and honorary titles of the Russian Federation;
r) Federal state service.

The joint jurisdiction of the Russian Federation and the subjects of the Russian Federation include (Article 72 of the Constitution):

a) Providing for the correspondence of the constitutions and laws of the republics, the charters and other normative legal acts of the territories, regions, cities of federal importance, autonomous regions or autonomous areas to the Constitution of the Russian Federation and federal laws;
b) Protection of the rights and freedoms of man and citizen; protection of the rights of national minorities; ensuring the rule of law, law and order, public security and the border zone regime;
c) Issues of possession, use and disposal of land, subsoil, water and other natural resources;
d) Delimitation of state property;
e) Utilization of natural resources, protection of the environment and ensuring ecological safety; specially protected natural territories, protection of historical and cultural monuments;

f) General questions of upbringing, education, science, culture, physical culture and sports;
g) Coordination of issues of health care; protection of the family, maternity, paternity and childhood; social protection, including social security;
h) Carrying out measures against catastrophes, natural calamities, epidemics, elimination of their aftermath;
i) Establishment of common principles of taxation and dues in the Russian Federation;
j) Administrative, administrative procedural, labour, family, housing, land, water, and forest legislation; legislation on subsoil and environmental protection;
k) Personnel of the judicial and law enforcement agencies; the Bar, notary offices;
l) Protection of the traditional habitat and way of life of small ethnic communities;
m) Establishment of common principles of organization of the system of bodies of state authority and local self-government;
n) Coordination of international and foreign economic relations of the subjects of the Russian Federation, fulfillment of international treaties and agreements of the Russian Federation.

Exclusive competence of the subjects of the Federation is described in the following way (Article 73 of the Constitution):

Outside the limits of authority of the Russian Federation and the powers of the Russian Federation on issues under joint jurisdiction of the Russian Federation and the subjects of the Russian Federation, the subjects of the Russian Federation shall possess full state authority.

Thus, it means that everything outside of the exclusive competence of the Russian Federation and joint competence of the Russian Federation and subjects of the Russian Federation falls under exclusive competence of the subjects of the Russian Federation, where they are empowered to legislate.

4. Structure of the Federation

The territory of the Russian Federation consists of *85 subjects*. *The Subject*–is the component of the federation. In different countries they can be named differently: province, state, republic, canton, etc. In Russia–the official name is "*the subject of the Russian Federation*". All subjects have their territory, population and borders. Subjects establish the system of their power in accordance with frameworks, introduced by federal laws. There are six types of subjects:

- ✓ Republic;
- ✓ Territory (oblast');
- ✓ Region (krai);
- ✓ City of federal importance (federal city);
- ✓ Autonomous region;
- ✓ Autonomous territory.

The Constitution incorporates the full list of all 85 subjects of the Russian Federation in article 65, chapter 3. The Constitution describes the status of the subjects and the status of the subjects is different.

Republics are named as the states; however they have no sovereignty, so this name "state" in relation to the republics is of a formal nature. Republics have their own Constitutions, coats of arms, anthems and flags. The main principle under which the republics are organized is the principle of compact inhabitance of people of certain nationality, thus republics are called "national subjects".

Territories and regions are not declared as states; however they are called "state formation", created on the basis of territorial principle.

A city of federal importance is a very specific territorial structural unit, which is applicable to only three cities in the Russian Federation–Moscow, St. Petersburg and Sevastopol.

Autonomous regions and autonomous territories are also "state formations", created on the basis of the national-territorial principle.

These subjects of the Russian Federation establish the system of regional power independently on the basis of frameworks, and adopted by federal legislation. All of them have a Charter, as the main legal document, adopted on the level of the subject. They have territory, borders, population and legislation.

The constitutional status of the subjects *is common* in the following aspects:

- ➢ Only the Russian Federation as a federation has sovereignty;
- ➢ No subject of the Federation has the right to leave the Federation;
- ➢ The rule of federal law applies to the whole territory of Russia, including any subject of the Federation;
- ➢ Subjects of the Russian Federation have no right to change their status independently.

5. System of the State Bodies of the Subject of the Russian Federation. Federal Intervention

The system of the state bodies on the level of subjects of the Russian Federation is determined in accordance with the Constitution, Federal law "On the General Principles of Organization of the Legislative (Representative) and Executive Bodies of the State Power of the Subjects of the Russian Federation" and legislation of the concrete subject of the Russian Federation.

This system of state bodies of the subject is constituted by the legislative (representative) body–the parliament, the highest executive body–the government, and other bodies, organized in accordance with adopted regulations. The Head of the subject may at the same time be the head of the executive body, thus this state official is included in the executive power of the subject.

There are different procedures of appointment of the *Head of the Subject (other official names are Governor, Head of Government, etc.)*. In accordance with the federal law, which entered into force from the June 1, 2012 the Head of the Executive power can be:

- ✓ Elected by the population of the subject of the Federation, having an active electoral right; or
- ✓ Elected by the legislative body of the subject of the Federation, in which case this procedure is directly approved by the legislation of the subject of the Federation.

The candidate should be over 30 years old and the candidature should be supported by local municipal deputies by voting for the candidate. The term of authority is defined in accordance with the legislation of the subject of the Federation.

Among the responsibilities it is worth mentioning the following:

✓ Representation of the subject in relations with Federal State Bodies;

✓ Formation of the higher executive body of the subject of the Federation;

✓ Representation of the subject in relations with foreign officials in external economic relations;

✓ Promulgation of the laws, adopted by the legislative body of the subject, etc.

The Head of the Subject forms the government–the highest executive body of the subject. Depending on the legislation of the subject, the Head of the Subject may lead the government himself or appoint another head of government.

The government of the subject leads the economic and social activity in the region, forms the budget and spends it, depending on the provisions approved. The structure of the government is defined by the legislation of the subject. The government of the subject coordinates its activity with the Government of the Russian Federation.

The legislative body–the parliament of the subject of the Russian Federation–is formed by the voting of the population of the subject with active electoral rights. Functions of the regional parliament can be divided in the following way:

- *Legislative function*–the parliament of the subject is the only authorized body of the subject to adopt laws and other legal regulations, having the force of law of the subject;
- *Representative function*–the parliament is the only official body of the subject, which represents the interests of the whole population of the subject;
- *Control function*–the parliament in accordance with legislation of the subject is empowered by certain control functions over the executive branch of power, for example approval of the budget, expressing non-confidence in the government, the control of appointment of different officers.

The term of authorities is defined by the legislation of the subject and normally constitutes from two to five years. Regional parliaments are elected on the basis of the electoral system established by the legislation of the subject. In most cases it is mixed system–a combination of proportional and majority electoral systems, when half of the members of parliament are elected on a majority system and the other half on a proportional system.

Most regional parliaments are unicameral; however several are bicameral, depending on the legislation of the subject. The structure of regional parliament is mostly similar to the structure of the Federal Assembly–the federal parliament and included committees, commissions, factions and Chairperson of the parliament.

While the Federation is a more complicated structure of the state, in some cases it becomes necessary to adopt mechanisms, preventing subjects of federation to violate the Constitution and federal legislation. *Federal intervention* is one of the constitutional effective mechanisms to guarantee the rights of all members of the Federation.

We may formulate *Federal intervention* as constitutional institution with the main purpose to protect constitutional order by intervention into the activity of the state officials and state bodies of the subjects of the Federation in case they are violating Constitution and federal laws. The need to include federal intervention measures into the legislation flows from the nature of the federative state, when the federal powers control and ensure that subjects of the Federation act in accordance with the Constitution and federal laws and do not infringe human rights in their activity. There is no special law on federal intervention; however there are several measures, already included into federal legislation, which may be used by federal bodies to ensure stability and compliance with the Constitution and federal laws.

In particular, the following federal intervention measures are established by the legislation of the Russian Federation:

- Dismissal of the Head of the Subject of the Federation by the President of Russia;
- Dissolution of the legislative body of the subject of the Federation by the President of Russia;
- Application of budget measures, when the federal executive power controls over budget spending, done by the subject of the Federation;
- Transfer of the police, internal troops and other force under the direct command of the federal bodies;
- Suspending and further cancellation of the unlawful decision of the bodies of the subject of the Federation in case this decision contradicts the federal Constitution, federal laws and international agreement or such decision violates human rights. The President of Russia has the right to suspend the unlawful decision and the Constitutional Court may further cancel the act.

Federal intervention measures may be introduced by court decisions or by the President of Russia or other duly authorized official person. The constitutional responsibility of the subjects of the Federation is one of the important elements of ensuring the integrity of the federal state, the protection of human rights and the defencee of the constitutional order.

6. Federal Districts and Plenipotentiary Representatives of the President in Federal Districts

The territory of the Russian Federation is also divided by nine federal districts. This structure was not established by the Constitution; however it is closely connected with the realization of Presidential power.

A federal district is the territory, where the President of Russia is represented by his plenipotentiary representative, whose goal is to facilitate interaction between the Head of State and authorities of the subjects of Russia. The purpose of this system is to support the realization of Presidential powers, the development of the control system over the regional authorities, and to increase the efficiency of federal bodies.

Division of federal districts and the legal status of the plenipotentiary representatives are regulated by the *Presidential Decree No. 849, dated by May 13, 2000.*

The plenipotentiary representative is appointed and dismissed by the President of the Russian Federation. The plenipotentiary representative is the federal civil servant and official employee of the Executive Office of the President and is accountable to the President. The term of authority is defined by the President; however it cannot be more than the official term of office of the President.

Among the main functions of the plenipotentiary representative are the following:

- ✓ To provide the coordination of activities of the federal executive bodies in the respective federal district;
- ✓ To analyze the efficiency of law enforcement bodies in the federal district as well as staff security of the mentioned bodies, make respective suggestions to the President of the Russian Federation;
- ✓ To organize the interaction of the federal executive bodies with the bodies of the government of subjects of the Russian Federation, institutions of local self-government, political parties, other public and religious associations;
- ✓ To organize control over the execution of federal laws, decrees and orders of the President of the Russian Federation, acts of the Government of the Russian Federation, over the realization of federal programs in the federal district;
- ✓ To take part in the work of the bodies of the government of subjects of the Russian Federation as well as the bodies of local self-government located within the federal district;
- ✓ To make suggestions to the President of the Russian Federation on the suspension of acts of the executive bodies of subjects of the Russian Federation located within the federal district in case these acts contradict the Constitution of the Russian Federation, federal laws international obligations of the Russian Federation or violate human and citizen rights and freedoms.

The plenipotentiary in duty status shall have the right of unimpeded access to any organizations located within the federal district.

7. Current Tendencies in the Development of Federalism in Russia

One of the most interesting processes in the development of federalism in Russia is the consolidation of regions, which started during the year 2003.

The consolidation of regions is a political, economic and legal process of integration of some subjects of the Russian Federation, which were highly integrated prior to this, having close connections, both in political and economic spheres. The consolidation process started in the "complex" subjects of the Russian Federation–territories and regions with autonomies.

Due to the consolidation process the number of subjects of the Russian Federation reduced on six units. One of the main reasons was the complicated and questionable status of the autonomic territories, which on the one hand were separate subjects of the Federation, but on the other hand were substantial parts of the other subjects.

The procedure of consolidation is established by the Federal Constitutional Law No. 6-FKZ "*About the Order of Acceptance to the Russian Federation and Creation of the New Subject of the Russian Federation*", dated by December 17, 2001.

The *initiative* of adoption of the new subject stays in the hands of the subjects, where the new region is presumed to be created. The proposal is delivered to the President of Russia.

Each subject of the Federation, where the new region is going to be created conducts a *regional referendum*, where the people of the subject of federation decide the question, if they agree for consolidation of their subjects. If the decision is positive, then this *information is transferred to the President of Russia*, who has sufficient constitutional rights to introduce to the State Duma the draft of Federal Constitutional Law on the new subject of Russia. This law draft is reviewed by the State Duma and later on by the Federation Council in accordance with legislative procedure, established by the Constitution. In the case that even one of the subjects does not approve the consolidation on referendum, this issue can be reviewed again not earlier than one year after the previous referendum took place.

After the draft is approved by the Parliament, the President signs it and the appropriate changes are introduced to Article 65 of the Constitution, where the full list of the subjects of the Russian Federation can be found.

Illustrating the process of already consolidated regions we may mention *Perm' territory (oblast') and Komi-Permiatsky autonomic region (krai)* and the creation of *Perm' region*; consolidation of *Krasnoyarsky region and Taimur and Evenki autonomic regions*, when the consolidated region left the name–Krasnoyarsky region; consolidation of *Kamchatka territory and Koryak autonomic region* into the Kamchatka region; consolidation *of Irkutsk territory and Ust'-Ordynsky Byriatsky autonomic region* with the same name to the new subject–*Irkutsk territory* and consolidation of the *Chita territory and Aginsky Buryatsky autonomic region* into *Zabaikalski region.*

CHAPTER FIVE

THE ELECTORAL SYSTEM IN RUSSIA

The legislation of the Russian Federation on the electoral system is comprised of the following regulations:

- *The Constitution of the Russian Federation;*
- *Federal Constitutional Law #5-FKZ "On Referendum in the Russian Federation", dated June 28, 2004;*
- *Federal Law #67-FZ "On Basic Guarantees of Electoral Rights and the Right of Citizens of the Russian Federation to Participate in a Referendum", dated June 12, 2002;*
- *Federal Law #19-FZ "On the Election of the President of the Russian Federation", dated January 10, 2003;*
- *Federal Law № 20-FZ "On elections of the Deputies of the State Duma of Federal Assembly of the Russian Federation", dated February 22, 2014;*
- *Federal Law #20-FZ "On the State Automated System of the Russian Federation "Vybory", dated by January 10, 2003.*

1. The Overview of the Electoral System in Russia and Principles of Electoral Law

Electoral system in Russia means the order of elections of the President of Russia, deputies of the State Duma and the order of elections to another state and municipal bodies, performed on the basis of the Constitution of Russia and federal laws.

Election is the form of direct expression of will by citizens that is realized in accordance with the state and municipal legislation.

Citizens of Russia and sometimes foreign citizens, are vested by both active and passive electoral rights, however these rights can be limited by special censuses, like age, permanent residence census, etc.

Electoral rights are the constitutional rights of citizens of the Russian Federation to elect and be elected to bodies of state power and bodies of local self-government and the right to participate in the nomination of candidates, lists of candidates, in election campaigning, in the observing of the conduct of elections, the work of election commissions, including the establishment of voting results and election results and in other election activities, in the procedure stipulated by the legislation of the Russian Federation.

The Constitution of the Russian Federation and other acts establish *guarantees of the electoral rights* and the right to participate in a referendum–conditions, rules, and procedures and are intended to assure the exercising of the electoral rights of citizens of the Russian Federation, and their right to participate in a referendum.

Principles of the electoral right and of conducting elections and referendum are established by the Constitution and Federal Law *"On Basic Guarantees of Electoral Rights and the Right of Citizens of the Russian Federation to Participate in a Referendum*". Citizens participate in elections on the basis of *universal, equal and direct* electoral right by *secret balloting*.

Universal right means that all citizens of Russia, despite their nationality, gender, language, religion and place of residence who are already 18 years old possess an *active electoral right*, having the right to elect and depending on age–have a *passive electoral right*–the right to be elected.

The minimum age for passive electoral right is established as 18 years old. The age to qualify for the State Duma elections is 21 years, and for participation in the President of Russian elections–35 years.

Equal right means that all voters participate in the elections on an equal basis. Each voter gets *one voice* and all voices are equal.

Direct electoral right means that the deputies or the President are elected by direct voting, when the voter gives the voice directly for the candidates, without any interim stages.

Secret balloting means that no one should have control over the choice which the voter makes during voting procedure. This principle is guaranteed by several procedures, established by law. Each voter provides his voice in person; voting for another person is not permitted, voting ballots are not numbered or marked with the name of the person; the voter makes the choice in the special place, like a special closed cabin. Administrative and criminal responsibility is fixed for the violation of the rules, described above.

No mandatory vote is permitted–participation in elections shall be free and voluntary. No one shall compel a citizen of the Russian Federation to participate or not to participate in elections and referendum or shall prevent free expression of his will. Citizens residing abroad also possess electoral rights of the same amount as citizens residing in Russia, despite the time period they have spent living abroad.

Foreign citizens are deprived of the voting right, except for the elections to municipal bodies, when permanently residing foreigners get an electoral vote. Foreign citizens shall not be engaged in activities which promote or impede the nomination of candidates (lists of candidates), the election of registered candidates, aninitiative to conduct a referendum, and the achievement of certain results in during elections or referenda.

As stated previously, electoral rights may be limited. Citizens declared incapable by a court or held in custody under a court sentence shall not be entitled to elect and be elected or to participate in a referendum.

The following citizens are deprived of the *passive electoral right*:

- Those sentenced to imprisonment for the commitment of a serious crime and (or) felony and having on the voting day a conviction that is not withdrawn or spent;
- Those sentenced for the commitment of extremist crimes stipulated by the Criminal Code and having on the voting day a conviction that is not withdrawn or spent;
- Those administratively punished for the commitment of an administrative offence related to extremist activity if the voting is conducted before the period during which such person is being administratively punished.

2. The System of Electoral Bodies in the Russian Federation

In accordance with Federal law the following list of election commissions shall function in the Russian Federation:

- The Central Election Commission of the Russian Federation;
- Election commissions of the subjects of the Russian Federation;
- Election commissions of municipal formations;
- District election commissions;
- Territorial (district, city, and other) election commissions;
- Precinct commissions.

Commissions shall ensure the exercising and protection of electoral rights, and prepare for and conduct elections in the Russian Federation.

Commissions shall, within the scope of their competence, consider appeals on violation of the law they received during the election campaign, verify such appeals and provide applicants with written responses within five days, but not later than on the day preceding the voting day, and with regards to appeals received on the voting day or on the day following the voting day–immediately. If the facts stated in such appeals require additional verification, decisions shall be taken thereon not later than within ten days.

The Central Election Commission of the Russian Federation is a federal state body organizing the preparation and conduct of elections and referendum in the Russian Federation.

It operates on a permanent basis and is empowered by the authorities for realization during the whole period of the elected state bodies' existence. The term of powers constitutes *five years*. The Central Election Commission of the Russian Federation consists of *fifteen members*.

Five members of the Central Election Commission of the Russian Federation shall be appointed by the State Duma of the Federal Assembly of the Russian Federation out of candidates proposed by the factions, other associations of deputies of the State Duma of the Federal Assembly of the Russian Federation, or by individual deputies of the State Duma of the Federal Assembly of the Russian Federation.

Five members shall be appointed by the Federation Council out of the candidates nominated by the legislative (representative) bodies of state power of the subjects of the Russian Federation and higher officials of the subjects of the Russian Federation (the heads of the high executive bodies of state power of the subjects of the Russian Federation).

Five members of the Central Election Commission shall be appointed by the President of the Russian Federation.

The Chairman of the Central Election Commission is elected by its members by secret balloting.

Among the authorities of the Central Election Commission we may mention the following:

- Exercise control over the observance of the electoral rights of citizens of the Russian Federation;
- Ensure the implementation of measures related to the preparation and conduct of elections, the improvement of the electoral system in the Russian Federation; the introduction, operation, and improvement of means of automation, the legal education of voters, professional training of commission members, and other individuals engaged in organization of elections, and the publication of required printed materials;
- Implement measures aimed at the organization of funding of the preparation and conduct of elections, distribute the funds allocated out of the federal budget as financial support of the preparation and conduct of elections, and control the proper use of the above funds;

- Provide legal, methodological, organizational, and technical support to commissions;
- Implement international cooperation in the field of electoral systems;
- Set standards by which lists of voters, referendum participants and other election documents and documents related to the preparation and conduct of referenda are to be produced;
- Consider complaints (appeals) related to decisions and actions (inaction) of subordinate commissions and take reasonable decisions in connection to these complaints (appeals);
- *The Central Election Commission of the Russian Federation* together with election commissions of the subjects of the Russian Federation check consolidated financial reports and data on the receipt and expenditure of funds of political parties, have control over sources and the volume of property received by political parties as entry or member fees, donations of citizens and legal entities, and inform citizens on the results of such checks;
- Within the scope of its competence, it shall be entitled to issue binding instructions in the sphere of electoral law;
- It is entitled to issue opinions on the compliance of laws and other regulations of the subjects of the Russian Federation with federal laws that govern the electoral rights of citizens of the Russian Federation and their right to participate in a referendum.

Election commissions of the subjects of the Russian Federation, election commissions of municipal formations, district election commissions and territorial precinct commissions are formed on the basis of proposals made by political parties that nominated lists of candidates admitted to the distribution of deputy seats in the State Duma of the Federal Assembly of the Russian Federation, the legislative (representative) body of state power of the corresponding subject of the Russian Federation.

Election commissions of subjects of the Russian Federation are the state bodies of subjects of the Russian Federation that organize the preparation and conduct of elections and referendum of the Russian Federation within the scope of their competence. They act on a permanent basis. The term of powers of election commissions of the subjects of the Russian Federation *constitutes five years*. The number of voting members of the election commission of the subject of the Russian Federation shall be set by the constitution (statute), the law of the subject of the Russian Federation; however this cannot be less than 10 and more than 14. The election commission of the subject of the

Russian Federation is formed by the legislative body and the head of the subject of the Russian Federation on the basis of proposals made by representative bodies of municipal formations, the election commission of the subject of the Russian Federation of the previous convocation, and the Central Election Commission of the Russian Federation.

Among their authorities are:

- Exercising control in the territory of the subject of the Russian Federation over the observance of the electoral rights of citizens of the Russian Federation and the right of citizens to participate in a referendum;
- Ensuring implementation in the territory of the subject of the Russian Federation of measures related to the preparation and conduct of elections, referenda, the improvement of the electoral system in the Russian Federation; the introduction, operation, and improvement of means of automation, the legal education of voters, professional training of commission members, and other individuals engaged in the organization of elections and the publication of required printed materials;
- Approving the list of territorial commissions;
- Providing legal, methodological, organizational, and technical support to subordinate commissions;
- Considering complaints (appeals) related to decisions and actions (inaction) of subordinate commissions and take reasoned decisions on these complaints (appeals); etc.

The role of the other election commissions of municipal formations, district election commissions, territorial election commissions and precinct commissions is to organize, control and perform realization of the elections' stages while conducting elections on different levels.

Commissions operate on a collegiate basis. A commission shall be qualified to start functioning if at least two-thirds of the total established number of its members was appointed. The first meeting takes place not later than on the fifteenth day after the decision on the appointment of its voting members is taken but not earlier than the term of powers of the previous commission expires. In this case, at least two-thirds of the total number of its members shall be appointed. The chairman of the election commission of the subject of the Russian Federation shall be elected by secret ballot at the first meeting of such commission out of voting members of the election commission on the basis of the proposal made by the Central Election Commission of the Russian Federation.

There are prohibitions for the appointment of the voting commission's members. In particular, the following categories cannot be appointed:

- ✓ Foreign citizens or citizens of the Russian Federation with citizenship of the foreign state or residence in the foreign state;
- ✓ Citizens of the Russian Federation declared legally incapable or with limited capability by the decision of a court that came into force;
- ✓ Citizens of the Russian Federation under the age of 18 years;
- ✓ Deputies of legislative (representative) bodies of state power, bodies of local self-government;
- ✓ Elective officials, as well as higher officials of the subjects of the Russian Federation;
- ✓ Judges, prosecutors.

3. The Stages of the Electoral Process

All elections should take place in time, which is specifically declared by the valid law. Elections are mandatory and cannot be postponed or cancelled. The date of voting is determined on the basis of the federal law. All elections are conducted on Sunday. It is not permitted to fix Election Day on a working day.

All elections are conducted in accordance with stages of electoral process. *All stages are essential* from a legal perspective. They are the following:

1) Registration of the Voters and Voters Lists;
2) Creation of electoral districts and polling stations;
3) Creation of electoral commissions;
4) Promotion of the candidate;
5) Registration of the candidate;
6) Information electoral campaign;
7) Election Day;
8) Calculation of the Results and Official announcement and publishing of the Results.

Registration of the Voters and Voters' Lists

All voters should be registered. The obligation for registration is performed by the Head of the municipal community or the Head of the City of Federal Importance (the subject of the Russian Federation). The State Bodies performing registration of the citizens (these bodies constitute part of the Ministry for Internal Affairs of the Russian Federation) provide the municipal bodies with the information about registered citizens and foreigners on a monthly basis. Voters have unconditional right to access the information in these lists.

The territorial election commissions consolidate the information from municipal bodies to the special Voters Lists. These Lists include citizens of Russia, who have active electoral rights on the date of Voting. This list is presented for public review 20 days before the Voting Date. If a person discovers discrepancies or mistakes in the List, he/she should inform the territorial election commission and proclaim the review and changes of the List. The List cannot be changed after the voting is finished and the calculation of votes has started.

Creation of electoral districts and polling stations

Elections are organized based on the territorial principle. The territory of the State is divided into the electoral districts. *An electoral district* is the territory determined in accordance with the law, from which citizens of the Russian Federation directly elect a deputy or an elective official. Electoral districts can be formed as single electoral districts; multi-seat electoral districts or single-seat electoral districts.

A single electoral district is the electoral district which includes the entire territory in which the election is held; a *multi-seat electoral district* is the electoral district in which several deputies are to be elected and in which voters vote for each of the deputies personally; a *single-seat electoral district* is the electoral district in which one deputy is to be elected.

The Electoral Commission, 80 days in advance of the Voting Date, defines the scheme of the electoral districts. Following this, 20 days prior to the Voting Date this scheme is approved by the legislative body of the subject of the Russian Federation or the municipal legislative body.

Polling stations are organized for the organization of voting and the calculation of votes. The polling stations are organized by the local municipal bodies to provide voters with comfort for voting. The obligation abroad is to organize polling stations at the embassies and consulates. The requirement for the creation of the polling station is not to exceed 3,000 voters for one polling station. Lists of the polling stations with their correct addresses are published not later than 40 days prior to the Voting Date.

Creation of electoral commissions

The role and status of the electoral commissions are described in paragraph two of this chapter. When analyzing the role of electoral commissions in the electoral procedure it is necessary to mention that electoral commissions perform their activity on an *open basis*, so that the candidates, their representatives, journalists and other interested people may receive information about their activity. Decisions of the electoral commissions are published by the press. Activity of the electoral commission is done on a *collective basis*, thus the quorum constitutes two-thirds of the total list of members. All commissions *are independent*.

Nomination of the Candidates

Candidates for the elections can be nominated by direct nomination and nomination in the list of candidates.

Direct nomination is possible in the following ways:

- ✓ By self-nomination;
- ✓ Nomination by election association.

Nomination of candidates in the list of candidates may be carried out by a political party entitled in accordance with federal law to participate in elections, or by its regional branch or other structural subdivision.

A citizen of the Russian Federation who is not entitled to a passive electoral right at a corresponding election shall not be nominated as a candidate. Also, the passive electoral right is ceased for former Presidents who were exposed to the procedure of dismissal and former Presidents after two consecutive terms of Presidency.

A candidate may be nominated only at one electoral district. This rule shall not apply when a candidate is nominated by one and the same election association at one and the same election in a single-seat (or a multi-seat) electoral district and in a list of candidates. A candidate (except candidates nominated in the list of candidates) shall personally submit documents and the Election Commission may verify the data on candidates.

Self-Nomination of Candidates shall be carried out by way of notification thereof of the election commissions where the candidates are to be registered, followed by the collection of signatures in support of such self-nominated candidates. Self-nomination of candidates may require the support of the active support group (up to 500 people).

Nomination of Candidates, Lists of Candidates by Election Associations. Election associations shall be entitled to nominate candidates and lists of candidates. In a single-seat electoral district an election association may nominate one candidate. In a multi-seat electoral district an election association may nominate a candidate for each deputy seat in this electoral district. In a single electoral district an election association may nominate one list of candidates, and at elections of an elective official–one candidate.

In accordance with the procedure established by law, signatures of voters may be collected in support of the nomination of candidates, lists of candidates or a referendum initiative. The number of signatures required for the registration of candidates and lists of candidates shall be established by law and shall not exceed 2 percent of the number of voters registered in the territory of the electoral district. The number of signatures required by law for the registration of candidates in a multi-seat electoral district shall not exceed 2 percent of the number of voters registered in the territory of the corresponding electoral district divided by the number of deputy seats but not less than 10 signatures. Each signature list shall be certified by the signature of a person collecting signatures of voters or referendum participants.

In accordance with Federal Law "On the Election of the President of the Russian Federation" the candidate, who is self-nominated should collect 300,000 signatures of the voters, so that not more than 7,500 signatures should be collected in each subject of the Russian Federation. If the candidate is nominated by the political party (except parties with places in the State Duma), it is necessary to get not less than 100,000 signatures of the voters, so that not more than 2,500 signatures should be collected in each subject of the Russian Federation.

Registration of a Candidate

A candidate or a list of candidates shall be registered by the corresponding election commission upon the availability of documents or upon the availability of a decision of the political party. If the corresponding election commission identifies that data on candidates is incomplete or requirements for the preparation of documents are not met, not later than three days before the meeting of such an election commission that shall consider the issue of the registration of a candidate, or the list of candidates, such an election commission shall notify a candidate or election association to this effect. This should occur not later than one day before the day of the meeting of the election commission that shall consider the issue of registration of a candidate or a list of candidates.

The number of signatures of voters or referendum participants collected in support of a candidate or a list of candidates for a referendum initiative and submitted for the purposes of the registration of a candidate or a list of candidates, for calling a referendum may exceed the number of signatures required for such registration, but not more than by 10 percent

Upon completion of the verification of a signature list a final protocol is prepared that states the number of declared signatures, the number of submitted signatures and the number of verified signatures of voters or referendum participants, as well as the number of signatures recognized as unauthentic and (or) invalid stating the grounds for such recognition.

The candidate may be refused registration, for instance in the following cases:

- A candidate is not entitled to a passive electoral right;
- Candidates nominated by a political party do not observe the requirements to nomination of a candidate specified by the Federal Law "*On Political Parties*";
- An insufficient number of submitted authentic and valid signatures of voters submitted for registration of the candidate, or identification of 10 and more percent of unauthentic and (or) invalid signatures out of a total number of signatures selected for verification;
- A candidate did not establish an electoral fund. A lack of funds in such an electoral fund shall not become the grounds for refusal to register a candidate;
- A candidate, his attorney, an authorized representative for financial issues and other person or organization acting by their order has bribed voters, which has been established by the court.

All candidates shall have equal rights and bear equal responsibilities.

Candidates who occupy state or elective municipal positions or are on state or municipal service and candidates who are officials, journalists, and other employees of organizations of the mass media, shall not abuse the advantages of their official positions during their election campaigning. Registered candidates occupying state or municipal positions or working in organizations of the mass media, shall for the period of their participation in elections, be relieved from their official duties.

Informational Election Campaign

Citizens of the Russian Federation and public associations shall be entitled to conduct election campaigning in the forms permitted by law.

The following shall be regarded as *an election campaign*:

- Calls for voting for or against a candidate (list of candidates);
- An expression of preference with regards to any of the candidates and election associations, in particular, statements indicating the

candidate or the list of candidates and election association for which a voter will vote;

- A description of possible consequences of the election or non-election of a candidate or the admittance or non-admittance of the list of candidates to the distribution of deputy seats;
- Distribution of information with an obvious predominance of information on a certain candidate or election associations in combination with positive or negative comments;
- Distribution of information on activities of a candidate unrelated to his professional activity or performance of his official duties;
- Activity promoting the formation of a positive or negative attitude of voters towards a candidate or an election association which nominated a candidate or a list of candidates.

Election campaigning may be conducted on television and by radio broadcasting organizations and in periodicals; by means of public campaigning events; by producing and distributing printed, audio-visual and other campaigning materials, etc.

Election campaigning expenditure shall be paid exclusively out of corresponding electoral funds.

There are limitations for participation in election campaigning, in particular it is prohibited for state and municipal officers to participate with usage of their professional position. Foreigners are also limited in campaigning.

A campaigning period commences from the day of nomination of a candidate or list of candidates and ends at midnight local time one day before the voting day. State and municipal mass media shall ensure equal conditions for the election campaigning of registered candidates, including the presentation of their election programs to voters.

Commissions shall monitor compliance with the established procedure for conducting election campaigning, referendum campaigning and take measures to remove committed violations. Law enforcement and other authorities shall take measures to stop unlawful campaigning activities, prevent production of and seize false and unlawful printed, audio-visual and other campaigning materials, identify the producers of such materials and the source of payment, and promptly inform the corresponding election commission or referendum commission about the facts established and measures taken.

Election Day, Calculation and Publishing of the Results

In order to participate in elections, a voter gets a ballot. The numbering of ballots shall not be allowed. It is also not allowed to personalize ballots by any means.

During voting for candidates, the surnames of registered candidates shall be arranged in the ballot in alphabetical order, and the ballot shall contain the following information about each registered candidate:

- ✓ Surname, first name, patronymic;
- ✓ Year of birth;
- ✓ Name of a Russian Federation subject, district, city, other settlement where the candidate resides;
- ✓ Main place of work or service, official position;
- ✓ If a candidate is a deputy and exercises his powers on a non-permanent basis, this fact and the name of the representative body;
- ✓ If a candidate was nominated by an election association–the words "Nominated by election association" with the abbreviated name of the election association;
- ✓ If a candidate is a self-nominated candidate–the word "self-nomination".

Ballots shall be printed in Russian. Subject to a decision of the commission specified by law, ballots shall be printed in the Russian language and in the official language of the given republic comprised in the Russian Federation.

Elections start at 8 a.m. on a Sunday. The duration of voting shall not be less than ten hours.

Each voter or referendum participant shall vote in person, and voting on behalf of other voters or referendum participants shall be prohibited. Electronic voting may be conducted instead of voting with the use of paper ballots.

Early voting is permitted, however not earlier than 15 days prior to the vote.

After the voting is finished, the commission starts the calculation of the resultsin the presence of the official representatives of the candidates. These results are formalized in the form of protocol.

Vote counting shall be open and transparent, with all actions and results of the counting of ballots and votes of voters carried out by the voting members of the precinct commission being consecutively announced and entered in the enlarged form of the protocol of voting results.

On the basis of the first original copies of the protocol of voting results received from subordinate commissions, a commission duly authorized by the law shall establish the results of elections.

It may be established by law that if more than two candidates were included in the ballot and neither of them received the number of votes required to be elected, the corresponding election commission shall call a repeat vote for two or more candidates who received the largest number of votes. The organization and conduct of a repeat vote, including the order in which information on the candidates for whom a repeat vote is to be conducted is arranged in the ballot, shall be carried out in accordance with the law.

The general results of elections and the information on the number of votes received by each candidate (list of candidates), votes cast for options "Yes" and "No" ("For" and "Against") shall be officially published by the corresponding commission in the order and terms established by law but not later than one month after the voting day.

While conducting elections and referenda the *State Automated Information System "Vybory" (GAS "Vybory")* is used. This is the only electronic official system which may be used for the calculation of votes and consolidation of the data.

4. Financing the Elections

Expenses related to the preparation and conduct of elections of a relevant level in the Russian Federation, the operation and improvement of means of automation, the training of election officials and voter education shall be paid for by election commissions out of the funds allocated for these purposes from an appropriate budget (the federal budget, the budget of the subject of the Russian Federation and (or) the local budget).

Candidates must establish their own electoral funds for funding their election campaigns to the relevant election commission in the period between the submission of a written notice of their nomination (self-nomination) and the submission of documents for their registration by this election commission. At elections to bodies of local self-government a candidate is not required to create an electoral fund, if the number of voters in the electoral district does not exceed five thousand people and the candidate does not finance his election campaign.

Electoral funds of candidates or election associations may be created using the following sources:

- ✓ Own money of a candidate or election association;

- ✓ Sums allocated to a candidate by the election association that nominated the candidate;
- ✓ Voluntary donations of citizens;
- ✓ Voluntary donations of legal entities;
- ✓ Funds that are allocated to a candidate or election association by the corresponding election commission in cases established by the law.

No donations to the electoral funds of candidates or registered candidates, and election associations to referendum funds shall be allowed from:

- ✓ Foreign states and foreign legal entities;
- ✓ Foreign nationals;
- ✓ People without nationality;
- ✓ Citizens of the Russian Federation under 18 years of age on the voting date;
- ✓ Russian legal entities with foreign participation if the foreign share exceeds 30 percent;
- ✓ International organizations;
- ✓ Bodies of state power, other state bodies and bodies of local self-government;
- ✓ State and municipal institutions, states and municipal unitary enterprises;
- ✓ Military units, military institutions and organizations and law enforcement authorities;
- ✓ Charity organizations and religious associations as well as organizations established by them;
- ✓ Anonymous persons and organizations, and some other sources, listed by federal law.

Depending on the level of elections there are limitations on the maximum amount of electoral funds.

In particular, in Presidential Elections the maximum amount of the electoral fund is 400,000,000 Russian Rubles, however in cases where the elections are held in two stages the maximum amount is increased to 500,000,000 Russian Rubles.

The authority to manage electoral funds belongs to candidates and election associations.

Electoral funds may only be used by candidates and election associations to cover expenses related to their election campaigns.

Before the voting day the corresponding election commission shall periodically provide information on the receipt and outgoings of electoral funds to the mass media for publication.

Not later than 30 days from the day of the official publication of the election results, the candidate or election association shall provide the corresponding commission with a final financial report on the size of their electoral fund, the sources used for its creation and on all expenditure out of such electoral fund. The final financial report shall be provided together with initial financial documents evidencing receipt and expenditure of the electoral fund.

Candidates and election associations shall transfer any unspent funds remaining on the special electoral account or referendum account after the voting day to citizens and legal entities that made donations to their electoral funds in proportion to the donations.

For the purposes of supervision over the proper spending of funds allocated to commissions for the preparation and conduct of elections, and over sources, proper accounting, and use of electoral funds, for the auditing of the financial documents of candidates and election associations, supervisory and auditing services shall be established under the Central Election Commission of the Russian Federation or election commissions of the subjects of the Russian Federation.

5. Electoral Disputes

In the process of elections any violations of the rules, established by laws are potentially possible. Russian legislation establishes the rules of appeal of decisions and actions, which violate the electoral rights of citizens.

Appeals of decisions and actions of state bodies and municipal bodies as well as of decisions and actions of commissions and their officials that violate the electoral rights of citizens may be submitted to the courts of general jurisdiction. The decisions and actions of the Central Election Commission are submitted to the Supreme Court of the Russian Federation.

The decisions and actions of the election commission may also be appealed to the superior election commission.

Appeals of decisions and actions that violate the electoral rights of citizens may be submitted by voters, candidates, their attorneys, election associations and their attorneys, or other public associations,

The registration of a candidate shall be annulled by the election commission that registered the candidate if the candidate has lost his passive electoral right or in any other case, described by federal law. A court of an appropriate level may cancel a decision of an election commission on the voting results and election results in an election precinct, territory, electoral district or municipal formation, in the subject of the Russian Federation, in the whole of the Russian Federation in different cases, as described by federal laws, for example in the cases of violation of the rules of preparation of voters' lists, the order of formation of election commissions, the voting and vote counting procedures (including interference with their observation), the establishment of election results, the unlawful refusal of the registration of a candidate, a list of candidates recognized as such after the voting day, and other violations of election legislation if these violations prevent the establishment of the real will of the voters. The cancellation of a decision on election results by an election commission or a court in cases where violations prevent the establishment of the real will of voters shall cause the invalidation of elections in this electoral district.

Citizens and state and municipal officials, who are deemed guilty by the court, will carry administrative, criminal and other types of responsibility as regulated by federal laws.

6. Referendum

A referendum of the Russian Federation is a vote by citizens of the Russian Federation having a participation right in the referendum, concerning an issue of State importance or local importance, depending on the level of the referendum.

The basic law, which regulates the referendum in the Russian Federation, is *Federal Constitutional Law #5-FKZ "On Referendum in the Russian Federation", dated June 28, 2004.*

There are several *types of Referendum* in Russia:

- ➢ Federal referendum;
- ➢ Referendum of the subjects of the Russian Federation;
- ➢ Local (municipal) referendum.

The referendum is carried out on the basis of general equal direct and free declaration of will of citizens of the Russian Federation in the case of a secret ballot. Citizens of the Russian Federation have the right to participate in the referendum irrespective of gender, race, nationality, language, origin, property, residence, and relation to religion, belief, and belonging to public associations. The participation of the citizen of the Russian Federation in the referendum is free and voluntary. Voting on the referendum is secret, thus excluding the possibility of any control of the declaration of will of the citizen of the Russian Federation, including the supervision of the completion of the voting bulletin with the participant of the referendum in the place allocated for the secret vote.

In the Russian Federation, the initiative to conduct a referendum belongs to citizens of the Russian Federation who are entitled to participate in a referendum. *This initiative to perform a referendum* on the federal level should be supported by not less than *2 million citizens* of the Russian Federation, taking into consideration that not more than 50 thousand should live in the territory of each subject of the Russian Federation.

The Constitutional Assembly also has the right to initiate a referendum in the case that this referendum concerns the adoption of the new Constitution of Russia.

In order to initiate a referendum an initiative group may be formed. Any citizen or group of citizens of the Russian Federation who are entitled to participate in a referendum shall have the right to form such an initiative group. The number of persons in such an initiative group for the conducting of a referendum of the Russian Federation constitutes at least 4,200 people, thus the initiative group should be divided by subjects of Russia–not less than 100 people from each subject of the Russian Federation, from more than half of the subjects;the number of persons in the initiative group for conducting a referendum of the subject of the Russian Federation, the local referendum is established by law of the subject of the Russian Federation.

For the initiative to conduct a referendum of the subject of the Russian Federation, a local referendum may also be exercised by an election association or another public association

For a referendum to be called, a referendum initiative shall submit signatures of referendum participants supporting the referendum initiative. A referendum of the Russian Federation shall be called in accordance with the Constitution of the Russian Federation or the federal constitutional law. A referendum of the subject of the Russian Federation shall be called by the legislative body of state power of the subject of the Russian Federation in accordance with federal laws and laws of the subject of the Russian Federation. A local referendum shall be called in accordance with federal laws, laws and the subject of the Russian Federation and the statute of a municipal formation.

Questions brought by a Referendum

The List of questions, permitted and not permitted to be brought by referendum is regulated by federal laws, acts of the subject of federation and local acts, depending on the level of the referendum.

It is important to mention that questions of a referendum of the subject of the Russian Federation should fall within the jurisdiction of the subject of the Russian Federation, or within joint jurisdiction of the Russian

Federation and subjects of the Russian Federation. Questions brought up to a local referendum should only be of local significance.

Questions to be brought up to a referendum shall not restrict or abolish generally recognized human and civil rights and constitutional guarantees for exercising thereof.

The following questions are prohibited from being brought up to a referendum of the subject of the Russian Federation or a local referendum:

- The early termination or prolongation of terms of powers of bodies of state power of the subject of the Russian Federation, bodies of local self-government, on suspension of their authorities, as well as on the conducting of early elections to bodies of state power of the subject of the Russian Federation or bodies of local self-government or the postponement of the said elections;
- A personal list of bodies of state power of the subject of the Russian Federation and bodies of local self-government;
- The election of deputies and officials; approval or appointment or removal of officials; consent to appointment or removal of such officials;
- The adoption or amendment of the corresponding budget; the fulfillment or modification of financial commitments of the subject of the Russian Federation or municipal formation;
- The adoption of extraordinary and urgent measures to ensure the health and security of the population.

This list is full and no other restrictions are established for questions to be brought up for a referendum.

There are limitations for calling a referendum, depending on the time period or situation in the country. Namely, it is not permitted to call the referendum, when:

- *A martial law or a state of emergency* has been established in the territory of the Russian Federation or in the territory in which the referendum is to be conducted or within a part of this territory, or within three months after the martial law or the state of emergency has been removed;
- *The regulations governing the preparation and conduct of the corresponding referendum were violated* in exercising the initiative to conduct such a referendum;
- As established by law, *two years after the referendum is held* it is *not permitted to initiate the other one*, when the wording of the referendum question (questions) is of the same meaning.

A decision adopted at a referendum shall be binding and shall not need any additional approval.

A decision adopted at a referendum of the subject of the Russian Federation or a local referendum may be cancelled or changed by adopting a different decision at a referendum of the subject of the Russian Federation or a local referendum, respectively, but not earlier than two years after the initial decision was adopted, or if the initial decision was invalidated (ceased to be in effect) by a court.

A decision made at a referendum of the subject of the Russian Federation or a local referendum may be *cancelled by a court* on the following grounds:

- The order of conducting a referendum has been violated making it impossible to establish the real will of the referendum participants;
- Non-compliance of the law of the subject of the Russian Federation on the basis of which the referendum of the subject of the Russian Federation was conducted with the Constitution of the Russian Federation;
- Non-compliance of the decision made at a referendum of the subject of the Russian Federation or a local referendum with the Constitution of the Russian Federation, the federal law, and for a local referendum with the law of the subject of the Russian Federation.

If the results of a referendum were invalidated, the commission organizing the voting at a referendum shall call for a repeat vote.

CHAPTER SIX

THE PRESIDENT OF THE RUSSIAN FEDERATION

1. Separation of Powers in Russia

The Constitution of the Russian Federation establishes the separation of powers' system by regulating in Article 11 that

> *State power in the Russian Federation shall be exercised by the President of the Russian Federation, the Federal Assembly (the Federation Council and the State Duma), the Government of the Russian Federation, and the courts of the Russian Federation.*

The three powers' system is fixed: the legislative is represented by the Federal Assembly, the executive is represented by the Government of the Russian Federation and the judiciary is represented by the courts of the Russian Federation.

The separation of powers is one of the main warranties from usurpation and is part of the democratic State system of the development of State Bodies. The Russian Constitution declared the *separation of powers* and moreover clearly fixed the volume of powers of each body.

But where is the President? *The President of the Russian Federation* does not enter into any branch of power, being the Head of State and having powers related to each of the three mentioned.

In accordance with the Russian Constitution the President of Russia is the solitary *Head of the State*, who is elected by the citizens with active voters' rights. The President issues legal regulations, discharges leadership duties, settles disputes and ensures that the Constitution is observed.

The President of the Russian Federation possesses immunity.

The President is responsible for ensuring that the constitutions and legislation of Russia's constituent territories do not contravene the Constitution of the country or federal laws. If they do, the President is empowered to demand from any governmental body of the Russian Federation or one of its constituent territories that it respects civil and human rights and liberties and, if they are violated, that they be restored in full.

The legal status of the President, his elections and the termination of the powers is regulated by:

- The Constitution of the Russian Federation, chapter 4;
- Federal Law #19FZ "On President of Russian Federation elections" dated by January 10, 2003.

The institution of Presidency first appeared in the USSR in the year 1990, by the adoption of the Law of the USSR "On the foundation of the President position". M. Gorbatchov was elected as the first President of the USSR, however by termination of the USSR in December 1991 this official position terminated its existence.

In the RSFSR–in such a way Russia was called as part of the Soviet Union (USSR) and the creation of the new state–the Russian Federation, the official position of the President of the RSFSR was adopted by the Law "On the President of RSFSR" on April 24, 1991 and June 12, 1991 the first President of Russia (RSFSR) was elected.

2. Elections of the President

The President of the Russian Federation is elected for a term of six years by the citizens of the Russian Federation as it is established by Article 81 of the Constitution of Russia. The requirements for the candidate are established as follows:

- Over 35 years old;
- A legally capable citizen of Russia, living permanently in Russia not less than 10 years;
- Not being in prison due to the court decision in force.

The term of Presidency is limited by the Constitution as follows: "One and the same person will not be elected the President of the Russian Federation for more than two terms running each after each".

This constitutional provision was clarified by the Constitutional Court of Russia by the decision, dated November 5, 1998, in accordance with which two terms there should be followed by a one term gap and only afterwards may the candidate participate in the following elections.

Elections are announced by *the Federation Council* in accordance with the Constitution. The day of elections is fixed as the second Sunday of the month after the expiration of the previous constitutional term of the President.

Candidates may be nominated as follows:

- Self-nomination provided the requirements, established by Law, are fulfilled.
- By political parties, empowered to participate in elections.

Self-nomination should be supported by the voters' group of not less than 500 citizens of Russia having active electoral right. A self-nominated candidate is entitled to collect not less than 300,000 signatures of voters, however each subject of Russia should give not more than 7,500 of voters' signatures.

The candidate, nominated by a political party should provide 100,000 signatures of voters and each region of Russia should give not more than 2,500 of voters' signatures. It is worth mentioning that this requirement is applied to the parties, which have no official representation *in the State Duma* (Parliament chamber) based on previous elections. In the case where the party is presented *in the State Duma* and decides to nominate a candidate for the Presidential elections, a collection of voters' signatures is not required.

After the candidate is registered by the Central Election Commission of the Russian Federation he may start an election campaign which consists of meetings with voters, speaking on television and radio, interviewing with mass media resources, etc.

Presidential elections may consist of one or two rounds. If one of the candidates gets more than 50 per cent of the votes in the first round he/she is the winner, however in the case of fewer votes, a second round becomes obligatory and the two candidates who had the majority of votes during the first round are entered into the second one. The winner of the second round and the elected President is the person who obtained a simple majority of votes.

The Central Election Commission has 10 days to calculate the results and announce the winner.

The next step after the elections is the *Inauguration* procedure.

The Constitution of Russia in Article 82 implements the text of the Presidential oath:

> *"I swear in exercising the powers of the President of the Russian Federation to respect and safeguard the rights and freedoms of man and citizen, to observe and protect the Constitution of the Russian Federation, to protect the sovereignty and independence, security and integrity of the State, to faithfully serve the people".*

This oath is taken in the presence of members of the Council of the Federation, members of the State Duma and judges of the Constitutional Court of the Russian Federation.

3. Termination of the Presidential Authorities

It is surely worth mentioning that normally the President's powers are expired by the newly-elected President of Russia taking of the oath of loyalty.

The Constitution of Russia limits early official termination of the President's authorities by the following grounds:

- Resignation;
- Inability to exercise the powers due to health reasons;
- Dismissal from the official position.

Let us review these grounds in more detail.

1. *Resignation* is the voluntary decision of the President to terminate his/her activity. There should be different reasons for this decision and the subsequent act of resignation, such as a health condition, family problem, fatigue, etc. There is no detailed regulation for the resignation procedure, it is just necessary for the President to declare the resignation. There is no legal requirement for any state body to accept this resignation.

In the period from the time that the Constitution of Russia was adopted in the year 1993 there has only been one case when the President of Russia declared his resignation. It was on December 31, 1999, when President Boris Yeltsin made his official speech informing the citizens of Russia about his resignation. At the same time he signed the Presidential Decree on his resignation and the empowerment of the new acting President. As it is regulated by the Constitution, when the President is incapable of fulfilling his duties, they shall be temporarily fulfilled by the Chairman of the Government of the Russian Federation; however the powers of the acting President are limited. There is no right to dissolve the State Duma, call a referendum, or to submit proposals on amendments to, and review of, the provisions of the Constitution of the Russian Federation.

2. *Inability to exercise the powers due to health reasons.* These grounds are listed only by the Constitution of Russia and have no detailed clarification in Russian legislation. On July 11, 2000 the Constitutional Court of the Russian Federation touched upon this issue in its decision and expressed the position, that this procedure requires additional clarification by Russian legislation. There is no a concrete procedure for a detailed explanation of health reasons and which bodies should participate in the procedure of settlement of the inability to exercise the powers of the President due to health reasons.

3. *Dismissal from the official position.* This ground for early termination of the President's authority has more clear and detailed

regulation in Russian law. It is necessary to mention that sometimes this procedure is mixedup with procedure of impeachment of the President of United States, however legally these procedures are not the same.

Dismissal of the President from the official position constitutes the measure of constitutional liability of the President of State. The details of this procedure are clearly described by the Constitution in Article 93.

The Constitution establishes the following *reasons for dismissal:*

1. *High Treason;*
2. *Grave Crime.*

In accordance with clause 93 of the Constitution the following bodies participate in the process of dismissal of the President:

- The State Duma;
- The Supreme Court of the Russian Federation;
- The Constitutional Court of the Russian Federation;
- The Federation Council.

Let us go into more detail into the roles of these bodies in the dismissal process and define the stages of the process.

1st Stage. Procedure is being initiated by the State Duma, when not less than *one-third of State Duma members* should support an initiative of accusing the President. The proposal of accusing the President should include the defined characteristics of the crime and a clear explanation of the President's role in the performance of this crime.

2nd Stage. The State Duma accepts an Order on formation of the special commission on the assessment of the case and the procedure of its performance. This commission is formatted on a temporary basis and its members are selected on the basis of equal representation from each party, presented in *the State Duma*. This commission reviews all the relevant documentation and finalizes its opinion in the form of a Conclusion, which should be supported by the majority of the commission. After acceptance this Conclusion is sent to the *Council of the State Duma*.

3rd Stage. The *State Duma* on its hearing meeting reviews the proposal of accusing of the President and all the supportive documentation, including the Conclusion of the special commission. It is necessary to get no less than two-thirds of the votes (300 member votes) of the *State Duma* members to get approval of the accusation.

4th Stage. In the case that the State Duma approves the proposal of accusation, the next stage is the review of the *Supreme Court*, which analyses if there is a crime in the actions of the President. Based upon the review of the case *the Supreme Court* issues a *Conclusion. The State Duma* applies to *the Supreme Court* at the same time that the Conclusion, adopted by the *State Duma,* is sent to *the Federation Council.*

5th Stage. When the Supreme Court issues a positive Conclusion, confirming the crime in the actions of the President, the case is transferred *to the Constitutional Court of the Russian Federation*. The involvement of the *Constitutional Court* is based upon the application issued by the *Federation Council* and sent to the *Constitutional Court*.

6th Stage. The Constitutional Court reviews the case and analyses the constitutionality of the procedure conducted. If it is fully in line with the Constitution, *the Constitutional Court* gives a positive Conclusion which is forwarded to *the Federation Council*.

7th Stage. Upon positive conclusion, provided by the Constitutional Court, *the Federation Council* starts an official review of the case and all supporting documents, consisting of the Conclusions, done by *the State Duma*, *the Supreme Court* and *the Constitutional Court,* and it is definitely *the Federation Council*that makes the final point in the procedure of dismissal. In the case that members of *the Federation Council* make a decision by two-thirds of the votes (it is necessary to get at least 111 member votes) and support the accusation, taking into account that from the date of the accusation by *the State Duma* to the date of the final decision taken by the Council of the Federation, no more than *three months* should have passed–then the President is dismissed. If the procedure is not finalized within three months the accusation against the President is treated as rejected.

In Russian history after the last Constitution of 1993 was adopted, there was only one case when the dismissal procedure was initiated, in 1999 members of the State Duma started an initiative to dismiss President Boris Yeltsin. The initiative to dismiss, based on five potential crimes conducted by Yeltsin, was supported by more than one-third of the members of the State Duma and a special commission was elected to review the case. After all the materials were prepared and transferred to the discussion of the State Duma it appeared that there were not enough votes to support this case.

4. Competence of the President

The competence of the President of the Russian Federation is based on the constitutional provision, which clearly describes his status as the Head of State. The President does not enter into any branch of power, being the regulating and balancing figure for the three known powers: legislative, executive and judiciary. Moreover the clear and full description of the President's status is given by Article 80 of the Constitution. The President is the Head of State, guarantor of the Constitution and the rights and freedoms of man and citizen. The competence of the President, which is described in detail by the Constitution, assists him to realize his status.

The scope of his competence is quite wide, assisting the President to act in almost any sphere of the political life in the country.

In accordance with the Constitution the President:

1) Acts as guarantor of the Constitution and the rights and freedoms of man and citizen;
2) Takes measures on the protection of sovereignty, independence and state integrity;
3) Performs unity of the power within the whole country and the functioning and interaction of all state bodies;
4) In accordance with the Constitution and federal laws definesthe main directions of internal and external policy;
5) Represents Russia in relations with other countries;
6) Solves issues in the area of citizenship;
7) Acts as the Supreme Commander-in-Chief of the Armed Forces of the Russian Federation.

Based on the nature of the competence and interaction with other state bodies the competence of the President of the Russian Federation can be separated into the following groups:

1st group: Competence in the area of interaction with Federal Bodies

The President of Russia is empowered with a wide range of authorities in the sphere of the formation of state bodies. We may separate them by the three branches of powers: interaction with Legislative power, interaction with Executive power and interaction with Judiciary power.

a) Interaction with the Legislative power–the Parliament.

- The President announces elections of the State Duma;
- The President has the right to dissolve the State Duma in some cases and according to the rules established by the Constitution of the Russian Federation.

These cases are the following:

o *As the result of the non-acceptance by the State Duma of the candidacy of the Chairman of the Government of the Russian Federation.*

In accordance with Article 111 of the Constitution the Chairman of the Government of the Russian Federation shall be appointed by the President of the Russian Federation with the consent of the State Duma. The proposal of the candidate is submitted by the President not later than two weeks after a newly-elected President has started the official job or after the resignation of the Government of the Russian Federation or one week after the State Duma has rejected the candidate.

The State Duma shall consider the candidate nominated by the President of the Russian Federation for the post of the Chairman of the Government of the Russian Federation during the week after the submission of the nomination. If the State Duma rejects the candidates three times for the post of the Chairman of the Government of the Russian Federation, the President should dissolve the State Duma and appoint new elections. There are no limitations in law for proposing the same candidate three times consecutively.

o *As the result of a motion of no-confidence, expressed by the State Duma to the Government of the Russian Federation.*

In accordance with the Article 117 of the Constitution, the State Duma may express noconfidence in the Government of the Russian Federation. A no-confidence resolution shall be adopted by a majority of votes of the total number of the deputies of the State Duma. After the State Duma expresses no-confidence in the Government of the Russian Federation, the President of the Russian Federation is free to announce the resignation of the Government or to reject the decision of the State Duma. If the State Duma again expresses no-confidence in the Government of the Russian Federation, then within *three months* the President of the Russian Federation *shall announce* the resignation of the Government or dissolve the State Duma.

The Chairman of the Government of the Russian Federation may raise before the State Duma the issue of confidence in the Government of the Russian Federation. If the State Duma votes no-confidence, the President shall adopt a decision within seven days on the resignation of the Government of the Russian Federation or dissolve the State Duma and announce new elections.

➢ The President promulgates federal laws adopted by the State Duma and the Federation Council.

Promulgation includes the signature of the Law and following official publication. In accordance with the Constitution the President may also use his suspensive veto right, when he is not in full agreement with the law which was adopted by the State Duma and the Federation Council, and does not want to sign such law. In this case, in accordance with Article 107 of the Constitution, the Parliament may overcome the suspensive veto by the qualified majority of votes or amend the law using the conciliation procedure.

➢ The President is empowered with the right of legislative initiative.

This right is not limited by competence and the President may initiate the law in any area, moreover, e.g. the President has the monopoly right to initiate Federal Constitutional Laws about the creation of the new subject of the federation.

- The President appoints his official representatives in the State Duma and in the Federation Council.

These official representatives facilitate interaction between the President and the deputies of the State Duma and members of the Federation Council, and they have the right to participate in plenary hearings, committee's discussions, etc.

- The President addresses the Federal Assembly annually with a message on the situation in the country, and on the guidelines for the internal and foreign policies of the State.

This practice has been known since 1994, when the President started addressing members of the Federation Council and deputies of the State Duma, presenting his assessment of the situation in the spheres of public life and formulating his views on fundamental aspects of state internal and international policy. There is no doubt, that this message becomes an important guideline for the Federal Assembly, the Government and the whole country. The President's position on issues of domestic policy is taken into account in law-making activities.

b) Interaction of the President with the Executive Power–the Government of the Russian Federation.

The President has a vast scope of responsibilities in relation with the Executive power. It is known that in accordance with the Constitution the President does not enter into any branch of powers; however there is the opinion that due to his competence he is the closest to the Executive power. The following are the competences, established by the Russian Constitution and other laws in the sphere of the interaction with the Government:

- Appointment of the Head of the Government, based on the agreement with the State Duma, as it was described earlier in this book;
- At the proposal of the Chairman of the Government of the Russian Federation, to appoint and dismiss the deputy Chairmen of the Government of the Russian Federation and federal ministers. The candidates are recommended by the Chairman of the Government;
- The President of Russia approves the system of the federal executive power. It is done by means of the President's Decree;
- The President manages several federal executive bodies.

Among them there are the following ministries: the Ministry for Internal Affairs, the Ministry for Civil Defence, Emergencies and Elimination of Consequences of Natural Disasters; the Ministry for Foreign Affairs, the Ministry of Defence, the Ministry of Justice, about 10 Services and Agencies.

- Chair meetings of the Government;

The President of Russia may chair meetings of the Government, especially when the most important issues of the State are being discussed;

- Adopt a decision on the resignation of the Government of the Russian Federation;
- Suspend acts of the Executive power bodies of the subjects of Russia.

The President has the right to suspend acts of the bodies of executive power of the subjects of the Russian Federation if these acts contradict the Constitution of the Russian Federation and the federal laws or international commitments of the Russian Federation or violate the rights and freedoms of man and citizen until the issue is settled using the court procedure.

- The President has the right to cancel acts and decisions, issued by the Government of the Russian Federation.

c) Interaction of the President with the Judiciary power–the courts of the Russian Federation

The President has rather wide responsibilities in the area of interaction with the Judiciary power. Most of these powers are connected with the formation of the judicial community, in particular the President:

- Presents to the Federation Council candidates for appointment as judges of the Constitutional Court of the Russian Federation and the Supreme Court of the Russian Federation;
- Appoints judges of other federal courts.

Not all state bodies could fall into the three branches of law. For instance the Central Bank, the Accounts Chamber and the Procurator Office are separate *independent State bodies*. The President of Russia has responsibilities in forming these bodies, since the President:

- Submits a candidate for the post of the Procurator-General of the Russian Federation to the Federation Council and a proposal to dismiss the Procurator-General of the Russian Federation;
- Submits the candidates of the Chairman of the Accounts Chamber of the Russian Federation and Deputy Chairman of the Accounts Chamber of the Russian Federation to the State Duma, and by the Federation Council;

➢ Participates in the formation of the Central Electoral Commission, appointing five of its members.

2nd group: Competence in the area of interaction with the Bodies of the subjects of the Federation

The President of Russia in accordance with the provisions of Article 78 of the Constitution is entitled to ensure the concerted functioning and interaction of all bodies of state power on the whole territory of the Russian Federation. The President performs this function in coordination with the Government of the Russian Federation. While describing this scope of competence it is necessary to mention what it entails.

a) Solving disputes between the federal State bodies and State bodies of the subjects of Federation

The President of the Russian Federation may use conciliatory procedures to solve disputes between the State bodies of the Russian Federation and bodies of State bodies of the subjects of the Russian Federation, as well as between bodies of state of the subjects of the Russian Federation. If no agreed decision is reached, he has the right to submit the dispute for the consideration of a corresponding court.

These procedures may be realized in the different forms, such as joint discussion of the arguable issues, creation of the conciliation commissions, public discussions, etc. It is important to mention that an initiative may come from different sides: the President, State Duma, state bodies of subjects of the Federation, or other bodies.

b) Appointment of the President's Plenipotentiary Envoys in the Federal Districts

Article 83 of the Constitution of the Russian Federation in its subclause "j" regulates the constitutional right of the President to appoint the plenipotentiary envoys in the federal districts. In execution of this constitutional right the President adopted the Decree, dated *by May 13, 2000 #849 "On the Plenipotentiary Envoy in the Federal District"*, which regulates in detail the status and role of plenipotentiary envoys. In accordance with these documents the purpose of these Envoys is to ensure a better performance by the President of his responsibilities, to support better coordination between the Head of the State and authorities of the subjects of the Federation in order to maintain stability and better performance of the duties of the President and regional authorities.

Currently in Russia there are nine Federal Districts: the Central Federal District, Northwestern Federal District, Southern Federal District, North Caucasian Federal District, Volga Federal District, Urals

Federal District, Siberian Federal District, Far Eastern Federal District and Crimean Federal District. Each of them is headed by the Plenipotentiary Envoy, appointed by the President of the Russian Federation. Plenipotentiary Envoys and their deputies are part of the President's Administration.

c)Participation in formation of the State Bodies of the subjects of the Russian Federation and control over their activity

In accordance with the provisions of the Constitution and State legislation, the President participates in the formation of the State Bodies of the subject. For instance, in accordance with internal regulations adopted by the concrete subject of the Federation the President has the right to nominate the candidacy for the post of the Head of the Subject (head of the Executive Power) and introduce this candidate to the local legislative body for approval.

Moreover, the President has the right to terminate the authority of the Head of the Subject in two cases:

- A loss of trust from the President to the Head of the Subject; or
- In the case of the legislative body of the Subject expressing a motion of no-confidence in the Head of the Subject.

After the authority of the Head of Subject is terminated by the President, he appoints a temporary Head until the new one takes up this position in accordance with the procedure, prescribed by law.

If the Head of the Subject issues an act which is contradictory to the provisions of the Constitution of the Russian Federation, the President is entitled to suspend this act until it is adjusted in line with current legislation and following this suspension to take out a warning on the Head of the Subject. In the case that the Head of the Subject proceeds with this unlawful activity the President has the right to release the Head of the Subject from his duties.

3rd group: Competence in the area of State defence and security

a)The President–is the Supreme Commander-in-Chief of the Armed Forces

In accordance with the Constitution the President is the Supreme Commander-in-Chief of the Armed Forces of the Russian Federation; approves the Military Doctrine, which means the plans for Armed Forces development and mobilization and covers all issues, related to the performance and development of the Army and its position in the modern world.

The President appoints and dismisses the High officers of the Armed Forces and forms and heads the Security Council of the Russian Federation.

b) The President is vested by exclusive right to impose martial law

In accordance with the Constitution of the Russian Federation the President is monopoly empowered to impose martial law. In accordance with adopted Federal Constitutional Law "On Martial Law" the President issues the Decree, which should be approved by the Federation Council.

c) The President approves the structure and quantity of the Armed Forces and related organizations

Federal Law "*On Defence*", dated April 24, 1996 defines more clearly the responsibility of the President in this area. The Head of State presides over the Armed Forces and other army bodies, forms and terminates state executive bodies within the period of war, approves federal programs on the development of army manufacturing, approves the list of army official positions, approves the structure of the Armed Forces and the total number of members.

4th group: Competence in the area of external affairs

a)The President governs foreign policy

The President governs the foreign policy of the Russian Federation and appoints and recalls diplomatic representatives, however after consultations with corresponding committees and commissions of the chambers of the Federal Assembly.

b) The President represents the Russian Federation in international relations

During foreign visits the President represents the Russian Federation; he conducts negotiations and signs international treaties and agreements without any prior approval from another State Body. He also represents the Russian Federation during the visits of foreign official bodies to Russia and signs relevant documents.

c) The President formulates foreign policy guidelines in his annual Message to the Federal Assembly

These foreign policy guidelines become a directive to the Minister for Foreign Affairs, who is a direct subordinate to the President. These guidelines also influence Parliament memberswhen drafting and adopting laws, and the Government in general during the execution of the laws in force and international treaties in force on the territory of the Russian Federation.

5th group: Competence in the area of citizenship, awarding State decorations and pardons

This area of competence seems to be traditional for the Head of State. The President decides the issues of citizenship and grants citizenship for those who have applied in accordance with federal laws. Citizenship in Russia is qualified as a stable legal connection between the State and the citizen, expressed in the combination of rights and duties. The President makes decisions on the admittance to citizenship, the exit from citizenship and the restoration of citizenship, when a person applies within common procedure. *The Commission for citizenship issues,* organized within the structure *of Presidential commissions*, assists the President to solve issues with citizenship. The President is empowered in the area of granting the *State Asylum*. These powers of the Head of State are regulated by the President's Decree, dated by July 21, 1997 "*On the granting of the State Asylum by the Russian Federation*". Granting of the State Asylum is in the President's power, which is formalized by a Decree of the President.

The President has the power to award State Decorations and honorary titles. Awarding Decorations and honorary titles is supported by a Decree issued by the President. The *Commission for State Decorations* is an advisory body established to assist the President in his constitutional duty.

The President of Russia has powers in the area of a pardon. A pardon means forgiveness by the State of a crime and conviction of a person, followed by the cancellation of the penalty imposed on that person. The President has the right to pardon in accordance with Article 89 of the Constitution of the Russian Federation. It is necessary not to mix *pardon*, which is individual act, with *amnesty* which is a collective act. An *Amnesty* is provided in Russia by the *State Duma* and applies to a certain group of people. Currently, applications for a pardon are analyzed on the level of subjects of the Federation and subsequent proposals are provided by the President of Russia. It is necessary to mention that this right is not very often used by the Head of State.

6th group: Competence in other spheres

There are other competences belonging to the President which cannot be grouped with others. For example, only the President is entitled to announce referendum at the state level. The procedure of referendum is regulated in detail by the Federal Constitutional Law "*On Referendum*", dated by June 28, 2004 #5-FKZ.

The President forms the Executive Office of the President of the Russian Federation (Administration) which acts as a support body to the President and assists him in the fulfillment of his constitutional duties and rights.

5. Acts of the President

As the Head of the State the President has the right to issue acts, which are statutory acts. In accordance with Article 90 of the Constitution of the Russian Federation the President issues *decrees* and *orders*. They are mandatory for the fulfillment of the whole territory of the Russian Federation.

Decrees–are mandatory statutory acts. They are expected to have a repeated usage and a non-defined list of subjects. Some of the Decrees are of an individual nature, when a Decree is issued on citizenship, for state decorations, the appointment of the Head of the Government, on political asylum, on a pardon, etc. Such acts are applied only to the person listed.

Orders–are of an individual nature, issued for special cases, for instance human resources, organizations, etc. Orders are issued while regulating the activity of the Executive Office of the President. Orders are issues mostly on current issues.

The legal force of the Decrees is higher than the Orders; however they should be in line with the Constitution, federal laws and international treaties, ratified in Russia.

Acts of the President do not require subsequent approval and enter into force on the expiration of seven days after the date of their first official publication.

Presidential Decrees should be published in the named *official resources*, which are the same as for the official resources for publishing federal laws and described in the chapter "Legislative Power" of this book, unless they consist of the information which constitutes a State Secret or are confidential. They are published within ten days after signature by the President.

The Federal Government controls the execution of the Decrees, signed by the President in accordance with Federal Constitutional Law #2-FKZ "*On the Government of the Russian Federation*", dated December 17, 1997.

The Presidential Executive Office monitors the enforcement of the Presidential decrees and orders, and reports back the results to the President.

Presidential Decrees and Orders cannot be cancelled by other state bodies. Only the Constitutional Court of the Russian Federation has the right to name them as not complying with the Constitution by the request of the relevant applicant.

6. State Institutions Connected with the President

While analyzing the status of the President it is very important to list the State institutions, which are interrelated with the President.

They can be classified into the following categories:

a) Supportive bodies

The Presidential Executive Office (Administration of the President) is a State Body, responsible for the provision of administrative support to the President in all areas of his activity as the Head of State.

The Status of the Presidential Executive Office is regulated by the Decree of the President, dated by April 6, 2004. It is formed by the President and consists of a list of subdivisions, such as:

- *Presidential State-Legal Directorate*, responsible for the provision of legal support to the Presidential Executive Office;
- *Presidential Control Directorate*, which oversees the federal laws and other statutory acts for implementation of the President's decision and supports the President in due implementation of Presidential policy;
- *Presidential Speechwriting Office*, preparing drafts of speeches for the President as well as other publishing activity;
- *Presidential Foreign Policy Directorate*, supporting the President with the main foreign policy rules and participating in the creation of general foreign policy strategy;
- *Presidential Domestic Policy Directorate*, which provides support to the President in outlining domestic policy and provides the President with information about the situation in the country;
- *Presidential Directorate for the Protection of Citizens' Constitutional Rights*, which provides support in realization of the President's constitutional rights in the area of human rights implementation, and *other directorates*.

The role of the Presidential Executive Office is rather high, since this body supports the President in drafting laws, Presidential Decrees and Orders, Presidential speeches and other documents, signed by the President. The Presidential Executive Office plays a serious role in the interaction between the President and other players of the political system, such as political parties, non-governmental organizations, foreign State

Bodies and their representatives, foreign politicians and members of international organizations.

Permanent Plenipotentiary Representatives of the President in nine Federal Districts are also part of the Presidential Executive Office.

b) Consulting bodies

The role of the consulting bodies is also very high. Mostly they provide consulting support to the President in performance of his duties; however, some of them participate in advising the President of the most important issues of Domestic and Foreign Policy.

The State Council

This consulting body was created in accordance with the Decree of the President, dated September 1, 2000. One of the reasons for its creation was the reform of the formation terms of the Federation Council, when governors of the Russian regions (subjects of the Federation) lost their right to represent the interests of their regions on a federal level, namely in the Federation Council. The State Council consists of the governors of the regions and other members directly appointed by the President, as for example, the Permanent Plenipotentiary Representatives in Federal Districts.

The main purpose of this body is to assist regions in realizing their policy on a federal level andto facilitate interaction between regional power and federal power. The meetings of the State Council are conducted once every quarter and include discussions on the most important issues of the relations between federal and regional powers. The President of Russia heads the State Council. The members of the State Council form the Presidium for deciding burning issues, and this consists of seven members, holding meetings once every month. All the decisions of this body are of a pure *consulting* nature.

The Security Council

In accordance with provisions of Article 83 of the Constitution the President of Russia formed the Security Council. The status of this body is regulated in details by the *Law of Russia "About security"*, dated by March 5, 1992 and the *Presidential Decree of June 7, 2004*.

The Security Council is a constitutional body supporting the President in the area of the realization of Presidential policy in the area of national security, which includes the security of the individual, society and the state from threats, arising both internally and externally.

The Structure *of the Security Council* includes the Head of the Security Council–the President of Russia, and permanent and other members. The President appoints members of the Security Council. The Security Council Office, which supports the activity of the Security Council, is a separate directorate of the Presidential Executive Office.

Permanent members of the Security Council are the Head of Government, the first deputy to the Head of Government, the Minister of Defence, the Head of the Presidential Executive Office, the Head of the Federation Council, the Head of the State Duma, the Secretary of the Security Council, the Minister for Foreign Affairs, the Minister for Internal Affairs, the Head of the Federal Security Service and the Head of the Service of External Investigation.

Among the members *of the Security Council* are the Head of the Minister of Finance, the Minister of Justice, the Head of the Army Headquarters, etc. The President has the right to amend the list of Security Council members. The Security Council prepares proposals on defending the State and its citizens from internal and external threats and participates in the formation of State Policy in the area of security. Meetings of the Security Council take place in accordance with a plan, adopted by the President of Russia; however extraordinary meetings are also possible, when it is necessary to discuss burning issues.

Presidential Commissions and Presidential Councils

While looking into the structure and list of the bodies which support the President in the realization of constitutional rights and duties it is necessary not to underestimate the role of Presidential Commissions and Presidential Councils. Within the term of performance of Presidential duties this list may change from time to time, among the list there are the following Commissions: the *Commission for Strategic Development of the Fuel and Energy Sector and Environmental Security, Commission for Civil Service and Management Personnel Pool, Commission for Military Technology Cooperation with Foreign States, Commission for Screening Candidates for Federal Judges, Interdepartmental Commission for the Implementation of the National Program to Assist the Voluntary Resettlement in Russia of Compatriots Currently Living Abroad, Commission for State Decorations, Commission for Rehabilitation of the Victims of Political Repression, Commission for Citizenship Issues, etc.*

Presidential Councils: *for Economic Modernization and Innovative Development, Council for Interethnic Relations, Council for Countering Corruption, Council for Civil Society and Human Rights, Council for the Financial Market Development, Council for the Local Self-Government Development, etc.*

The main purpose of these Councils and Commissions is to advise the President on different issues within his scope of competence. These bodies are formed by specialists in different areas and well-known respected experts.

CHAPTER SEVEN

THE LEGISLATIVE POWER: THE FEDERAL ASSEMBLY LEGISLATIVE PROCESS

The Russian Constitution regulates that legislative power in Russia shall be exercised by the *Federal Assembly*–the Parliament of the Russian Federation–which is the representative and legislative body of the Russian Federation.

The legal Status of the *Federal Assembly*, its formation, rules and competences are regulated by the following laws and regulations:

- ✓ *The Constitution (chapter 5);*
- ✓ *Federal Law № 20-FZ "On elections of the Deputies of the State Duma of the Federal Assembly of the Russian Federation" dated February 22, 2014;*
- ✓ *Federal Law № 229-FZ "On Formation Procedure of the Federation Council of the Federal Assembly" dated December 3, 2012;*
- ✓ *Regalement of the State Duma;*
- ✓ *Regalement of the Federation Council.*

1. History of the Russian Parliament

The history of the representative body in Russia goes back to ancient times, when *Veche* was functioning as a form of power, permitting common people to participate in the decision of important issues. Strictly speaking, *Veche* cannot be named as a predecessor of the Parliament, since it was a meeting of all free people having a right to vote, however the "*law-making*" function was very close to the modern parliament.

Later on, in the middle ages, in different parts of Russia the Boyar duma and then Zemskysobor started to function, playing a serious role in making laws and in other important issues.

At the beginning of the 19th century a new body was founded–the State Council which was named as a legislative and consulting body and which participated in law-procedure in the Russian Empire. It certainly cannot be qualified as a parliament, since members were appointed by the Tsar and Chairman of the State Council the same time combined his duties as the Chairman of the Government; however the State Council participated in the discussion of the laws in Russia.

The beginning of the 20th century is known as the transformation of the monarchy in Russia, as the State Duma was created in 1906. The State Duma and the State Council practically constituted the Parliament of Russia, being the chambers of this Parliament. Laws which were signed by the Tsar required prior approval from both chambers–the State Duma and the State Council.

The revolution of 1917 changed the political system and the form of ruling in Russia. Russia transferred from the monarchy to the State of Soviets. Soviets meant the new system of representative power.

On the State level, when the USSR as the new state was created in 1922 the highest legislative and representative body became the Supreme Soviet. According to the Constitution, the Supreme Soviet was empowered to elect the Presidium of the Supreme Soviet, to form the Government and the Supreme Court of the USSR and to appoint the General Prosecutor. The Supreme Soviet consisted of two chambers: the Council of Union and the Council of Nationalities.

The Constitution of Russia, dated December 12, 1993 in its Chapter 5, regulated the legislative branch of power as the two chamber parliament–the Federal Assembly, where the *State Duma* and *Federation Council* are the two chambers. The *State Duma* is formatted as a result of elections and represents the whole nation, whereas the *Federation Council* is formatted by two representatives from each subject of the Federation and represents the interests of the subjects. The Federal Assembly has its permanent place in Moscow.

2. Status of the Federal Assembly

The Federal Assembly–the Parliament of the Russian Federation is the highest legislative body, which acts on a federal level. The Parliament is bicameral, which is typical for federative states.

The features of the Federal Assembly, which are specific due to its nature as the parliament of the country, are the following:

1) The Federal Assembly is the national representative body acting on the level of federal power;

2) It is a legislative body, which possesses the exclusive right to adopt laws on the federal level;

3) This State body is permanently acting;
4) Activity is done in the special procedural forms.

Analyzing the activity of the Russian Parliament we may separate three main functions, as:

➢ *Legislative function*

Legislative function means the absolute exclusive right of Parliament to adopt laws, through usage of the formalized legislative procedure. Only the Federal Assembly is empowered to adopt acts with the status of laws by consecutive review by both chambers in accordance with procedure regulated by the Constitution and federal laws. Elimination of the Parliament from the legislative procedure will never give the act status of federal law in Russia. Delegated legislation is not present in the Russian Federation.

➢ *Control function*

The control function results from the separation of powers and the performance of the "checks and balances" system in Russia. The legislative branch of power plays an important role in this system and acts in several aspects: control over the Government, for example expressing non-confidence, it has control of the appointment of different state officers, like the State Duma it provides approval to the President of the appointment of the Head of Governments, and the Federation Council approves the candidacies of the High courts' judges, etc.

➢ *Finance function*

The State Duma plays an important role in the adoption of the state budget and control over budgetary performance. The Government develops and initiates the draft of the state budget, which should be reviewed and approved by the State Duma and subsequently by the Federation Council and the President. The Government provides the State Duma with the detailed yearly report of the State Budget performance. The Federal Assembly as the Parliament of the Russian Federation participates in the formation of the Accounts Chamber and the appointment of the Head of the Central Bank of Russia.

We will review these functions in detail later in this chapter.

3. The Federation Council

The Federation Council is the permanently acting body–the chamber of the Russian Parliament. It consists of the 170 members and represents interests of the subjects of the Russian Federation in the Russian Parliament. It is formed by two representatives from each subject: one representative from the executive power and one representative from the legislative power.

Formation of the Federation Council

The formation of the Federation Council is regulated by the *Federal Law № 229-FZ "On Formation Procedure of the Federation Council of the Federal Assembly" dated December 3, 2012.*

The following are the requirements of the candidate to the Federation Council:

- ✓ A citizen of the Russian Federation with a permanent residence for five years on the territory of the subject of the Federation which he will represent in the Federation Council as a general rule;
- ✓ To be 30 years old;
- ✓ Having a faultless reputation;
- ✓ Completely capable;
- ✓ Having no connections with foreign countries, like foreign citizenship or residence in other countries;
- ✓ For the representatives from the legislative body there is the additional requirement to be the deputy of this legislative body.

Representatives of different branches of power acquire the position in the Federation Council by different means.

Candidate of the Representative of the legislative body of the subject of Russia is proposed by the Chairman, deputies group more than one-fifth of the total list of deputies or deputies' factions. The decision is made by the majority of the deputies of the legislature within one month, starting from the date of the first session of the legislative body.

*Candidates to the position of the Representative of the executive body of the subject of Russia*are nominated by the candidate to the position of the Head of the subject of the Russian Federation, at the same time Head of the executive power. Each candidate to the position of the Head of the subject nominates three different names. After the elections are completed the person who becomes the Head of the subject, within one day from the date of empowerment, selects one candidate from this list of three candidates and this person is vested with the powers of the member of the Federation Council. The term of authority of each member of the Federation Council depends on the term of authority of the body which nominated him to the Federation Council.

Competence of the Federation Council

Competence of the Federation Council is defined by *the Constitution of the Russian Federation* (Art.102) and clarified in *the Regalement of the Federation Council,* dated January 30, 2002. It flows from the status of the Federation Council as the body representing the interests of the subjects of the Russian Federation, thus concentrating responsibilities interrelated with the area of federalism.

- *Participation in the legislative procedure*

One of the core functions is participation in the legislative procedure.The Federation Council participates in the development oflegislative acts and adopts laws and amendments. Moreover, the Federation Council possesses the legislative initiative right, which may be used by the Federation Council as a state body and by its members personally.

The Federation Council participates in the legislative procedure and reviews laws, after adoption by the State Duma. The Federation Council has the right not to express its opinion regarding several types of laws; however there is a constitutional list of laws which is mandatory for review and approval by the Federation Council. This mandatory list includes federal laws, concerning the State budget; federal taxes; finance, currency, credit and customs' regulations, monetary emission; ratification and denunciation of the international agreements; status and defence of the state border; issues of war and peace.

- *Approval of the change of subjects' borders*

Subjects of the Federation in Russia have the inalienable right to agree with changes of the borders between the subjects. It is done in the form of a local referendum, which later on goes through the approval (in the form of law) process by the Federation Council.

- *Approval of Presidential Decrees on the introduction of martial law and of a state of emergency*

Martial law is introduced by the President of the Russian Federation in a case of aggression against the State or the threat of aggression. The Federation Council assesses the basis for the decree and approves it or declines. Such a mechanism is treated as an additional warranty in the sphere of the defence of human rights.

- *Deciding on the possibility of using the Armed Forces of the Russian Federation outside the territory of the Russian Federation*

Armed Forces of the Russian Federation may participate in peacekeeping and other types of operations abroad only when they comply with constitutional provisions and are approved by the Federation Council.

- *Appointment of elections of the President of the Russian Federation*

In accordance with Federal Law #19-FZ "*On President of Russian Federation elections*" dated by January 10, 2003 and the Constitution of the Russian Federation the Federation Council appoints elections of the President of Russia.

The decision on current elections should be taken not earlier than 100 days, and not later than 90 days, before the voting date. The voting date in Presidential elections is the second Sunday of the month, when the previous elections took place and the President was elected six years ago. If the Federation Council does not appoint the election date–the Central Elections' Commission should make this decision.

In case of the early termination of the Presidential authorities the Federation Council should appoint elections within 14 days after such early termination. In this case the voting day will be the last Sunday before the date that the Presidential authorities expired.

- *Dismissal of the President of the Russian Federation*

The Federation Council plays an important role in the process of dismissal of the President, making the final decision on the dismissal in accordance with Article 93 of the Constitution of Russia. This decision should be accepted by at least two-thirds of the total list of members of the Federation Council and adopted within three months from the initiative, accepted by the State Duma.

- *Appointment of judges of the high courts of Russia: the Constitution Court, the Supreme Court of the Russian Federation*

The President of Russia proposes to the Federation Council candidates for the position of the high court's judges. The Federation Council appoints the judges.

- *Appointment and dismissal of the Procurator-General of the Russian Federation*

Appointment of the Procurator-General of the Russian Federation is done on the basis of the Presidential proposal. When the Federation Council does not approve a candidate, the President proposes another candidate within thirty days. The general term of authority for the Procurator-General is *five years.*

- *Appointment and dismissal of the Deputy Chairman and half of the auditors of the Accounts Chamber*

The Accounts Chamber is established in accordance with Article 101 of the Constitution of Russia, which says that "*For the purpose of exercising control over fulfillment of the federal budget the Federation Council and the State Duma of the Federal Assembly of the Russian Federation establish the Accounts Chamber of the Russian Federation*". The Federation Council appoints the Deputy Chairman and half of the auditors of the Accounts Chamber. The legal status of the Accounts Chamber is regulated by the Federal Law #41-FZ "*On Accounts Chamber of the Russian Federation*", dated by April 5, 2013.

The Federation Council may have other authorities regulated by federal laws. For example the Federation Council analyses the proposals of the President for the appointment of the diplomatic representatives in different countries.

Internal Structure of the Federation Council

The internal structure and activity of the Federation Council is defined by *the Constitution*, federal laws and the *Regalement of the Federation Council*. The basis for the decisions taken by the Federation Council is open to collective discussion of the different issues. Parliament's Chamber conducts hearings which may be both open and closed as defined by the Regalement.

The Federation Council elects the Chairman and several Deputy Chairmen. The Chairman and deputies should represent different subjects of the Federation. Most functions of the Chairman and his deputies are of a procedural nature: they conduct sessions, manage the apparatus of the Federation Council and conduct other procedural activity.

The Council of the Chamber, which is a permanent collective body, is organized to arrange the activity of the Federation Council. It is formed by the Chairman of the Federation Council, his deputies, chairperson of all committees and several commissions. The Council of the Chamber conducts a lot of activity related to the performance of the smooth activity of the Federation Council.

It is a true statement that the most important bodies of the Federation Council are committees and commissions, since the majority of the work is done within these structural bodies. Committees function on a permanent basis, whereas commissions are more *ad hoc* bodies; however, there are still several permanent commissions. All members of the Federation Council except for its Chairman and Deputy Chairmen participate in the activity of one committee. Currently there are ten committees in the Federation Council:

✓ *Committee on Constitutional Legislation, Legal and Judicial Affairs and Civil Society Development;*

✓ *Committee on Federal Structure, Regional Policies, Local Self-Governance and Affairs of the North;*

✓ *Committee on Defence and Security;*

✓ *Committee for Foreign Affairs;*

✓ *Budget and Financial Markets' Committee;*
✓ *Committee on Economic Policy;*
✓ *Committee for Agrarian and Food Policy and Environmental Management;*
✓ *Committee on Social Policy;*
✓ *Committee on Science, Education, Culture and Information Policy;*
✓ *Committee on House Rules and Parliamentary Performance Management.*

Committees and permanent commissions are equal in their rights and obligations. In particular, they prepare opinions on laws and draft laws, organize parliamentary hearings and have other functions. Commissions on an *ad hoc* basis are created for deciding concrete issues. When an issue is solved, the commission terminates its existence.

The Federation Council performs two sessions during the year: the *spring session* is from January 25 to July 15 and *the autumn session* is from September 16 to December 31. Hearings are conducted at least twice a month; however these can take place more often. The quorum for hearings is more than half of the members of the Federation Council. A decision is made by means of open or secret voting.

The Federation Council acts on a permanent basis and does not terminate its activity after the expiration of the certain term.

4. The State Duma

Formation of the State Duma

The State Duma is one of the chambers of the Federal Assembly which is formed by national elections. There are 450 (four hundred and fifty) members, called "the deputies", representing the interests of the Russian population. The Chamber's term of authority constitutes 5 (five) years. In accordance with the *Federal Law № 20-FZ "On elections of the Deputies of the State Duma of the Federal Assembly of the Russian Federation" dated February 22, 2014* the deputies are elected on the basis of a mixed electoral system, combining both proportional and majority systems. *225 deputies* are elected on the basis of the proportional system: from federal lists under a proportional representation system. Only registered political parties can participate in the elections with some limitations and independent candidates are not permitted. To qualify for the allocation of mandates, political parties need to receive 5 percent of the valid votes. The federal electoral district in which deputies of the State Duma are elected includes the entire territory of the Russian Federation. Voters living outside the territory of the Russian Federation are included in the federal electoral district. *225 deputies* are elected based on the majority electoral system on one mandate electoral districts.

Candidates on one-mandatory districts may be:

- o *Proposed by political parties.* A political party may propose candidates who are members of this party, but also candidates who are non-party, however the number of such candidates cannot be more than 50 percent of the total number of candidates in the list, proposed by this party.
- o *Self-proposed.* Such candidates should collect not less than 0.5 per cent of signatures of the total quantity of the voters, registered in the relevant one-mandatory district.

The above-mentioned law introduced serious changes to the procedure of the formation of the State Duma. The State Duma, elected in the year 2011, was elected on the basis of the pure proportional system. The next elections, which are planned for the year 2016, will take place on the basis of the new regulations, adopted by the law of 2014.

There are the following requirements of the candidates:

- ➢ To be 21 years old;
- ➢ Citizen of the Russian Federation;
- ➢ Legally capable citizen of Russia;
- ➢ Not being in prison due to the court decision in force.

Competence of the State Duma

The scope of competence of the State Duma is regulated by *the Constitution* in Article 103 and clarified in the *Regalement of the State Duma*, dated byJanuary 22, 1998.

In particular, the State Duma:

o *Provides agreement to the President of the Russian Federation for the appointment of the Chairman of the Government;*

The proposal of the candidate is submitted by the President to the State Duma. The State Duma shall consider the candidate nominated by the President of the Russian Federation for the post of the Chairman of the Government of the Russian Federation during the week after the submission of the nomination. If the State Duma rejects the candidates three times for the post of Chairman of the Government of the Russian Federation, the President shall dissolve the State Duma and appoint new elections.

o *Makes decision on the motion of non-confidence to the Government;*

In accordance with Article 117 of the Constitution, the State Duma may express no-confidence in the Government of the Russian Federation by a majority of votes of the total number of the deputies of the State Duma. The President of the Russian Federation is free to announce the resignation of the Government or to reject the decision of the State Duma. If the State Duma again expresses no-confidence in the Government of the Russian Federation within *three months*, the President of the Russian Federation *shall announce* the resignation of the Government or dissolve the State Duma.

o *Appoints and terminates the responsibilities of the Head of the Central Bank;*

The term of authority of the Head of the Central Bank constitutes 4 (four) years. The Candidacy is proposed by the President of the Russian Federation to the State Duma during the session of the Duma, which is the lastbefore the expiration of the current Head of the Central Bank. The candidate is discussed within the Committee of the State Duma on budget, taxes, banks and finance prior hearings in the Chamber. The candidate is elected when more than 50 per cent of the State Duma deputies agree with the candidature. If the State Duma does not agree, the President provides the candidate within the next two week. It is important, that one candidate cannot be proposed more than twice.

The State Duma has powers to terminate the position of the Head of the Central Bank after the President has introduced such proposal to the State Duma. The decision is made by the majority of voice of the deputies.

o *Appoints and terminates the responsibilities of the Chairman of the Accounts Chamber and half of the Accounts Chamber auditors;*

The State Duma establishes the Accounts Chamber of the Russian Federation for the purpose of exercising control over the fulfillment of the federal budget, the composition and the order of the activities of which are determined by federal law. The Chairman of the Accounts Chamber is appointed and released from duty by the State Duma on the proposal of the President of the Russian Federation. One half of the auditors of the Accounts Chamber are appointed and released from their duties by the State Duma as advised by the President of the Russian Federation. The term of office of the Chairman of the Accounts Chamber, the Deputy Chairman of the Accounts Chamber and Auditors is 6 years.

o *Appoints and terminates the responsibilities of the Commissioner for Human Rights of the Russian Federation;*

The Commissioner for Human Rights of the Russian Federation is the official State Body, which was established in the year 1997 to ensure the performance of the State guarantees in the sphere of the State defence of rights and freedoms. The overall activity of the Commissioner for Human Rights is regulated by the Federal Constitutional Law *"On the Commissioner for Human Rights of the Russian Federation"*.

The candidate for the position of the Commissioner for Human Rights may be proposed by the President, the Federation Council, deputies of the State Duma and their communities not later than one month prior to the expiration of the authorities of the previous Commissioner. The State Duma gives approval by a majority of member voices. The term of authority of the Commissioner is five years. The State Duma is also empowered to resign the Commissioner.

- *Announces an amnesty;*

Amnesty–is a collective act, which adopts the State Duma and means official forgiveness of past offences. The Amnesty Act is adopted by the State Duma in the form of the Resolution on Amnesty. Commonly the Amnesty Act is associated with special events or holidays.

- *Accuses the President within the procedure of the official dismissal of the President from his official position;*

There are two main reasons for the dismissal of the President established by the Constitution: high treason and grave crime. The State Duma accepts the position of the initiator of the procedure. The proposal for accusing the President should include the defined characteristics of the crime and a clear explanation of the President's role in the performance of this crime and *one-third of State Duma members* should support the initiative of accusing the President. Afterwards, the State Duma forms the special temporary commission on the assessment of the case and the procedure of its performance, which reviews all the relevant documentation and finalizes its opinion in the form of a Conclusion, which should be supported by the majority of the commission. After acceptance, his Conclusion is sent to the Council of the State Duma. The role of the State Duma is finished when not less than two-thirds of the votes (300 member votes) of the *State Duma* members approve the accusation.

- *Performs activity in the sphere of international relations;*

The State Duma has rather vast powers in the sphere of international relations. The State Duma ratifies and denounces international agreements, adopts decisions on different aspects of international relations, explaining the State Duma position. An international agreement is introduced to the State Duma by the President with the request for ratification thereof. The State Duma reviews and adopts the ratification in the form of federal law, which then, passes to the Federation Council and the President for promulgation.

The State Duma actively participates in inter-parliamentary relations, signing the agreements with foreign parliaments and parliamentary organizations. The Chairman of the State Duma represents its interests in relations with other organizations.

Internal Structure of the State Duma

The *Constitution of the Russian Federation*, in Article 101, regulates that both chambers of the Russian Parliament form internal committees and commissions.

The overall structure of the State Duma is regulated by federal laws. The *Chairman of the State Duma* is the head of the Chamber. The Chairman is elected from the deputies of the State Duma by secret voting. It is necessary to gain more than half the votes of the members of the Chamber. Normally such elections are held after the new State Duma has been elected by the voters. Simultaneously with the Chairman the deputies elect the First Vice Chairman and other Vice Chairpersons. The number of Vice Chairpersons is established by the State Duma Regalement. It is worth mentioning that all these people should represent the interests of different party factions.

The *Council of the State Duma* is created for the preliminary preparation and decision of organizational issues. This structural unit is permanently acting. The permanent members with the decision vote are the Chairman of the State Duma, the first Vice Chairmen, Vice Chairmen and leader of the party fractions. The heads of the Committees and Commissions can participate in the activity of the Council, however only with advising votes.

Another structural element of the State Duma *is the deputies' faction,* which is the organized community of the deputies, belonging to the one party. In the State Duma, elected in 2011, there are four deputies' factions (*Edinaya Rossia, Communist Party of the Russian Federation, LDPR and Spravedlivaya Rossia*). Their main purpose is to develop a unified party policy and thereafter implement it while making laws and realizing other deputies' functions. All deputies' factions act on the basis of strict party discipline.

Finally, there are *committees and commissions*. Strictly speaking they are the main structural units in the State Duma, where most internal work is done.

As a general rule–the committee is the permanent structural unit; the commission is formed on a temporary basis for the decision of certain issues. However, there are still permanent commissions as well, like the

Commission on Deputies' Ethics. Committees are formed on the basis of equal representation of the deputies from different deputy factions. All deputies should be members of the committees. This rule applies in such a way, that a deputy should be member only in one Duma committee, however the Chairman of the Duma and Vice Chairmen do not enter into any committee. Committees and commissions work in the form of meetings, so that there should be not less than two meetings within the month, once two weeks. A quorum constitutes more than half of the deputies.

Currently there are 30 committees in the State Duma and 6 commissions, for example the following committees:

- ✓ *Committee on Agrarian Issues;*
- ✓ *Committee on Security and Anti-Corruption activity;*
- ✓ *Committee on Budget and Taxes;*
- ✓ *Committee on Property Issues;*
- ✓ *Committee on Constitutional Legislation and State Construction;*
- ✓ *Committee on Defence, etc.*

The State Duma starts its first hearings on the thirtieth day after it was elected. The President may call for hearings earlier. The first hearing opens with the oldest deputy and until the Chairman and his deputies are elected; representatives of each faction chair the meetings on the basis of mutual agreement.

There are two sessions within the year: *the spring session* from January 12 until June 20 and *the autumn session* from September 1 until December 25.The State Duma conducts hearings twice a week. The President, Chairman of the Government, ministers, members of the Federation Council, the Commissioner for Human Rights, judges of the Constitutional Court and Supreme Court, Chairman and auditors of the Accounts Chamber, the Procurator-General, and the Head the Chief Elections Commission may present on the hearings. Members of the Government may be invited to participate and provide answers to deputies' questions.

Termination of the State Duma Authorities

The activity of the elected deputies of the State Duma is terminated in the following situations:

- ➢ Expiration of the 5th year term of authorities;
- ➢ Early termination of the authorities by the President of the Russian Federation.

Early termination is possible in two situations: when the State Duma is in conflict with the President or in conflict with the Government.

One situation of the *conflict between the President and the State Duma* is possible, when, in accordance with the Constitution *the President proposes the nominee for the position of the Chairman of the Government* and the State Duma rejects this proposal three times, done by the President. The President dismisses the State Duma and appoints the Chairman of the Government by himself.

A second situation *of the conflict between the Government and the State Duma* takes place when the State Duma votes for non-confidence in the Government. In this situation if the State Duma votes for non-confidence twice within three months the President should make a decision and choose, whether the State Duma or the Government is dismissed. If the President dismisses the State Duma new elections should take place within four months after the dismissal date.

The Constitution of Russia proclaims the following limitations for the dismissal of the State Duma: its activity cannot be terminated within one year of the elections, within the period of the President's official dismissal, starting from the announcement of the charge of the President by the State Duma and until the Federation Council confirms the charge and within six months up to the expiration of the President's authority.

5. Parliamentary Control

On May 7, 2013 the President of Russia signed *Federal Law #77-FZ "On Parliamentary Control"*. This law became the first law which regulates in detail mechanisms which are possessed by the Federal Assembly in the sphere of its control functions, thus making the "*checks and balances*" principle function even stronger.

Parliamentary control is a widely used mechanism of control by the legislative power of the executive power. The Federal Law "*On Parliamentary Control*" systematized all the forms of control in Russia and clarified the principles and forms of application.

Parliamentary control pursues several purposes. It is a valuable mechanism in the revealing of key problems in government activity; it assists in the support of the constitutional rights of a person, helps to strengthen legality and acts as an instrument in corruption mitigation.

Parliamentary control can be applied in *the following forms:*

- Review by the State Duma of the question of confidence in the Government of the Russian Federation;

- Taking measures by Chambers of the Parliament, committees of the Parliament and the Accounts Chamber on parliamentary control in the sphere of budget relations;
- Hearings by the State Duma of the yearly reports by the Government on the performed activity, including answers to the questions from the members of Parliament;
- Review by the State Duma of the annual reports by the Central Bank of the Russian Federation;
- Hearings by the State Duma of the reports, done by the Chairman of the Central Bank;
- Making Parliamentary inquiries, done by the Chambers;
- Arranging deputies' inquiries, done by the deputies of the State Duma and members of the Federation Council;
- Hearings of the reports, done by the ministers and other governmental officials within "governmental hour";
- Hearings of the Chairman of the Government, deputies of the Chairman of the Government, the Procurator-General, Chairman of the Central Bank, other state officials in review of the extraordinary situations;
- Appointment and dismissal of the Chairman of the Accounts Chamber, his deputy and its auditors;
- Coordination between members of the Parliament and auditors of the Accounts Chamber;
- Coordination between members of the Parliament and the Commissioner for Human Rights in the Russian Federation;
- Hearings by the Federation Council of the annual reports of the Procurator-General of the Russian Federation on legality and law and order maintenance in the Russian Federation;
- Invitation of Government officials and other state officials to the Parliamentary committees and commissions;
- Sending representatives of the Federal Assembly for the participation in the current activity of the organizations of different forms;
- Conducting Parliamentary hearings;
- Conducting Parliamentary investigations.

It is worth discussing several of them in more detail.

The Parliamentary and deputies' inquiry serves as an important instrument in control by the legislative branch of power over the executive branch. Parliamentary and deputies' inquiries may be directed to the Chairman of the Government, members of the Government, the Procurator-General, the Chairman of the Central Bank of Russia, the managers of other federal state bodies, state off-budget foundations, state bodies of the subjects of the Federation or municipal bodies. The inquiry should include only those issues which are covered by the competence of the relevant body. The state official should provide an oral reply to the inquiry during the parliamentary session or in writing within 15 days upon receipt of the inquiry or later, if agreed with the parliamentary chamber.

Hearings of members of the Government and other state officials which provide answers to questions from members of the Federation Council or the State Duma are organized within the so-called "governmental hour", taking place in one of the Chambers of the Federal Assembly. Simultaneously with the relevant governmental official, a member of the Accounts Chamber who is responsible for the analogous issues can be invited. Issues of budget spending and the fulfillment of core governmental programs may be discussed within the "governmental hour". Governmental officials may also be invited to the discussions within parliamentary committees and commissions.

Parliamentary investigation. Rules of the Parliamentary investigation are regulated by the *Federal Law "On parliamentary investigation",* dated December 27, 2005 #196-FZ. In particular, the Parliamentary investigation is conducted for situations and cases with negative influence on society and the state, such as serious violations of human rights, guaranteed by the Constitution; serious violations of finance discipline in budget spending; cases of serious emergency situations, etc. In this list there are several limitations, since the activity of the President and the activity of the court and State investigation bodies is not subject to Parliamentary investigation. The term of investigation cannot be more than one year. An investigation is initiated by a group of deputies or Federation Council members not less than one-fifth of the total number of members of the Chamber. A Parliamentary investigation may be also initiated by the responsible industry branch committee. An investigation may also be initiated on the basis of a proposal by the Commissioner for Human Rights.

As a result of the initiation of the Parliamentary investigation a special commission is created. This commission has vast powers in conducting the investigation: it can request and obtain the necessary documents from state and municipal bodies; invite involved officials and other people to give explanations and share information, etc.

Resulting from the Parliamentary investigation the commission prepares a final report which is shared between the Chambers of the Federal Assembly, the Government and the President and is published for open discussion. The Government should analyze the report and reply for the measures taken to improve the situation.

Parliament is empowered to control Governmental activity in the adoption of legal acts, which should be accepted in accordance with the laws, prior to adoption by Parliament.

As a result of the measures taken for parliamentary control the Chambers of the Russian Parliament are empowered to:

- Entrust the committee or commission of the Chamber to develop a relevant draft of federal law;
- Propose the relevant state body or state officials to take measures for the mitigation of the violations of law and elimination of the reasons for such violations;
- Review an issue of confidence in the Government;
- Apply to the Procurator's office or the Investigative Committee of the Russian Federation;
- Dismiss officials, whose dismissal is with the participation of the legislative body.

6. Status of the Member of Parliament in Russia

The status of the members of the Federation Council and the deputy of the State Duma is defined by the Federal Law "*On the Status of Members of the Federation Council and the Status of the Deputy of the State Duma of the Federal Assembly of the Russian Federation", dated March 8, 1994 #3-FZ.*

Under the term "members of Parliament" we understand members of the Federation Council and deputies of the State Duma collectively. The procedure of the vesting of powers is different: while the deputy of the State Duma is elected by the citizens of the Russian Federation and thus, represents the interests of the whole nation, the members of the Federation Council represent the interests of only one subject of the Russian Federation, which has delegated a member of the Federation Council. The same person has no right to combine positions in both Chambers simultaneously. The term of authority of the deputy of the State Duma is fixed at *five years* and the terms of authority of the members of the Federation Council depends on the terms of authority of the State body, which has delegated a representative to the Federation Council.

Members of Parliament have no right to perform any other activity, or combine posts with other paid positions, except scientific, teaching or creative activity. Members of Parliament perform their duties on a professional basis, having indemnification for the activity. The activity of a Member of Parliament may be separated into the following parts: work in Chambers, work in committees and commissions and interaction with voters, which is also applicable to the deputies of the State Duma. Deputies of the State Duma possess *free representational mandate*, which means that they are not bound by their promises to the voters and the latter have no right to withdraw them. Deputies' authorities can be terminated upon the initiative, expressed by the deputy; upon receipt of any other citizenship by the deputy, death and announcement of death and loss of legal capacity, confirmed by court decision.

Both deputies of the State Duma and members of the Federation Council possess immunity, which prevents arrest and prosecution, until they are deprived of immunity by the relevant Chamber, which the person is a party to. It means that the party can be arrested and prosecuted only when the person is detained on the crime scene. Deprivation of immunity is performed by the relevant Chamber upon application by the Prosecutor-General.

7. Legislative Process

The competence of the Federal Assembly is realized in the form of laws, which are adopted by the Chambers. The Federal Assembly reviews the following types of laws: laws on amendments to the Constitution, Federal Constitutional laws and Federal laws.

Law on amendment to the Constitution–means the special act, which introduces the amendments to *chapters three to eight* of the Constitution of the Russian Federation. The procedure of its adoption is different from other laws. It is adopted as a Federal Constitutional Law and further should be approved by two-thirds of the legislative bodies of the subjects of the Russian Federation. The amendment to the Constitution is subsequently entered into the text of the Constitution.

Federal Constitutional Laws are adopted for the regulation of the most important relations, which are clearly mentioned in the Constitution. This type of law mostly regulates the status of the federal state bodies or other issues of vital importance to the state (for example Federal Constitutional Law "*On the Constitutional Court of the Russian Federation*", Federal Constitutional Law "*On the Government of the Russian Federation*", Federal Constitutional Law "*On creation of the new subject of the Russian Federation*", etc.) The procedure of adoption of such laws is more complicated, comparing to ordinary federal laws. They should be approved by *two-thirds of the deputies of the State Duma* and *three-quarters of the Members of the Federation Council* and the Federation

Council has no right to refrain from the review. *The President* should sign this type of law *without any veto right.*

Federal laws constitute the most numerous group of laws on the federal level. They regulate issues of the status of the state bodies, human rights, democratic institutions, etc. The procedure of adoption includes the State Duma and the Federation Council, however the Federation Council may refrain from the review, except for several issues, where it should provide the position. This procedure is described later in this chapter. The President may use the *suspensive veto* right while approving this type of law.

The legal force of the *Law on amendments to the Constitution* and *Federal Constitutional Law* is higher than the legal force of the ordinary federal laws and in case of controversy between them the first ones prevail.

The Legislative process means the process, which is regulated by the Constitution, federal laws and Regalements of the Federal Assembly Chambers on the discussion, adoption and publication of the federal laws.

The Legislative process includes several mandatory stages, which are important and follow in a certain sequence. Only completion of one stage permits transfer to the next one. All the stages are formalized and duly documented; all the rights and obligations of the participants are fixed by the constitutional regulations.

The Legislative Process Stages

As grounding on the types of review of the federal law draft we may select the following main stages of the legislative process:

1. *Legislative initiative;*
2. *Review by the Federal Assembly;*
3. *Promulgation by the President of the Russian Federation.*

These stages are divided into smaller stages.

1. Legal initiative

Legal initiative means the stage of the legislative process, when authorized bodies, empowered by the rights concretized by the Constitution, initiate drafts ofconstitutional and ordinary federal laws.

In accordance with Article 104 of the Constitution of Russia, the right for legal initiative belongs to:

- ✓ The President of Russia;
- ✓ The Federation Council;
- ✓ Members of the Federation Council;
- ✓ Deputies of the State Duma;

- ✓ The Government of Russia;
- ✓ Legislative bodies of the subjects of the Russian Federation;
- ✓ The Constitutional Court of Russia, the Supreme Court of Russia, within the scope of competence of these courts, which is limited by the Constitution and federal legislation.

When the subject of the legislative initiative introduces the draft of law, it is necessary to supply this draft with the following documents:

- ➢ Explanatory note, clarifying the purpose of the law and the concept of the law;
- ➢ Full text of the draft;
- ➢ List of the federal laws, which will be amended or terminated, due to the new law;
- ➢ Financial report, clarifying the budget side of the new law;
- ➢ Governmental conclusion, when the draft of the law touches upon budgetary spending, introduces, amends or terminates current taxes, duties, or regulates the financial liabilities of the State.

2. Review by the Federal Assembly

Review by the Federal Assembly includes the review by the State Duma and a further review by the Federation Council. In Russia the only way for the law to go through Parliament is to be introduced to the State Duma and afterwards move for review by the Federation Council, but not vice versa.

➢ *Review by the State Duma*

Preliminary review

The draft of the Law is introduced by the subject of the legislative initiative to the State Duma and is forwarded to the Chairman of the State Duma. Regalement of the State Duma envisages mandatory registration of the draft by the administration of the State Duma. After the registration, the Chairman of the State Duma directs the draft to the profile committee of the State Duma, specializing on the issue. Within *fourteen days* this committee reviews the draft and transfers it to the Council of the State Duma for further actions.

The Council of the State Duma reviews the draft and confirms conformity with the Constitution and the Regalement of the State Duma. If the draft is in line with the listed legal acts, so that:

a) The initiating party has constitutional legislative initiative rights;
b) The realization of the initiative is in line with the rules, established by the Constitution and the Regalement of the State Duma, and then the Council nominates the Committee, which is responsible for this draft.

In the case of non-conformity the draft is returned to the body which initiated it for completion. After completion the draft can once again be initiated to the State Duma.

When the Council of the State Duma nominates the responsible Committee, at the same time the Council makes a decision on the inclusion of the draft to the State Duma agenda. Simultaneously the draft with the supporting documentation is forwarded for review to the relevant committees, to the President, the Government, the Federation Council, High courts of the Russian Federation, in case the law touches upon their competence.

Readings in the State Duma

Readings are the legal form of the discussion and approval of the law draft. The legal draft considers the review in the State Duma in three readings. There is still a possibility for the draft to be approved after the first reading and we will review this procedure in this chapter in more detail.

The First reading is the primary review of the draft by the State Duma deputies. Within the primary review the main provisions of the draft are being discussed. Also, the question of the general necessity of the law is discussed and the overall concept and compliance with constitutional provisions. The discussion is started by the speech of the subject of legislative initiative or its representative. The responsible committee provides its position as well.

As the result of the First reading the following decisions may be taken:

1) Accept the draft in the First reading and proceed with readings in the State Duma; or
2) Decline the draft; or
3) Accept the law. This acceptance means that the law is adopted in the first reading without any changes and will be passed to the Federation Council for further review and acceptance. Such a situation is possible only when there are no objections to the law both in full and in detail; and the competent committee have provided a positive position.

Within *five days* after acceptance in the first reading the draft is sent to the subjects of the legislative initiative. Within the first and second readings the subject of the legislative initiative may propose amendments to the law, which are further consolidated and provided for discussion during the *second reading*.

The Second reading means the discussion of the draft in detail by the deputies of the State Duma. This is the most detailed discussion of the draft within the State Duma, when the proposed amendments are being discussed and voted on. This reading starts with the message from the competent Committee, where it provides a position about the draft and informs about the amendments obtained. Initiators of the amendments may make a public speech with clarification of their amendments and their purpose. The competent Committee gives advice on the list of amendments for rejection. In the case that the deputies agree with them–they reject such amendments. The discussion concerns the amendments for approval, the deputies vote on them and as the result of the discussion the list of the approved amendments is created. After the second reading is finished the deputies vote on acceptance of the draft in the second reading. *The decision may be as follows:*

1) *Accept the draft* in the Second reading and proceed with further reading in the State Duma;

2) *Decline the draft.*

If the draft is declined its review in the State Duma is terminated.

The draft, accepted in the Second reading, is sent to the competent Committee for further adaptation in accordance with the amendments accepted. As the result–the final text of the law is created. The Council of the State Duma appoints the Third reading of the law draft.

The Third reading is the final reading of the draft of the law. It means the general discussion on the law with all amendments, agreed on the Second reading and incorporated into the draft text. It is not permitted to introduce any changes on the stage of the third reading, however in some situations, if supported by the majority of the deputies, the draft may be returned to the Second reading, where it can be discussed in more detail. In accordance with the Regalement of the State Duma the draft of law can be voted in Second and Third readings on the same day, in which case the final law draft is ready and legal and linguistic expertise of the draft has taken place.

As the result of the Third reading the following decisions may be taken:

1) *Accept the draft* in the Third reading;

2) *Decline the draft.*

If the draft is accepted it means that the law is approved by the State Duma. Draftswhich are declined are not approved and their existence is terminated. The draft which is approved by the State Duma is called a federal constitutional or federal law, depending on the nature of the law.

For approval by the State Duma the federal constitutional law should get two-thirds of the deputies' votes (301 votes). For approval of the ordinary federal law it is necessary to get a majority of votes (226 votes). This rule is applied to all readings in the State Duma.

After the review and approval of the law in the State Duma the law is transferred to the Federation Council within five days.

➢ *Review and Approval by the Federation Council*

The Federation Council plays an important role in the legislative process in the Russian Federation; however its participation varies, depending on the type of law and type of question, covered by the concrete law.

In accordance with Article 106 of the Constitution of the Russian Federation the Federation Council is obliged to review the following types of federal laws:

✓ On the federal budget;

✓ On federal taxes and duties;

✓ On finance, currency, credit, customs' regulations, monetary emission;

✓ On the ratification and denunciation of international agreements;

✓ On the question of the status of the State border;

✓ On issues of war and peace.

The Federation Council *is obliged* to review the *Laws on Amendments to the Constitution* and the *Federal Constitutional Laws.*

The Law, which was adopted by the State Duma after transfer to the Federation Council is registered within 48 hours and is distributed to all members of the Federation Council for the review.

The Federation Council should review the law *within fourteen days* of its provision to the Federation Council by the State Duma. After the law is registered in the Federation Council the Chairman of the Chamber nominates the Committee which is responsible for this law and prepares the report on the law for provision to the Chamber. If the law is not listed as the law, which should be mandatorily reviewed by the Federation Council, the nominated Committee may mention in the report that it advises that the law should not be reviewed. In this situation the law is further forwarded for Presidential approval. In the other case–the law should be reviewed by the Federation Council.

When the law is entered into the plenary meeting of the Federation Council it is reviewed during one discussion. Upon discussion the Federation Council makes the decision on whether to approve or to decline the law. Federal law is approved by the majority of votes; Federal Constitutional Law is approved by a qualified majority (*three-quarters of the voices*). If the Federation Council is late with the review and does not provide its opinion within 14 days, the term is prolonged to the next meeting of the Federation Council.

If the Federation Council approves the Law it is transferred further for review by the President of the Russian Federation. If the Federation Council declines the Law it is returned to the State Duma for consideration. The rejected law is supported by the official resolution by the Federation Council with clarification of the list of articles and parts opposed by the Federation Council, which is necessary to conciliate with the State Duma. The proposal to create the Conciliation Commission to solve all the disagreements may also be part of this official resolution.

Recurring Review by the State Duma and the Conciliation Procedure

After the Federation Council declines the law it is returned to the State Duma. The Council of the State Duma forwards the documents to the responsible committee of the State Duma for review and opinion. After the review this committee may recommend the following to the State Duma:

- ✓ To create the Conciliation Commission; or
- ✓ To leave the law in the same edition as it was adopted by the State Duma earlier; or
- ✓ To disqualify the law.

The Conciliation Commission is created by both Chambers: the State Duma and the Federation Council. Representatives of the State Duma are elected at the plenary meeting of the State Duma; representatives of the Federation Council are elected by the members of the Federation Council. This Commission reviews every non-agreed part of law and proposes new variants per each statement. After the review and discussion is finished the Conciliation Commission provides the protocol and table, containing old and new proposed wordings of the law. These documents are provided to the Duma deputies and the whole package is reviewed by the State Duma on the readings. In the case that new proposals are accepted–the draft is transferred to the Federation Council; if even one proposal is not accepted, then the State Duma may propose that the Conciliation Commission should continue the process of conciliation.

The State Duma may *overcome the objection and opinion of the Federation Council* by the voting of the qualified majority, when two-thirds of the State Duma vote for the edition of the law, adopted by the State Duma; the objections of the Federation Council are treated as overcome and the law is transferred to the President for signature within five days.

Promulgation by the President of the Russian Federation

Promulgation means the sanctioning of the law by the Head of State–the President of the Russian Federation. Promulgation consists of two stages: *signature by the President and publication of the law.*

Promulgation is very important on the way to the full legal force of the law and all the stages should be competed in full.

Signature by the President

In accordance with Article 107 of the Constitution of the Russian Federation the President signs the law and publishes it. The President should sign it within fourteen days of receipt of the law from the Federation Council or use his *veto right*. Veto is one of the control functions of the President, permitting him to influence the legislative process on the stage of promulgation. The President of the Russian Federation possesses a *suspensive veto right*, which he may use for *ordinary federal laws*. A veto right cannot be applied for the Federal Constitution laws as well as for the laws of amendments to the Constitution. When the President agrees with the law–he signs it within fourteen days and sends it for official publication. If the President uses his veto right, the law is treated as rejected and is returned to the Federal Assembly for further review.

When the rejected law comes to the Federal Assembly it is forwarded to the Council of the State Duma, which in its turn sends it to the responsible committee for review. This committee *within ten days* should provide a position in respect of the rejected law:

- ✓ Whether the proposal of the President should be accepted (this Presidential proposal can be done in the form of a recommendation to reject the law or to amend the law as advised by the President);
- ✓ To create the Conciliation Commission for settling the dispute; or
- ✓ To adopt the law in the initial edition.

The first variant requires participation of the whole Chamber in the review and voting of the draft. If accepted as advised by the President, than the law turns for approval of the Federation Council and further signature by the President.

The second variant leads to the creation of the Conciliation Commission, with the participation of the representatives from the Federation Council, the State Duma and official representatives of the President. This Commission tries to find the compromising variant and proposes a new draft of the law, which will be acceptable by the President as well. Afterwards, this draft should be approved by the State Duma and the Federation Council and signed by the President.

The third variant is also possible when the law is adopted in the initial edition. It means the overcoming of the Presidential veto by the qualified majority (*two-thirds*) of votes by both Chambers of Parliament. In this situation the President is obliged to sign such law even if he does not agree with it.

Official publication

The procedure of official publication is regulated by the *Federal Law "On the way of publication and entrance into legal force of the federal constitutional laws, federal laws, acts of the Chambers of the Federal Assembly", dated by June 14, 1994 #5FZ.* Federal law should be published within seven days after the President has signed it. Official publication means publication in printed and internet sources, directly mentioned in the law. Currently they are the following: "Parliamenskaya gazeta" (Parliament newspaper), "Rossiyskaya gazeta" (Russian newspaper), "Sobranie Zakonodatel'stva Rossiyskoy Federatsii" (Collection of the legislation of the Russian Federation). These mentioned resources are written paper resources. There is also one internet resource– *www.pravo.gov.ru*, where the laws are also being officially published.

Federal laws enter into force on the expiration of *ten days* after the law has been officially published, until another term is directly mentioned in the law.

Ratification of international agreements

This chapter would not be complete without mentioning the procedure of ratification of international agreements, since both Chambers of the Federal Assembly take part in this procedure.

In accordance with the Constitution the ratification is done by the Federal Assembly in the form of the law. As regulated by the *Federal Law "On International agreements of the Russian Federation", dated by July 15, 1995 #101FZ*, the following international agreements should be ratified in the Russian Federation:

a) Performance of which requires changes in the current laws or the adoption of new federal laws and which establishes the rules which differ from the rules, established by current laws;
b) The subject of which are the main rights and freedoms of the person and citizen;
c) On territorial separation of the Russian Federation from other countries, including agreements on the state border and the separation of the continental shelf of the Russian Federation and exclusive economic region;
d) On the basis of the interstates' relations on the issues, covering the defence of the Russian Federation, issues of disarmament or international control over arms, on issues of world peace and security and peace agreements and agreements on collective security;
e) On participation of the Russian Federation in interstate unions, international organizations and other interstate communities, in

case these agreements envisage the transfer of part of the authorities of the Russian Federation or fix a legal binding nature of them to the bodies of the Russian Federation;

f) In case the parties of international agreement previously agreed for further ratification.

The international agreements are introduced to the State Duma by the official body which has signed this agreement. The State Duma reviews the ratification proposals and after consultations with committees and commissions of the State Duma ratifies the international agreement in the form of federal law. This federal law goes to the Federal Assembly for further review. After both Chambers have provided their position the law on ratification goes to the President for signature and publication. If the international agreement includes provisions which are contradictory to the provisions of the Constitution, such international agreement may be ratified only if the relevant amendments are done to the Constitution in advance.

8. Accounts Chamber

The legal status of the Accounts Chamber of the Russian Federation is regulated by *the Constitution of Russia* and the *Federal Law "On the Accounts Chamber of the Russian Federation", dated by April 5, 2013, #41-FZ.*

The Accounts Chamber is a permanently acting State Body of external state audit, which is organized with the participation of the President and the Federal Assembly and is accountable to the Federal Assembly. The Accounts Chamber is a financially, organizationally and functionally independent body. The Accounts Chamber determines its internal structure by itself. The activity of the Accounts Chamber may be suspended, for example when the activity of the Chamber of the Parliament is suspended as well.

In analyzing the status of the Accounts Chamber it is necessary to mention that it is not formally included into any branch of power in Russia and as the Central Bank, Commissioner for Human Rights, the Procurator's office and Central Election Committee it forms a separate group of bodies with special status.

Among the main goals of the Accounts Chamber are the following:

✓ Organization and control over the federal budget and state non-budget funds spending;

✓ Audit of the results of the social and economic development goals of the Russian Federation;

- ✓ Analysis of findings and violations on budgetary spending;
- ✓ Assessment of the level of efficiency of tax and other preferences and other financial privileges;
- ✓ Assessment of the reliability of the budgetary reports;
- ✓ Control over the legality of the budget money flow.

Functions of the Accounts Chamber are fully described by the federal law. The Accounts Chamber cannot hold any function, which is not included in the list. Among the most important functions we may name the following:

- ✓ External state finance control in the sphere of budget relations;
- ✓ Legal expertise of the drafts of federal laws on federal budget and state non-budgetary funds of the Russian Federation;
- ✓ Expertise of the state reports on federal and regional budgets' spending;
- ✓ Assessment of the efficacy of management of federal resources;
- ✓ Conducting of audits of spending of State resources in different objects;
- ✓ Expertise of international agreements and federal law drafts, which may lead to budget spending;
- ✓ Audit of the internal and external debt of the Russian Federation;
- ✓ Coordination with the prosecutors' offices in the different aspects, related to budget spending and control over them.

The Accounts Chamber includes the Chairman, Deputy Chairman, auditors of the Accounts Chamber and the assisting body. The Chairman of the Accounts Chamber is appointed by the State Duma on the proposal of the President for the term of six years. The same person cannot stand in this position for more than two successive terms. The candidates are proposed to the President by the deputies' factions and the President chooses from three candidatures. The decision is made by the majority of deputies' votes.

Requirements of *the candidate* are as follows:

- ➢ Citizen of the Russian Federation;
- ➢ No connections with foreign countries, such as foreign citizenship, permanent residence, etc;
- ➢ Higher education (University);
- ➢ Five years of professional experience in the area of state management, state audit, economics, finance, jurisprudence.

The Chairman of the Accounts Chamber is not permitted to have family relations with the President of the Russian Federation, Chairman of the Federation Council, Chairman of the State Duma, Chairman of the Government, Chairman of the Constitutional Court of the Russian

Federation, Chairman of the Supreme Court, Head of the President Executive Office, Procurator-General of the Russian Federation or the Head of the Investigative Committee of the Russian Federation.

In accordance with clause 39 of the law "*On the Accounts Chamber*" the Chairman of the Accounts Chamber, the Deputy and auditors possess immunity, so that they cannot be arrested and criminal proceedings cannot be initiated without approvalby the Federal Assembly Chamber, which appointed them. Moreover, criminal proceedings can only be initiated by the Head of the Investigative Committee of the Russian Federation.

The Accounts Chamber is vested with vast *powers,* permitting implementation of the goals, established by current law.

Among these powers are the following:

- ✓ Control, analytical, information and other types of activity;
- ✓ Provides instructions and notifications resulting from the performed audits;
- ✓ Requests and receives documents and other materials, necessary to perform audits;
- ✓ Involves representatives from the relevant state bodies, experts, specialists, other auditor and scientific organizations to perform audits;
- ✓ Organizes interaction with relevant account state bodies of the subjects of Russia;
- ✓ Assists state and municipal bodies in conducting budget activity, participates in different educational programs for providing relevant knowledge to the state and municipal officials.

For performance of the powers of the Accounts Chamber it is vested by certain *methods of activity*. The Federal law regulates the following methods: check, revision, analysis, inspection and monitoring.

Check is used for the documentary review of several actions or operations which are specifically mentioned in the decision of the Check performance.

Revision is used for a more complex audit of the activity, which includes a documentary and factual audit of the legality of actions, operations and correctness of the accounting papers.

As a result of both check and revision the Accounts Chamber produces the document, named the Act.

Analysis is used to investigate the specific parts and activity of the auditing objects with further systematization of the results of investigation.

Inspection is used for the analysis and review of the specific part of the objects under investigation. Both the results of the analysis and inspection are formalized as *a conclusion.*

Monitoring is used to perform the collection and analysis of the information on the activity of the audited subject and is used on a permanent and systematic basis.

All the materials resulting from the inspections, monitoring, analysis, revisions and checks are provided to the Federal Assembly Chambers as it is regulated by federal law.

CHAPTER EIGHT

THE EXECUTIVE POWER IN RUSSIA

In accordance with Article 110 of the Russian Constitution the Executive power in Russia shall be exercised by the Government of the Russian Federation. The composition, nomination and rules of activities of the Government of the Russian Federation are regulated by:

- ✓ *The Constitution (chapter 6);*
- ✓ *Federal Constitutional Law № 2-FKZ "On the Government of the Russian Federation" dated December 17, 1997;*
- ✓ *Decrees of the President;*
- ✓ *Regulations of the Government of the Russian Federation № 260 dated June 1, 2004 which were sanctioned by the decision of the Government.*

1. Federal Executive Bodies

The specific characteristic of the executive power in Russia is its dualism which appears in the division of this power between the President and the Prime Minister. It should be mentioned, however, that the Russian President does not formally belong to any branch of power, including executive power. As provided in the Constitution the President is the Head of State but not the head of the Government. At the same time, the Constitution provides that the President shall adopt measures to ensure the coordinated functioning and interaction of all bodies of state power, including executive power. It is quite obvious that the President plays a significant role in all spheres and branches. Although the Prime Minister is considered to be the head of the Government there are several federal ministries, agencies and services which are under the direct subordination of the President, at present among them are: the Ministry of the Interior; Ministry of Defence; Ministry of Emergencies and Disaster Relief; Ministry of Foreign Affairs and its agency (Federal Agency for the Commonwealth of Independent States, Compatriots Living Abroad, and International Cultural Cooperation); Ministry of Defence and its two services and two agencies (Federal Service for Military-Technical Cooperation, Federal

Service for Technical and Service Control; Federal Agency for Special Construction and Federal Agency for the Procurement of Armaments, Military and Special Equipment, and Logistical Resources–Rosoboronpostavka); Ministry of Justice and two of its services (Federal Penitentiary Service and Federal Bailiff Service); State Courier Service; Foreign Intelligence Service; Federal Security Service; Federal Drug Control Service; Federal Guard Service; Federal Service for Fiscal Monitoring; Chief Directorate for Special Programs of the Russian President; Administrative Directorate of the President). This list is made on the basis of the decree of the President of the Russian Federation № 636 dd. May 21, 2012 "*On the structure of federal bodies of the executive power*". In accordance with this decree there are 20 ministries, 34 federal services and 25 federal agencies in the Russian Federation.

Other federal ministries, agencies and services are under the subordination of the Government.

Formation of the federal bodies of the executive power, their reorganization and liquidation are to be proceeded by the President at the suggestion of the Prime Minister. The statutes regulating the activity of the federal bodies of the executive power being under the direct authority of the President are to be approved by the President. The statutes regulating the activity of the federal bodies of the executive power being under the subordination of the Government are to be correspondingly approved by the Government.

The structure of the federal bodies of the executive power is as follows. First of all, this structure includes *federal ministries* which are federal bodies of the executive power with functions for the development of state policy and legal regulation in a specific sphere (financial, defence, educational, social, economic, etc.). Federal ministries are headed by federal ministers who are appointed by the President at the suggestion of the Prime Minister. Federal ministries ensure legal regulation in a specific sphere, and also coordinate and supervise federal services and federal agencies subordinated to them. It should be mentioned that neither the Constitution, nor the Federal Constitutional Law "*On the Government of the Russian Federation*" stipulates the concrete number of ministries which may exist. This issue is a subject of presidential decrees, namely the decrees on the structure of federal bodies of the executive power, which every newly-elected President shall adopt after inauguration and may revise at any time if necessary.

In the second place, the structure of federal bodies of the executive power consists of *federal services* which are federal bodies of the executive power with the functions of control and supervision in a specific sphere of activity, and also with special functions in ensuring defence, public and state security, and protection of the state boundaries and combat of crimes. Federal services are headed by heads (directors). Federal services are entitled to adopt individual legal acts on the basis of the Constitution, federal constitutional laws, and federal laws, legal acts of the President, the Government, and the federal ministry which coordinates and supervises the activity of the corresponding federal service. At the same time, federal services are not entitled to ensure normative regulation in a specific sphere if not otherwise stipulated in the decrees of the President or in the decisions of the Government.

Finally, *federal agencies* are forming the third part of the structure of federal bodies of Russian executive power. Federal agencies are federal bodies of the executive power whose function is to render state services. Federal agencies have much in common with federal agencies: as well as federal services, federal agencies are headed by heads (directors); they may adopt individual legal acts on the basis of the Constitution, federal constitutional laws, federal laws, legal acts of the President, the Government, and the federal ministry which coordinates and supervises the activity of the corresponding federal agency; however, they are not empowered to ensure legal regulation in a specific sphere if this is otherwise not stipulated in the decrees of the President or in the decisions of the Government.

As previously mentioned, the structure of the federal bodies of executive power may be revised by the decision of the President. For example, during 2000-2004 there used to be *state committees* (the State Committee of the Russian Federation on Physical Culture, Sport and Tourism, State Statistical Committee of the Russian Federation, State Customs Committee of the Russian Federation, State Fishery Committee of the Russian Federation, etc.) and *federal commissions of the Russian Federation* (the Federal Commission on the Security Market of the Russian Federation, Federal Energy Commission of the Russian Federation) in the structure of the federal bodies of executive power. They were the federal bodies of executive power which were responsible for intersectional cooperation on the issues referring to their competence, and also for functional regulation in a specific sphere.

2. Composition and Nomination of the Government of the Russian Federation. Structure of the Government

The Government of the Russian Federation consists of the Chairman, Deputy Chairmen and federal ministers.

The Chairman of the Government (Prime Minister) shall be appointed by the President of the Russian Federation with the consent of the State Duma (the lower chamber of the Russian Parliament–the Federal Assembly). The proposal for the candidate to the office of the Prime Minister shall be submitted not later than two weeks after a newly-elected President of the Russian Federation takes office or after the resignation of the Government or one week after the State Duma rejects the candidate. The State Duma shall consider the candidate nominated by the President to the office of Prime Minister within one week after the submission of the nomination. If the State Duma rejects the candidates to the office of Prime Minister three times, the President must dissolve the State Duma and appoint new elections. These rules are stipulated in Article 111 of the Constitution.

In 1998 when the former Russian President Boris Yeltsin proposed the same candidate several times to the office of Prime Minister the dispute between the President and the members of the State Duma arose on the content of paragraph 4 of Article 111 of the Constitution. The MEPs considered that the content of the above-mentioned paragraph did not provide a clear answer to the question whether the President is every time obliged to submit to the State Duma another (new) candidate or whether he has the right to submit the same candidate for the second and third times. This dispute became the subject of consideration in the Russian Constitutional Court which took the decision that the President has the right to submit the same candidate to the office of Prime Minister three times, and after the rejection of the same or different candidates to this office three times by the State Duma the latter is to be dissolved by the President (the decision of the Constitutional Court of the Russian Federation № 28-П dated December 11, 1998 on the interpretation of Article 111 of the Constitution).

Not later than within one week after his/her appointment the Chairman of the Government shall submit to the President proposals on the structure of the federal executive bodies. A newly-appointed Prime Minister shall propose to the President candidates to the offices of deputies to the Prime Minister and federal ministers who shall be appointed to their offices and dismissed from them by the President on the proposal of the Prime Minister.

The Chairman of the Government shall be released from office in the following cases:

- In the case of a personal decision on resignation from the office;
- In the case of acceptance of the resignation of the Government by the President.

Only once in Russia in September 2007 did the Government headed by Prime Minister Mikhail Fradkov apply for a resignation. This resignation obviously took place in anticipation of the presidential elections with the purpose of providing the President Vladimir Putin with the full freedom in making important decisions including decisions on personnel.

- In the case of the impossibility of the performance of his/her duties.

The resignation of the Prime Minister leads to the resignation of the whole Government.

If the Chairman of the Government is temporarily absent his duties shall be performed by one of his deputies under his decision, and if the Chairman of the Government is not able to take such a decision it shall be taken by the President on the proposal of the Prime Minister.

3. Structure of the Government of the Russian Federation

The Government's structure is as follows:

✓ *The Presidium of the Government;*

✓ *The Government Executive office;*

✓ *Coordinating and advisory governmental bodies.*

The functioning of *the Presidium of the Government* is not provided by the Constitution. This organ was founded in accordance with the Resolution of the Government № 371 "*On Foundation of the Presidium of the Government of the Russian Federation*", dated May 16, 2008 with the purpose of taking decisions on different operative issues on the proposal of the President. The decisions of the Presidium are to be taken by the majority of its members and cannot contradict the legal acts adopted by the Russian Government itself. Moreover, the Government is empowered to cancel any decision of its Presidium (Article 29 of the Federal Constitutional Law № 2-FKZ "On the Government of the Russian Federation").

The Government Executive office is a state body whose purpose is to ensure the activity of the Russian Government and its Chairman and also to organize control over the implementation of the decisions taken by the executive bodies. The Government Executive office is being regulated by the Instructions *"On the Government Executive Office of the Russian Federation*" sanctioned by the Resolution of the Government № 260 dated June 1, 2004, later revised in 2007 and 2008.

The Government Executive office includes:

✓ The secretariat of the Prime Minister;

- ✓ The secretariat of the first deputies of the Prime Minister secretariat of the deputies of the Prime Minister; plenipotentiary representatives of the Russian Government at the State Duma, the Federation Council, the Constitutional Court, the Supreme Court of the Russian Federation;
- ✓ Departments (altogether 22 departments for the time being, among them being: the Administrative Department; Department of Culture; International Cooperation Department; Department of State Government, Regional Development and Local Government; Department of Defence Policy; Department of Industry and Infrastructure; Agriculture Department; Department of Social Development and Environmental Protection; Department of Economics and Finance; Legal Department, etc.)

Coordinating and advisory bodies may be created by the Government if necessary in the form of various *governmental commissions* and *councils* (Ex.: *Governmental commission on control under foreign investments to the Russian Federation, Governmental commission on regional development, Council on competitiveness and entrepreneurship, etc.*)

There are several institutions, universities and organizations which are functioning under the Government of the Russian Federation (the Academy of National Economy; State University–the Higher School of Economics; Financial Academy; Research Institute of Legislation and Comparative Law; Information Telegraph Agency; Russian State Military Historical-cultural Centre; Federal State Institution "Analytical Centre under the Government of the Russian Federation").

4. Responsibility of the Government of the Russian Federation

The Government of the Russian Federation is accountable to the President and the State Duma. In accordance with Article 116 of the Constitution the Government shall resign after new President of the Russian Federation has been elected. In such a case the latter starts the process of nomination of a new Government. Moreover, the President may take a decision on the resignation of the Government or any of its members at any time.

Since 1993 the Government has been resigned by the decision of the President five times: four times by the decisions of President Boris Yeltsin (*in 1998 President B. N. Yeltsin at first resigned the Government headed by Prime Minister Victor Chernomyrdin, and secondly the Government headed by Prime Minister Sergey Kirienko; in 1999 President B. Yeltsin at first resigned the Government headed by Prime Minister Yevgeny Primakov and later the Government headed by Prime Minister Sergey Stepashin), and one time by the decision of President Vladimir Putin (in February 2004 he resigned the Government headed by Prime Minister Mikhail Kasyanov).*

The responsibility of the Government before the State Duma may take place in one of two forms stipulated by the Constitution:

1) In the form of acceptance by the deputies of a non-confidence resolution, and
2) In the form of a rejection in confidence in the Government by the deputies. These two forms of responsibility differ from each other in two aspects:
   (i) In the subjects initiating the procedure;
   (ii) In the legal consequences of each of the forms of responsibility.

When we are talking about the first form of responsibility of the Government the initiator of it will be the deputies of the State Duma (a majority of them, i.e. at least 226 deputies), and the legal consequences will be as follows: after the State Duma adopts a non-confidence resolution by a majority of votes of the total number of its deputies, the President shall be free to announce the resignation of the Government or to reject the decision of the State Duma. In the case in which the State Duma again expresses no-confidence in the Government within three months, the President shall take a decision either on the resignation of the Government or on the dissolving of the State Duma. Thus far, the President may for the first time ignore the decision of the State Duma and is obliged to take the decision in the case of a second non-confidence resolution adopted by a majority of the deputies within three month from the first non-confidence resolution adoption.

The attempts to adopt a non-confidence resolution against the Government happen very seldom in the parliamentary work of the Russian deputies. *Such attempts took place in October 1994, in June 1995 (against the Government headed by Prime Minister Victor Chernomyrdin), in March 2001 and in June 2003 (against the Government headed by Prime Minister Mikhail Kasyanov), in February 2005 (against the Government headed by Prime Minister Mikhail Fradkov). All these attempts failed. So far, there has been no case of the adoption of a non-confidence resolution against the Government in Russian parliamentary practice. However, in 1995 after the terrorist attack in Budyonovsk the deputies of the State*

Duma adopted a non-confidence resolution against three ministers. As a result they were sacked by President Boris Yeltzin.

When we are talking about the second form of responsibility of the Government before the State Duma the initiator will be the Prime Minister who may raise before the State Duma the issue of a refusal of confidence in the Government. If a majority of the deputies vote for such a refusal, the President within seven days shall take a decision on the resignation of the Government or will dissolve the State Duma and announce new parliamentary elections. It should be noticed that in this case the President does not have any right to ignore the decision of the State Duma and must solve the conflict within seven days.

In the case of a resignation of the Government it shall continue to work on the instruction of the President until a new Government is formed.

5. Competence of the Government of the Russian Federation

The Government of the Russian Federation has vast powers in various spheres. These powers are described in the Constitution (Article 114) and in more detail in the Federal Constitutional Law № 2-FKZ "*On the Government of the Russian Federation*".

The Constitution provides that the Government of the Russian Federation shall:

a) Work out and submit to the State Duma the federal budget and ensure its implementation, submit to the State Duma a report on the implementation of the federal budget;
b) Ensure the implementation in the Russian Federation of a single financial, credit, and monetary policy;
c) Ensure the implementation in the Russian Federation of a single state policy in the spheres of culture, science, education, health protection, social security, and ecology;
d) Manage federal property;
e) Carry out measures to secure the defence of the country, state security, and the implementation of the foreign policy of the Russian Federation;
f) Implement measures to ensure the rule of law, human rights and freedoms, protection of property and public order, and crime control;
g) Exercise other powers vested in it by the Constitution, the federal laws and decrees of the President of the Russian Federation.

The Federal Constitutional Law № 2-FKZ "*On the Government of the Russian Federation*" regulates in detail the competence of the Government, stipulating in the following spheres:

- *General competence of the Government:*
  - Realization of internal and external policy of the Russian Federation;
  - Legal regulation of a social-economic sphere;
  - Ensuring the unity of the system of executive power in Russia, and with the control of its bodies;
  - The development and realization of various federal programs.
- *Competence of the Government in the economic sphere:*
  - Regulation of economic processes in the country;
  - Ensuring a unity of the economic space and the freedom of economic activity, free movement of goods, services and finances;
  - Prognostication of the social and economic development of the Russian Federation;
  - development and realization of the programs concerning the development of the priority branches of the economy;
  - Development of the structural and investment policy and taking measure for its realization;
  - Managing federal property;
  - Development and realization of state policy in the spheres of international economic, financial and investment cooperation;
  - General guidance of customs' business;
  - Carrying out measures in defending the interests of domestic manufacturers, etc.
- *Competence of the Government in the budget sphere, financial, credit and monetary policy:*
  - Ensuring the implementation in the Russian Federation of a single financial, credit and monetary policy in the country;
  - Elaboration and presentation of the federal budget to the State Duma, and its enforcement;
  - Providing the State Duma with a report concerning the federal budget's enforcement;
  - Developing of tax policy;
  - Regulation of the equity market;
  - Management of the internal and external debts of the Russian Federation;
  - Implementation of currency regulation, currency control;

- Development of measures which concern the ensuring of a single pricing policy;

-Management of the currency and financial activities of the Russian Federation with foreign countries, etc.

- *Competence of the Government in the social sphere:*
- Ensuring the implementation in the Russian Federation of a single state social policy, realization of rights and Freedoms in the social security sphere;
- Promotion of the development of social security and charity;
- Carrying out measures in realization of people's labour rights;
- Developing the programs of reduction and liquidation of unemployment;
- Ensuring the implementation in the Russian Federation of a single state migration policy;
- Carrying out measures related to the realization of people's health-care rights;
- Cooperation with public and religious organizations;
- Carrying out measures relating to the developing of sport activities, tourism and health resorts, etc.

- *Competence of the Government in the cultural, scientific and educational spheres:*
- Development and taking measures of state support of the development of science;
- Ensuring state support for fundamental science;
- Ensuring the implementation of a single state policy in the sphere of education, defining of the basic directions of the development and improvement of general and professional education, the development of the system of free education;
- Ensuring state support of culture and preservation of cultural heritage of both the state and different peoples living in Russia, etc.

- *Competence of the Government in nature management and the environmental sphere:*
- Ensuring the implementation of a single state policy in the environmental sphere and ecological security;
- Carrying out measures related to the realization of people's right to a healthy environment;
- Organization of activities related to the protection and rational use of natural resources, regulation of nature management and development of mineral-raw-material base;

- Coordination of activities related to the prevention of natural disasters, accidents and catastrophes, liquidation of their consequences, etc.

• *Competence of the Government in the spheres of enforcement of law, observance of rights and freedoms, and combating crimes:*

- Taking part in the development and realization of state policy in the sphere of ensuring security to people, society and state;
- Carrying out measures related to ensuring people's rights and freedoms, protection of property and public order, combating crimes;
- Carrying out measures related to activity of the courts, etc.

• *Competence of the Government in defence and state security spheres:*

- Carrying out necessary measures related to the ensuring of defence and state security;
- Providing the Armed Forces with armaments, military equipment, material resources and all necessary services;
- Ensuring enforcement of state programs and plans which concern armament development;
- Ensuring social guarantees to armed forces personnel;
- Carrying out measures related to guarding the state borders;
- Manual of civil defence, etc.

• *Competence of the Government in external policy and international relations:*

- Carrying out measures related to realization of external policy of the Russian Federation;
- Ensuring representation of the Russian Federation in foreign countries and international organizations;
- Concluding international treaties, ensuring implementation of international obligations of the Russian Federation provided by the concluded international treaties, and also surveillance of the implementation by other partners of the international treaties of their obligations;
- Defending the geopolitical interests of the Russian Federation, protection of the Russian people abroad;
- Regulation and control in the spheres of external economic activities, cultural and scientific and technical cooperation, etc.

• *Competence of the Government in the law-making sphere:*

- Introduction of bills into the State Duma;

- Providing both the State Duma and the Federation Council with its official opinions on the draft laws which are subject to discussion in the chambers;
- The members of the Government are entitled to be present at the meetings of the chambers, their committees and commissions;
- Appointment of the governmental official representative at the chambers of the parliament.

The Government issues *decisions* and *orders* on the basis and for the sake of implementation of the Constitution, the federal laws and normative decrees of the President (§1 Article 115 of the Constitution).

6. The Central Bank of the Russian Federation (Bank of Russia)

The Central Bank of the Russian Federation (Bank of Russia) was founded on July 13, 1990, on the basis of the Russian Republic Bank of the State Bank of the USSR. It was accountable to the Supreme Soviet of the RSFSR, and was originally called the State Bank of the RSFSR.

On December 2, 1990, the Supreme Soviet of the RSFSR passed the Law on the Central Bank of the RSFSR (Bank of Russia), which declared the Bank of Russia to be a legal entity and the main bank of the RSFSR, accountable to the Supreme Soviet of the RSFSR. The law specified the functions of the bank in organizing money circulation, monetary regulation, foreign economic activity and regulation of the activities of joint-stock and co-operative banks.

In November 1991, when the Commonwealth of Independent States was founded and Union structures dissolved, the Supreme Soviet of the RSFSR declared the Central Bank of the RSFSR to be the only body of state monetary and foreign exchange regulation in the RSFSR. The functions of the State Bank of the USSR in issuing money and setting the ruble exchange rate were transferred to it. The Central Bank of the RSFSR was instructed to assume before January 1, 1992, full control of the assets, technical facilities and other resources of the State Bank of the USSR and all its institutions, enterprises and organizations.

On December 20, 1991, the State Bank of the USSR was disbanded and all its assets, liabilities and property in the RSFSR were transferred to the Central Bank of the RSFSR (Bank of Russia), which several months later was renamed the Central Bank of the Russian Federation (Bank of Russia).

In 1991-1992 an extensive network of commercial banks was created in the Russian Federation under Bank of Russia guidance through commercialization of the specialized banks' branches. The disbandment of the State Bank of the USSR was followed by changes in the chart of accounts, the establishment of a network of Central Bank cash settlement centres and their provision with computer technology. The Central Bank began to buy and sell foreign exchange in the currency market it established and to set and publish the official exchange rates of foreign currencies against the ruble.

In December 1992, as a result of the establishment of a single centralized federal treasury system, the Bank of Russia was no longer required to provide cash services for the federal budget.

The Bank of Russia carries out its functions, which were established by the Constitution of the Russian Federation (Article 75) and the Law "On the Central Bank of the Russian Federation (Bank of Russia)" (Article 22), independently from the federal, regional and local government structures.

In 1992-1995, to maintain stability of the banking system, the Bank of Russia set up a system of supervision and inspection of commercial banks and a system of foreign exchange regulation and foreign exchange control. As the agent of the Ministry of Finance, it organized the government securities market, known as the GKO market, and began to participate in its operations.

In 1995, the Bank of Russia stopped extending loans to finance the federal budget deficit and centralized loans to individual sectors of the economy.

To override the consequences of the 1998 financial crisis, the Bank of Russia took steps towards restructuring the banking system in order to improve the performance of commercial banks and increase their liquidity. Insolvent banks were removed from the banking services market, using the procedures established by the applicable law. Of great importance for the post-crisis recovery of the banking sector was the creation of the Agency for Restructuring Credit Institutions (ARCO) and the Inter-Agency Co-coordinating Committee for Banking Sector Development in Russia (ICC). Thanks to the effective measures implemented by the Bank of Russia, ARCO and ICC, by the middle of 2001 Russia's banking sector had on the whole overcome the aftermath of the crisis.

The Bank of Russia monetary policy was designed to maintain financial stability and create conditions conducive to sustainable economic growth. The Bank of Russia promptly reacted to any change in the real demand for money and took steps to stimulate positive economic dynamics, cut interest rates, damp down inflationary expectations and slow the inflation rate. As a result, the ruble gained somewhat in real terms and financial market stability increased.

There are some problems to which the Bank of Russia pays special attention. One of them is that specific risks connected with the dynamics of the prices of some financial assets and the price situation on the real estate market, have recently begun to play an increasingly important role. The practice of lending to related parties led to high risk concentrations in some banks, compelling the Bank of Russia to upgrade the methods of banking regulation and supervision by putting greater emphasis on substantive (risk-oriented) supervision.

Fictitious capitalization of banks is another matter of serious concern for the Bank of Russia. To prevent banks from using all sorts of schemes designed to artificially overvalue or undervalue the required ratios, the Bank of Russia in 2004 issued a number of regulations, including the Regulation "On the Procedure for Creating Loan Loss Reserves by Credit Institutions" and the Instruction "On Banks' Required Ratios".

As the number of credit institutions extending mortgage loans to the public increased, in 2003 the Bank of Russia issued the Ordinance "On Conducting a One-off Survey of Mortgage Lending", which set the procedure for compiling and presenting data on housing mortgage loans extended by credit institutions.

With the adoption of the Federal Law "On Mortgage Securities", credit institutions which ensured the observance of the requirements for the protection of investors' interests received the lawful opportunity to refinance their claims on mortgage loans by issuing mortgage securities.

In pursuance of the Federal Law "On the Central Bank of the Russian Federation (Bank of Russia)" and Federal Law "On Mortgage Securities", the Bank of Russia issued the Instruction "On the Required Ratios for Credit Institutions Issuing Mortgage-Backed Bonds", which specified the calculation and established the values of the required ratios and the values and methodology of calculating additional required ratios for credit institutions issuing mortgage-backed bonds.

In December 2003, the Federal Law "On Insurance of Personal Bank Deposits in the Russian Federation" was adopted. The law stipulated the legal, financial and organizational framework for the mandatory personal bank deposits' insurance system, and also the powers and procedure for the establishment and operation of an institution implementing mandatory deposit insurance functions and set the procedure for paying deposit compensation.

At present, an overwhelming majority of banks participate in the deposit insurance system. They account for almost 100 percent of total personal deposits placed in Russian banks.

In April 2005, the Russian Government and Bank of Russia adopted the Banking Sector Development Strategy for the Period up to 2008, a document which set as the main objective of banking sector development in the medium term (2005-2008) the enhancement of the banking sector's stability and efficiency.

The principal goals of banking sector development are as follows:

- Increasing the protection of interests of depositors and other creditors of banks;
- Enhancing the effectiveness of the banking sector's activity in accumulating household and enterprise sector funds and transforming them into loans and investments;
- Making Russian credit institutions more competitive;
- Preventing the use of credit institutions in dishonest commercial practices and illegal activities, especially the financing of terrorism and money laundering;
- Promoting the development of the competitive environment and ensuring the transparency of credit institutions;
- Building up investor, creditor and depositor confidence in the banking sector.

Banking sector reform will help implement Russia's medium-term social and economic development program (2005-2008), especially its objective to end the raw materials' bias of the Russian economy by rapidly diversifying it and utilizing its competitive advantages. At the next stage (2009-2015), the Russian Government and Bank of Russia will attach priority to effectively positioning the Russian banking sector on international financial markets.

Article 75 of the Constitution of the Russian Federation establishes a special legal status of the Bank of Russia, gives it the exclusive right to issue currency (§ 1) and protect the ruble and ensure its stability, which is the main function of the Bank of Russia (§ 2). The status, purposes, functions and powers of the Bank of Russia are also spelled out in Federal Law № 86-FZ, dated July 10, 2002, "*On the Central Bank of the Russian Federation (Bank of Russia)*" (Bank of Russia Law) and other federal laws.

According to Article 3 of the Bank of Russia Law, the purposes of the Bank of Russia are to protect the ruble and ensure its stability, promote the development of and strengthen the Russian banking system and ensure the efficient and uninterrupted functioning of the payment system.

A key element of the legal status of the Bank of Russia is its independence, which implies, above all, that the Bank of Russia is a special public and legal institution that has the exclusive right to issue currency and organize its circulation. The Bank of Russia is not a body of state power, but its powers are, in effect, the functions of a body of state power, because their implementation implies the use of state compulsion. The Bank of Russia performs the functions and exercises the powers stipulated by the Constitution of the Russian Federation and the Bank of Russia Law independently from the federal bodies of state power, regional authorities and local governments. Its independent status is codified in Article 75 of the Constitution of the Russian Federation and Article 1 and Article 2 of the Bank of Russia Law.

The legislative powers of the Bank of Russia imply its exclusive right to issue directives, regulations and instructions binding on the federal bodies of state power, regional authorities, local governments and all legal entities and natural persons on matters placed within its competence by the Bank of Russia Law and other federal laws. Bank of Russia legal acts shall come into force within 10 days after their official publication in *The Bank of Russia Bulletin*, except for the cases stipulated by the Board of Directors.

The Constitution of the Russian Federation does not give the Bank of Russia the power to initiate legislation, but it is involved in the law-making process not only by virtue of issuing its own regulations, but also owing to the fact that the drafts of federal laws and statutory acts of federal bodies of executive power concerning the performance by the Bank of Russia of its functions must be submitted to the Bank of Russia for consideration and approval.

The Bank of Russia is a legal entity. Its authorized capital and other property are federal property. Nevertheless, the Bank of Russia has both proprietary and financial independence. It exercises its powers to own, use and manage its property, including international reserves, in compliance with the purposes and according to the procedure established by the Bank of Russia Law. Bank of Russia property may not be seized or encumbered without its consent, unless the federal law stipulates otherwise. The financial independence of the Bank of Russia implies that it covers its expenses from its own incomes. The Bank of Russia may defend its interests in court, including international courts, the courts of foreign states and courts of arbitration.

The state is not liable for Bank of Russia obligations, just as the Bank of Russia is not liable for state obligations, unless they have assumed such obligations or unless federal laws stipulate otherwise. The Bank of Russia is not liable for the obligations of credit institutions, while the credit institutions are not liable for the obligations of the Bank of Russia, except the cases in which the Bank of Russia or credit institutions assume such obligations.

The Bank of Russia is accountable to the State Duma of the Federal Assembly of the Russian Federation (hereinafter referred to as the State Duma), which appoints and dismisses the Bank of Russia Chairman (on the proposal of the President of the Russian Federation) and members of the Bank of Russia Board of Directors (on the proposal of the Bank of Russia Chairman, agreed with the President of the Russian Federation), sends and recalls its representatives on the National Banking Board within its quota and considers the guidelines for the single state monetary policy and Bank of Russia annual report and takes decisions on them. On the proposal of the National Banking Board, the State Duma may take the decision to get the Accounts Chamber of the Russian Federation to audit the financial and economic activities of the Bank of Russia and its divisions and establishments. In addition, the State Duma holds parliamentary hearings on the Bank of Russia activities with the participation of its representatives and hears the reports by the Bank of Russia Chairman about the Bank of Russia activities in the course of presenting the annual report and guidelines for the single state monetary policy.

The Bank of Russia performs its functions in compliance with the Constitution of the Russian Federation, the Bank of Russia Law and other federal laws. According to Article 75 of the Constitution, the principal function of the Bank of Russia is to protect the ruble and ensure its stability. The Bank of Russia is the sole issuer of currency. Pursuant to Article 4 of the Bank of Russia Law, the Bank of Russia performs the following *functions:*

- In collaboration with the federal government it elaborates and implements a single state monetary policy;
- It is the sole issuer of cash and organizer of cash circulation;
- It approves the graphic designation of the ruble as a sign;
- It is the creditor of last resort for credit institutions and it organizes the credit institution refinance system;
- It sets the settlement rules in the Russian Federation;
- It sets the rules for conducting banking operations.
- It services budget accounts on all levels of the Russian budget system, unless the federal laws stipulate otherwise, by effecting settlements at the instruction of the authorized bodies of executive power and government extra-budgetary funds, which are assigned the task of organizing the execution of and executing the budgets;
- It efficiently manages the Bank of Russia international reserves;

- It takes the decision on the state registration of credit institutions, issues banking licences to credit institutions and suspends and revokes them;
- It supervises the activities of credit institutions and banking groups;
- It registers securities' issues by credit institutions in compliance with federal laws;
- It conducts independently or at the instruction of the Russian Government all types of banking operations and other transactions necessary for the performance of Bank of Russia functions;
- It organizes and exercises foreign exchange regulation and control pursuant to federal legislation;
- It sets the procedure for effecting settlements with international organizations, foreign states and legal entities and natural persons;
- It sets accounting and reporting rules for the Russian banking system;
- It sets and publishes official exchange rates of foreign currencies against the ruble;
- It takes part in the compiling of Russia's balance of payments' forecast and organizes the compiling of Russia's balance of payments;
- It sets the procedure for and conditions of foreign exchange purchases and sales by currency exchanges and issues, suspends and revokes permits for the currency exchanges to organize foreign exchange purchases and sales (the Bank of Russia will issue, suspend and revoke permits for the currency exchanges to organize foreign exchange purchases and sales as of the day of the coming into force of the corresponding amendments to the Federal Law on the Licensing of Individual Types of Activities);
- It analyses and makes forecasts for the situation in the Russian economy as a whole and by region, especially the monetary, financial and price relations, and publishes the corresponding materials and statistical data;
- It pays compensation for household deposits with bankrupt banks uncovered by the compulsory deposit insurance system in the cases and according to the procedure established by the federal law;
- It is the depository of the International Monetary Fund in the Russian currency and it conducts operations and transactions provided by the Articles of Agreement of the International Monetary Fund and the agreements with the International Monetary Fund;
- It performs other functions in compliance with federal laws.

CHAPTER NINE

THE JUDICIAL POWER AND PROSECUTION OFFICE IN RUSSIA

1. The Judicial System of the Russian Federation

The Constitution of the Russian Federation does not contain the detailed provisions related to the system of courts in the state. It has only provisions related to the high courts, existing in Russia:

- The Constitutional Court of the Russian Federation;
- The Supreme Court of the Russian Federation.

These high courts may be set up and abolished only upon amendment of the Constitution.

The Constitution, however, also stipulates that other federal courts may be established in the state. So far, the Russian Basic Law does not have any provisions concerning concrete types of judicial instances. However, it provides that the judicial system of the Russian Federation shall be instituted by the Constitution and the federal constitutional law. This provision means that any type of federal court in the Russian Federation may be established only if it is clearly provided by the federal constitutional law.

A single judicial system exists as opposed to other federations (the USA, Switzerland and Germany). The subjects of the Russian Federation are not entitled to have their own judicial systems. However, currently, there are two types of courts that the subjects of the Russian Federation may set up in accordance with their own laws:

(i) Constitutional courts of republics and charter courts of other subjects of the Russian Federation;

(ii) Justices of the Peace.

All other courts existing in the Russian Federation are considered to be federal courts.

There are *different types of courts* in the Russian Federation:

(1) The Constitutional Court of the Russian Federation;

(2) Courts of general jurisdiction, including military courts;

(3) Arbitration courts.

The Constitutional Court of the Russian Federation which is considered to be the organ of constitutional control is quite a unique court. It is a single court in the Russian Federation which is not at the head of the system of constitutional courts. Such a kind of courts' system does not exist in Russia at all. It should be emphasized that constitutional courts of republics and charter courts of other subjects of the Russian Federation do not form a single system of constitutional courts along with the Constitutional Court of the Russian Federation. The same rule applies among other federations, for example in Germany.

Courts of general jurisdiction form the whole system of courts of general jurisdiction which is headed by the Supreme Court of the Russian Federation. Military courts which are set up in the Russian Federation are considered to be the part of the system of courts of general jurisdiction.

Arbitration courts also form a separate system of courts which had been headed by the High Arbitration Court of the Russian Federation until 2014 when it was abolished by the constitutional amendment (Law of the Russian Federation dated February 5, 2014 № 2-FKZ "*On the Supreme Court of the Russian Federation and Prosecution Office of the Russian Federation*").

2. The Constitutional Provisions on the Judicial Power in the Russian Federation

Legal Basis

The Constitution of the Russian Federation provides that judicial power is one of the branches of state power which will perform justice in the Russian Federation. Pursuant to Article 118 §1 of the Constitution, justice in the Russian Federation shall be administered by courts alone. Pursuant to Article 1 of Federal Constitutional Law, "*On the judicial system of the Russian Federation*" of December 31, 1996, № 1-FKZ judicial power in the Russian Federation shall be administered solely by courts as represented by judges and jury members, as well as by people's and arbitration jurors invited in accordance with the procedure established by the law for administering justice. No other bodies and persons shall have the right to undertake the administration of justice. Judicial power shall be separate and shall act independently of the legislative and executive powers.

Chapter 7 of the Russian Constitution is dedicated to judicial power and includes the provisions which stipulate the structure and competence of different courts in Russia, the system of courts, legal status of the judges and principles of their activity. In general, the judicial system of the Russian Federation has been instituted not only by the Constitution, but also by numerous federal constitutional and federal laws, among them are:

1) *Federal Constitutional Law dated December 31, 1996, № 1-FKZ "On the Judicial System of the Russian Federation";*
2) *Federal Constitutional Law dated February 7, 2011, № 1-FKZ "On the Courts of General Jurisdiction";*
3) *Federal Constitutional Law dated April 28, 1995 № 1-FKZ "On the Arbitration Courts in the Russian Federation";*
4) *Federal Constitutional Law dated July 21, 1994, № 1-FKZ "On the Constitutional Court of the Russian Federation";*
5) *Federal Constitutional Law № 1-FKZ of June 23, 1999, "On Military Courts of the Russian Federation";*
6) *Federal Law dated August 20, 2004, № 113-FZ "On Jury of the Federal Courts of General Jurisdiction in the Russian Federation";*
7) *Federal Law dated December 17, 1998, № 188-FZ "On the Justice of the Peace in the Russian Federation";*
8) *Law of the Russian Federation dated June 26, 1992, № 3132-I "On the Status of Judges in the Russian Federation";*
9) *Civil Procedural Code dated November 14, 2002, № 138-FZ;*
10) *Criminal Procedural Code dated December 18, 2001, № 174-FZ (came into force as of July 1, 2002);*
11) *Code of the Russian Federation on Administrative Violations dated December 30, 2001, № 195-FZ;*
12) *Arbitration Procedural Code dated July 24, 2002, № 95-FZ.*

Principles of Justice

Justice in the Russian Federation is based on the following principles:

1. *Justice in the Russian Federationis to be administered by the courts alone*. This principle means that there cannot be any other than the court bodies entitled to resolve civil, criminal and other cases. It is specifically stipulated in the Constitution that the creation of any extraordinary courts shall not be allowed in the Russian Federation (§3 Art. 118 of the Constitution).

2. *Judicial power shall be exercised by means of constitutional, civil, administrative, and criminal proceedings.* Judicial power is being realized in accordance with the procedural order prescribed by the law. This order is generally universal and is being based on such universally recognized

principles as *the equality of all persons before the law and court, protection of the rights and freedoms of man and citizen in court proceedings, national language of the hearings, competitiveness and equality of the parties during the trial, the right to file appeals against procedural actions and decisions*. However, depending on the nature of the relationships legal proceedings have their peculiarities which allow the classification of legal proceedings as constitutional, civil, administrative, and criminal. Each type of legal proceeding is subject to regulation by the separate law, for example, constitutional procedure is stipulated in the Federal Constitutional Law "On the Constitutional Court of the Russian Federation" (1994), the civil proceeding–in the Civil Code of the Russian Federation (2002), the criminal proceeding–in the Criminal Code of the Russian Federation (2002) and the administrative proceeding–in the Code on administrative law infringements (2001). There is one more kind of legal proceeding in the Russian Federation–the arbitration proceeding which is close to the civil procedure but is stipulated in the Arbitration Procedure Code of the Russian Federation (2002).

3. Principle of equality of all persons before the law and the courts. Pursuant to Article 7 of the Federal Constitutional Law dated December 31, 1996, № 1-FKZ "On the Judicial System of the Russian Federation" courts shall not display preference towards any bodies, persons or parties in a litigation by their state, social, gender, race, national, language or political belonging or depending on their origin, property or position status, residence, birth place, attitude to religion, beliefs, membership in public associations and equally on other grounds not provided in the federal law.

Pursuant to Article 11 §1 of the Criminal Code of the Russian Federation (2001), persons committing offences on the territory of the Russian Federation involving the use of torture (irrespective of the citizenship of the victim) shall be held criminally liable under the applicable articles of the Criminal Code of the Russian Federation. In this way, Russian criminal law protects both its own citizens and foreign citizens, and also stateless persons, from the use of torture.

The criminal liability of the diplomatic representatives of foreign States and of other citizens who enjoy immunity, in the event of their commission of offences on the territory of the Russian Federation, is determined in accordance with the rules of international law (Article 11 §4 of the Criminal Code).

Pursuant to Article 12 §1 of the Criminal Code, citizens of the Russian Federation and stateless persons permanently resident in the Russian Federation who commit offences outside the territory of the Russian

Federation involving the use of torture incur criminal liability under the Criminal Code of the Federation if the acts perpetrated by them are deemed to be offences in the State on whose territory they were committed and if the perpetrators have not been convicted thereof in that foreign State.

When such persons are being convicted, their punishment may not be more severe than the most severe punishment prescribed by the law of the foreign State on whose territory the offence was committed.

Foreign citizens and stateless persons not permanently resident in the Russian Federation who have committed offences outside the territory of the Russian Federation may be subject to criminal prosecution provided either of the conditions specified in Article 12 §3 of the Criminal Code are attested, namely:

(a) Where the offence was intended to harm the interests of the Russian Federation;

(b) In cases covered by an international treaty of the Russian Federation (the principle of universal jurisdiction).

§1 of Article 2 of the Code of Criminal Procedure also stipulates that criminal proceedings conducted on the territory of the Russian Federation, regardless of where the offence itself was committed, shall follow the rules of the Code of Criminal Procedure of the Russian Federation, unless provided otherwise by an international treaty of the Russian Federation.

Military servicemen of the Russian Federation serving in units deployed outside the territory of the Federation shall be held liable under the Criminal Code of the Russian Federation for offences committed on the territory of a foreign State, unless provided otherwise by an international treaty of the Russian Federation.

4. Principle of open trial is stipulated in Article 123 §1 of the Constitution which is providing that examination of cases in all courts shall be open. Examination in camera shall be allowed only in cases envisaged by the federal law. First of all these cases are listed in Article 241 of the Criminal Procedure Code of the Russian Federation (2002) which says that conducting the judicial proceedings in camera shall be admissible on the grounds of a court ruling or resolution, if:

1) The judicial proceedings on a criminal case in court may lead to an indulgence of the state or of another kind of secret, protected by federal law;
2) The criminal cases under examination concern the crimes, perpetrated by the persons who have not reached 16 years of age;
3) An examination of the criminal cases on the offences of the sexual immunity and sexual freedom of the personality and on other

crimes may lead to an indulgence of the information on the intimate aspects of life of the participants in the criminal court proceedings or of information humiliating their honour and dignity;

4) This is called forth by the interests of guaranteeing security for the participants in the judicial proceedings, for their close relatives, relations or near persons.

Concrete, actual circumstances shall be indicated in the court ruling or decision on the hearing in camera which were used by the court as the grounds for the given decision to be adopted. The persons, attending an open court session, shall have the right to carry out audio recording and to make records of it in writing. Taking photographs, video recording and/or cinema shooting shall be admissible only with the permission of the presiding justice of the court session (§5 Article 241 of the *Criminal Procedure Code of the Russian Federation*).

5. Examination of a case in absentia is not to be allowed if it is not otherwise stipulated by federal law. In general, a case is to be examined in the presence of a defendant. However, the federal laws may provide situations when a case may be examined by the court in absentia. Pursuant to Article 247 §4 of the Criminal Procedure Code of the Russian Federation judicial proceedings in the absence of a defendant may be permitted, if the defendant files a petition on a crime of minor or medium gravity for an examination of the given criminal case in his absence.

6. Principle of controversy and equality of the parties. This principle is provided in Article 123 §3 of the Constitution of the Russian Federation which says: "*Judicial proceedings shall be held on the basis of controversy and equality of the parties*". The principle of controversy means that legal proceedings may be started only if there is a plaintiff's statement, a request of the state body or official, a complaint of a victim or an accusation of a public prosecutor claiming the court to consider their claims. The functions of defence, accusation and consideration of the case are separated from each other and may not be entrusted to the same organ or official. The courts in Russia are not considered to be the bodies of persecution. They are to provide all the necessary conditions for performance by the parties of their procedural obligations and rights.

7. Principle of presumption of innocence in criminal court proceedings. The accused shall be regarded as non-guilty until his being guilty of committing the crime is proved in accordance with the procedure, stipulated by the federal law, and is established by court sentence, which has entered into legal force. The suspect or the accused is not obliged to prove his innocence. The burden of proving the charge and of refuting the arguments cited in defence of the suspect or of the accused shall lie with the party of the prosecution. All doubts concerning the guilt of the accused, which cannot be eliminated in accordance with the procedure established by the present Code, shall be interpreted in favour of the accused. The verdict of guilty cannot be based on suppositions.

8. Justice in the Russian Federation shall be administered by a court of jury in cases provided by the federal law (Article 123 §4 of the Constitution). Pursuant to Article 8 of the Federal Constitutional Law "*On the judicial system of the Russian Federation*", citizens of the Russian Federation shall have the right to participate in the administration of justice in accordance with the procedure provided in the federal law. Participation of jury members in the administration of justice is a civic duty. The requirements of citizens participating in the administration of justice are to be set forth in the federal law. There is the Federal Law dated August 20, 2004, № 113-FZ "On Federal Jurors in Federal Courts of General Jurisdiction". In accordance with the Federal Act on the entry into force of the Code of Criminal Procedure of the Russian Federation of November 22, 2001, as set out in version No. 181-FZ of December 27, 2002, jury trials are gradually being introduced into courts throughout the Federation. On January 1, 2003, they were introduced in 60 regions, on July 1, 2003 in 14 regions, on January 1, 2004 in 5 regions, and on January 1, 2007, they were introduced in the remaining region–the Chechen Republic.

Courts of jurors in the Russian Federation are established at the Supreme Court of the Russian Federation, regional courts of general jurisdiction (Supreme Courts of the Russian republics, courts of the territories of the Russian Federation, regions, cities of federal importance, autonomous region and autonomous areas) and district (fleet) military courts. Courts of jurors in the Russian Federation consider only the criminal cases, namely felonies such as for example, treason, terrorist acts, gangsterism, propaganda of war, divulgence of state secrets, kidnapping, etc.

In conformity with the above-mentioned Federal Law 113-FZ of August 20, 2004, lists of candidates for jurors (general and reserve) are compiled every four years by the supreme executive bodies of the constituent entities of the Russian Federation from among citizens residing permanently in those constituent entities. The Law specifies the procedures and time frame for compiling the lists, the requirements made of jurors and the conditions for removing citizens from the general and reserve lists, and deals with issues relating to jurors' subsistence and so forth. In accordance with the Law the following citizens cannot be appointed as jurors:

- ✓ Citizens who are under 25 years old;
- ✓ Citizens with previous convictions not removed;
- ✓ Citizens who are legally incapable and who have restricted capability;
- ✓ Citizens who are registered in narcological or psycho-neurologic dispensaries;
- ✓ Citizens who are suspected or accused in the commission of a crime;
- ✓ Citizens who do not speak the language which is used in the legal proceedings;
- ✓ Citizens who suffer physical and mental diseases which prevent fully-fledged participation in consideration of the criminal case.

The citizens who have been included in the lists of jurors' candidates are to be excluded from such lists by the supreme executive bodies of the constituent entities of the Russian Federation in the following cases:

(1) If the citizens do not meet the requirements provided to the jurors;
(2) If the citizens deliver a written application stating that there are circumstances which prevent them from performing the jurors' duties;
(3) And, if these citizens:
 (i) do not speak the language which is used in the hearings;
 (ii) are not capable of performing the juror's duty because of their state of health proved by medical certificate;
 (iii) are older than 65 years;
 (iv) are replacing public officials or elective office in self-government;
 (v) are military personnel;
 (vi) are retired from the bodies of the federal security service, state guard service or foreign intelligence service–within five years from their retirement;
 (vii) perform the duties of the judges, public prosecutors, investigators, attorneys, public notaries, bailiffs or private detectives within the time of performance of such duties and within 5 years hereinafter;
 (viii) have special rank of an official of the bodies of internal affairs, drug control, customs office, and law-enforcement system;
 (ix) perform the duties of a priest.

9. Judges are persons vested with the powers to administer justice and perform their duties on a professional basis. There are *general* and *specific* requirements for the candidates for the positions of judges in the Russian Federation.

General requirements mean that judges may be only persons who:

- ✓ are Russian citizens;
- ✓ have a higher legal education;
- ✓ do not have and have not before had any criminal records;
- ✓ do not have foreign citizenship or a residence permit in a foreign country;
- ✓ are neither incapable or have restricted capability;
- ✓ are not registered in narcological or psycho-neurologic dispensaries;
- ✓ do not suffer physical and mental diseases which prevent them from performing the duties of a judge.

Specific requirements are being provided by the law to the candidates for different judges:

- Judges of the arbitration courts of the subject of the Russian Federation, constitutional (charter) court of the subject of the Russian Federation, district courts, justice of the peace, and also the garrison military courts may be citizens of the Russian Federation over 25 years of age with a higher education in law and a law service record of not less than 5 years.
- Judges of the supreme courts of republics, of territorial, regional courts, courts of cities of federal importance, courts of autonomous regions and autonomous areas, district (fleet) military courts, federal circuit arbitration courts, arbitration appellate courts, specialized arbitration courts may be citizens of the Russian Federation over 30 years of age with a higher education in law and a law service record of not less than 7 years.
- Judges of the Supreme Court of the Russian Federation may be citizens of the Russian Federation over 35 years of age with a higher education in law and a law service record of not less than 10 years.
- Finally, judges of the Constitutional Court of the Russian Federation may be citizens of the Russian Federation over 40 years of age with a higher education in law and a law service record of not less than 15 years with an unblemished reputation and a highly recognized reputation in the legal sphere.

All the judges in the Russian Federation shall have a unitary status and shall differ among themselves solely by powers and competence. The specifics of the legal status of specific categories of judges shall be determined by the federal laws and, should there be provision therein, they shall be determined also by the laws of the constituent members of the Russian Federation. Candidates for the offices of judges shall be selected on a competitive basis.

Judges of the Constitutional Court of the Russian Federation and the Supreme Court of the Russian Federation are to be appointed by the Federation Council upon proposals by the President of the Russian Federation.

Appointment of any judge may take place only if there is a positive conclusion of the correspondent Qualification College of Judges.

Judges of military courts are to be appointed by the President of the Russian Federation upon the proposals of the Chairman of the Supreme Court of the Russian Federation if there is a decision of the High Qualification College of Judges of the Russian Federation on appointment of the recommended candidate to the post of the judge of the correspondent military court.

In accordance with Russian legislation judges are not entitled:

- to be engaged in entrepreneurial activities and undertake any paid work except for scientific, teaching, literary and other creative activity;
- to replace other state positions, positions of state service, municipal positions, or to be an arbitrator;
- to be the members of any political party, support them and take part in political actions and political activity;
- to express publicly their attitude to the political parties and other public organizations;
- to express publicly their attitude to the subject of the case which is under consideration of these judges, etc.

Pursuant to Article 120 of the Constitution of the Russian Federation judges shall be *independent* and *submit only to the Constitution and the federal laws*. If after considering a case, a judge decides that an act of a state or other body contradicts the law, it shall pass on an appropriate decision according to the law.

The Constitution of the Russian Federation, the Federal Constitutional Law "On the Judicial System" of December 31, 1996, the Law *"On the Status of Judges in the Russian Federation"* of July 26, 1992, the Federal Law "*On Jurors in Federal Courts of General Jurisdiction*" and the procedural legislation currently in force in the Russian Federation provide the following guarantees to ensure judicial independence:

- ✓ Establishment of special procedures for the appointment of judges, and their appointment for life;
- ✓ Special procedures for administering justice;

- ✓ Prohibition (under threat of prosecution) of interference by any person in the administration of justice by judges;
- ✓ Special standards governing the procedures for suspending judges and removing them from office;
- ✓ Inviolability of judges;
- ✓ Existence of professional judicial bodies;
- ✓ Payment to judges by the State of a salary and benefits in keeping with their high status;
- ✓ Provision of special State protection for judges and members of their families, as well as for their property.

In the Russian Federation, no law or regulation may be promulgated that abolishes or curtails the autonomy of the courts or the independence of judges (Article 5 of the Federal Constitutional Law "*On the Judicial System of the Russian Federation*").

The powers of judges of the federal courts *shall not be limited to a definite term* except as otherwise established by the Constitution of the Russian Federation or the federal law on the status of judges adopted in compliance with them. The maximum age for holding the office of a judge of a federal court shall be 70 years.

No judge shall be removed from office. A judge may not be appointed (elected) to another position or to another court without his/her consent. The office of a judge shall be terminated or suspended by the decision of the relevant Qualification College of Judges. A decision of the relevant Qualification College of Judges on the early termination of the powers of judges for the commission of disciplinary offences may be appealed against to the Disciplinary Judgment Seat in accordance with federal constitutional law. Pursuant to Article 13 of the Federal Law "On the Status of Judges in the Russian Federation" (1992) the powers of judges may be terminated under the following conditions:

1) If a judge is recognized by the court's decision as a missing person;
2) If a criminal case is initiated against a judge;
3) If a judge takes part in the presidential, parliamentary elections, elections to the legislative body of any subject of the Russian Federation or municipal representative body as a candidate.

Judges are *immune*. Immunity of the judges means the inviolability of person, inviolability of the dwelling and office premises of the judges, transport, documentation, luggage and other property belonging to the judges, and also the secrecy of their correspondence.

Judges cannot be brought to criminal responsibility for their decisions taken upon consideration of the cases.

A decision on initiating *a criminal case* shall be taken:

- Against judges of the Constitutional Court of the Russian Federation–by the Chairman of the Inquiry Committee of the Russian Federation upon the consent of the Constitutional Court of the Russian Federation;
- Against judges of the Supreme Court of the Russian Federation, the supreme courts of republics, of territorial, regional courts, courts of cities of federal importance, courts of autonomous regions and autonomous areas, military courts, federal arbitration courts–by the Chairman of the Inquiry Committee of the Russian Federation upon the consent of the High Qualification College of Judges of the Russian Federation;
- Against judges of other courts–by the Chairman of the Inquiry Committee of the Russian Federation upon the consent of the Qualification College of Judges of the correspondent subject of the Russian Federation.

A decision on initiating of *an administrative case* shall be taken upon receipt of the report of the Prosecutor General of the Russian Federation:

- Against judges of the Constitutional Court of the Russian Federation, the Supreme Court of the Russian Federation, the supreme courts of republics, of territorial, regional courts, courts of cities of federal importance, courts of autonomous region and autonomous areas, military courts, federal arbitration courts–by the panel of judges consisting of three judges of the Supreme Court of the Russian Federation (the composition of this panel is to be renewed every year by the High Qualification College of Judges of the Russian Federation);
- Against judges of other courts–by the panel of judges consisting of three judges of correspondingly supreme courts of republics, of territorial, regional courts, courts of cities of federal importance, courts of autonomous region and autonomous areas (compositions of these panels are to be renewed every year by the Qualification College of Judges of the correspondent subject of the Russian Federation).

10. The courts shall be financed only from the federal budget. This principle ensures financial independence of all courts in the Russian Federation and the possibility of complete and independent administration of justice shall be ensured in keeping with the requirements of federal law.

3. The Constitutional Court of the Russian Federation

Composition and the Procedure for the Formation of the Constitutional Court of the Russian Federation

The authorities and procedure for the formation and activity of the Constitutional Court of the Russian Federation shall be determined by the Constitution of the Russian Federation and the Federal Constitutional Law № 1-FKZ of July 21, 1994 "*On the Constitutional Court of the Russian Federation*".

The Constitutional Court of the Russian Federation consists of *19 judges*, appointed to the position by the Federation Council upon a submission from the President of the Russian Federation. The Constitutional Court of the Russian Federation shall have the right to carry out its activity in the presence of not less than three-quarters of the total number of judges. The authorities of the Constitutional Court of the Russian Federation shall not be limited by a specific term.

Citizens who have are at least *40 years of age* as of the day of appointment, with an irreproachable reputation, having a legal higher education and work experience in the legal expression of at least fifteen years, with recognized high qualifications in the sphere of law, may be appointed Judges of the Constitutional Court of the Russian Federation. The maximum age for occupying the post of judge of the Constitutional Court of the Russian Federation is 70 years, except for the Chairman of the Constitutional Court for whom this provision does not apply.

Proposals of candidates to the post of judge of the Constitutional Court of the Russian Federation may be submitted to the President of the Russian Federation by members (deputies) of the Federation Council and deputies of the State Duma, as well as by the legislative (representative) bodies of constituent entities of the Russian Federation, supreme court bodies and federal legal agencies, all-Russia legal societies, legal scientific and educational institutions. The Federation Council shall consider the question of the appointment to the post of judge of the Constitutional Court of the Russian Federation within fourteen days from the time of receipt of a submission from the President of the Russian Federation. Each judge of the Constitutional Court of the Russian Federation shall be appointed individually to the post by secret ballot. The person appointed to the post of judge of the Constitutional Court of the Russian Federation shall be considered to be the person who has received votes from a majority of the total number of members (deputies) of the Federation Council. Should a judge leave the composition of the Constitutional Court of the Russian Federation, the submission on the appointment of another person to the vacant position of judge shall be submitted by the President of the Russian Federation to the Federation Council within one month from the day of the vacancy. A judge of the Constitutional Court of the Russian Federation whose term of authority has expired shall continue to fulfill the obligations of a judge until the appointment of a new judge to the post or until the adoption of a final decision on a case has begun with his participation.

Status of Judges of the Constitutional Court of the Russian Federation

Judges of the Constitutional Court enjoy *equal rights.*

A judge of the Constitutional Court of the Russian Federation may not be a member (deputy) of the Federation Council, a deputy of the State Duma, or of any other representative bodies, occupy or retain other state or public posts, have a private practice, engage in entrepreneurial or other paid activity, other than teaching, scientific or other creative activity, and such activity must not hinder the performance of his obligations as a judge of the Constitutional Court of the Russian Federation and may not serve as a legitimate reason for absence at a session, unless the consent of the Constitutional Court of the Russian Federation is given for this.

Judges of the Constitutional Court of the Russian Federation shall have immunity. They may not be brought to criminal or administration liability applied through court proceedings, be detained, arrested, subject to search without the consent of the Constitutional Court of the Russian Federation, with the exception of cases of detention at the place of a crime, with the exception where this is envisaged by federal law to ensure the safety of other persons.

The authorities of a judge of the Constitutional Court of the Russian Federation shall be terminated by virtue of: 1) a violation of the procedure for his appointment to the post of judge of the Constitutional Court of the Russian Federation, as established by the Constitution of the Russian Federation and this Federal Constitutional Law; 2) expiration of the term of authority of the judge or the judge reaching the maximum permissible age for the post; 3) a personal written application from the judge on retirement prior to reaching the maximum permissible age for the post; 4) the loss of Russian citizenship by the judge; 5) a guilty sentence handed down against the judge, which has entered into lawful force; 6) commission by the judge of an action which compromises the honour and dignity of a judge; 7) continuation by the judge, despite a warning from the Constitutional Court of the Russian Federation, of engaging in activities or committing actions not compatible with his office; 8) the judge's failure to participate in sessions of the Constitutional Court of the Russian Federation or evasion of voting more than two consecutive times without legitimate reasons; 9) the declaration of a judge as being incapable by a court decision which has entered into lawful force; 10) the declaration of a judge as missing by a court decision which has entered into lawful force; 11) the announcement that the judge has died by a court decision which has entered into lawful force; 12) the death of the judge. The authorities of a judge of the Constitutional Court of the Russian Federation may also be terminated by virtue of incapacity for health or other legitimate reasons over the course of an extended time (no less than 10 consecutive months) to fulfill the duties of a judge. The termination of the authorities of a judge of the Constitutional Court of the Russian Federation shall be implemented by a decision of the Constitutional Court of the Russian Federation, which shall be sent to the President of the Russian Federation and to the Federation Council and shall be the official notification of the opening of the vacancy.

Principles for the Activity of the Constitutional Court of the Russian Federation

The fundamental principles for the activity of the Constitutional Court of the Russian Federation are independence, collegiality, openness, adversarial procedures and the equality of parties.

Decisions of the Constitutional Court of the Russian Federation are binding throughout the territory of the Russian Federation for all representative, executive and judicial bodies of state authority, bodies of local self-government, enterprises, institutions, organizations, officials, citizens and their associations.

Authorities of the Constitutional Court of the Russian Federation

For the purposes of defending the foundations of the constitutional order, fundamental human and civil rights and liberties, ensuring the supremacy and direct effect of the Constitution of the Russian Federation in the entire territory of the Russian Federation, the Constitutional Court:

1) Resolves cases concerning conformity to the Constitution of the Russian Federation of:

a) Federal laws, legal acts of the President of the Russian Federation, the Federation Council, the State Duma and the Government of the Russian Federation;
b) The constitutions of republics, charters, and laws and other legal acts of the Subjects of the Russian Federation issued on questions under the jurisdiction of bodies of state authority of the Russian Federation and joint jurisdiction of bodies of state authority of the Russian Federation and bodies of state authority of subjects of the Russian Federation;
c) Agreements between bodies of state authority of the Russian Federation and bodies of state authority of constituent entities of the Russian Federation, agreements between bodies of state authority of constituent entities of the Russian Federation;
d) International agreements of the Russian Federation which have not entered into force.

2) Resolves disputes concerning competence between:
a) Federal bodies of state authority;
b) Bodies of state authority of the Russian Federation and bodies of state authority of constituent entities of the Russian Federation;
c) The higher state bodies of constituent entities of the Russian Federation.

3) In response to complaints against the violation of constitutional civil rights and liberties and in response to requests from courts tests the constitutionality of law applied or applicable in a specific case;
4) Gives interpretations of the Constitution of the Russian Federation;
5) Gives conclusions on compliance with the established procedure for accusing the President of the Russian Federation of treason or the commission of another grave crime;
6) Exercises legislative initiative on issues within its competence;
7) Exercises other authorities granted to it by the Constitution of the Russian Federation, the Federative Agreement and federal constitutional laws.

The Constitutional Court of the Russian Federation shall exclusively address questions of law. The Constitutional Court of the Russian Federation, during the implementation of constitutional court proceedings, shall refrain from the established study of actual circumstances in all cases where this is under the competence of other courts or other bodies. On questions concerning its internal activity, the Constitutional Court of the Russian Federation shall adopt the Regulations of the Constitutional Court of the Russian Federation.

Structure and Organization of Activity of the Constitutional Court of the Russian Federation

The Constitutional Court of the Russian Federation shall consider and decide cases in plenary sessions.

Currently, the chairpersons of the Constitutional Court of the Russian Federation are a Chairman of the Constitutional Court and his/her two Deputy Chairmen. All of them are appointed by the Federation Council on the submission of the President of the Russian Federation for the period of *6 years*. Upon the expiry of the term of their authority the same persons may be appointed for a new term.

Previously the chairpersons of the Constitutional Court of the Russian Federation were a Chairman of the Constitutional Court, one Deputy Chairman and a Judge-Secretary who were elected on an individual basis for a term of three years at a plenary session of the Constitutional Court of the Russian Federation judges by secret vote with a majority of the total number of votes.

The Chairman of the Constitutional Court of the Russian Federation shall: 1) oversee the preparation of plenary sessions of the Constitutional Court of the Russian Federation, convene them and preside over them; 2) submit for discussion by the Constitutional Court of the Russian Federation questions subject to consideration at plenary sessions and sessions of the chambers; 3) represent the Constitutional Court of the Russian Federation in relations with state bodies and organizations, public associations, and upon the authorization of the Constitutional Court of the Russian Federation make statements on its behalf; 4) carry out the general management of the administration of the Constitutional Court of the Russian Federation, present for approval by the Constitutional Court of the Russian Federation the candidatures of directors of the Secretariat of the Constitutional Court of the Russian Federation and other subdivisions of the administration, other services of the Constitution Court of the Russian Federation, as well as the Statute on the Secretariat of the Constitutional Court of the Russian Federation and the staff list of the administration; 5) exercise other authorities in accordance with this Federal Constitutional Law and the Regulations of the Constitutional Court of the Russian Federation. The Chairman of the Constitutional Court of the Russian Federation issues orders and directives.

The Deputy Chairmen of the Constitutional Court of the Russian Federation perform with the authorization of the Chairman of the Constitutional Court of the Russian Federation certain of the latter's functions, and also perform their duties, as assigned to them by the Constitutional Court of the Russian Federation.

Principles of Constitutional Court Proceedings

Independence

Judges of the Constitutional Court of the Russian Federation are independent and shall take guidance in the exercise of their authority solely from the Constitution of the Russian Federation and this Federal Constitutional Law. In their activity, judges of the Constitutional Court of the Russian Federation shall act individually and shall not represent any state or public bodies, political parties or movements, state, public, other enterprises, institutions or organizations, officials, state or territorial formations, nations or social groups. Decisions and other acts of the Constitutional Court of the Russian Federation shall express the legal position of judges which conforms to the Constitution of the Russian Federation and is free from political convictions. Judges of the Constitutional Court of the Russian Federation shall adopt decisions under conditions excluding the possibility of outside influence on freedom of their expression of intention. They shall not be permitted to request or receive from anyone any instructions with respect to issues accepted for preliminary study or examined by the Constitutional Court of the Russian Federation. No interference in the activity of the Constitutional Court of the Russian Federation shall be permitted and give rise to the liability stipulated by law.

Confidentiality

The consideration of cases and issues and the adoption of decisions thereon shall be carried out by the Constitutional Court collegially. The decision shall be adopted solely by those judges who participated in the consideration of the case in a court hearing.

Openness

The examination of cases at sessions of the Constitutional Court of the Russian Federation shall be open. The conducting of closed sessions shall be permitted only where envisaged by the Federal Law. Decisions adopted at both open and closed sessions shall be announced publicly.

Oral Proceedings

Proceedings at sessions of the Constitutional Court of the Russian Federation shall be oral. During the consideration of cases the Constitutional Court of the Russian Federation shall hear the explanations of the parties, testimony of experts and witnesses, and shall disclose available documents. At a session of the Constitutional Court of the

Russian Federation documents which were presented for review to the judges and parties or the content of which was stated at the session for that case need not be disclosed.

Language of Constitutional Court Proceedings

Proceedings at the Constitutional Court of the Russian Federation are to be conducted in the Russian language. Participants in proceedings who do not know Russian are to be provided with the right to give explanations in another language and to use the services of an interpreter.

Continuity of Court Sessions

The session of the Constitutional Court of the Russian Federation for each case shall occur without interruption, with the exception of the time allocated for rest or necessary for the preparation of participants of the proceedings for further proceedings, as well as for the elimination of circumstances hindering the normal course of the session.

Adversarial Nature and Equality of Parties

The parties shall enjoy equal rights and opportunities to support their positions on the basis of adversarial principles in a session of the Constitutional Court of the Russian Federation.

Constitutional Court Proceedings

The grounds for the examination of a case in the Constitutional Court of the Russian Federation shall be *a petition* to the Constitutional Court of the Russian Federation in the form of:

- A request,
- An application, or
- A complaint.

Petitions shall be sent to the Constitutional Court of the Russian Federation in writing and shall be signed by an authorized person(s). Petitions to the Constitutional Court of the Russian Federation shall be paid for by state duty.

- *Preliminary Consideration of Petitions*

Petitions received at the Constitutional Court of the Russian Federation shall be subject to compulsory registration. In cases where a petition: 1) clearly is not under the jurisdiction of the Constitutional Court of the Russian Federation; 2) based on its format does not conform to the requirements of the Federal Constitutional Law; 3) originates from an improper body or person; 4) is not paid for by state duty, unless otherwise established by this Federal Constitutional Law, the Secretariat of the Constitutional Court of the Russian Federation shall inform the applicant of the non-conformity of his petition to the requirements of the Federal Constitutional Law.

The Chairman of the Constitutional Court of the Russian Federation shall, in accordance with the procedure established by the Constitutional Court of the Russian Federation, assign to one or several judges the preliminary study of the petition, which must be completed within two months from the time of the registration of the petition. The preliminary study of a petition by a judge (judges) shall be a compulsory stage of the proceedings in the Constitutional Court of the Russian Federation. A conclusion of a judge (judges) of the Constitutional Court of the Russian Federation based on the results of preliminary study of a petition shall be reported in a plenary session of the Constitutional Court of the Russian Federation.

A decision to accept a petition for consideration must be adopted by the Constitutional Court in a plenary session within one month from the time of the conclusion of the preliminary study of the petition by a judge (judges).

The Constitutional Court of the Russian Federation shall adopt a decision to refuse to accept a petition for consideration in cases where:

(1) The resolution of an issue is stated in a petition, which is not under the jurisdiction of the Constitutional Court of the Russian Federation;

(2) A petition is not permissible in accordance with the requirements of this Federal Constitutional Law;

(3) For the subject of the position the Constitutional Court of the Russian Federation had previously issued a ruling which has retained its force.

Moreover, a petition may be withdrawn by the applicant prior to the commencement of the consideration of the case at a session of the Constitutional Court of the Russian Federation. In the event that a petition is withdrawn, proceedings on the case shall be terminated.

- *Preparation of Cases for Hearings*

In order to prepare a case for a hearing, compose a draft decision of the Constitutional Court of the Russian Federation and set forth materials in a session, the Constitutional Court of the Russian Federation shall appoint one or several judges to give reports. During the study of the petition and preparation of the case of hearing, the judge giving the report may in accordance with the powers of the Constitutional Court of the Russian Federation demand necessary documents and other materials, order the performance of audits, investigations, expert reviews, obtain advice from specialists or send requests. The judge giving the report and the presiding judge at the session shall determine which persons to invite or call to the session, give instructions on the notification of the place and time of the session, and also send necessary materials to participants in the process.

- *Hearings of the Case*

Sessions of the Constitutional Court of the Russian Federation shall be conducted openly, except where envisaged by the Federal Constitutional Law. The Constitutional Court of the Russian Federation may schedule a closed session where this is necessary to protect a secret protected by law, or to ensure the safety of citizens or preserve public morality. Closed sessions shall be attended by judges of the Constitutional Court of the Russian Federation, parties and their representatives.

At the appointed time the presiding judge, having ascertained the presence of a quorum shall open the session of the Constitutional Court of the Russian Federation and announce which case is to be considered. The presiding judge shall ascertain the appearance of participants in the process, and verify the authorities of the parties' representatives. In the event that any of the participants in the process fail to appear or a representative of duly executed authorities is absent, the presiding judge shall pose the question of the possibility of considering the case. In the event that the Constitutional Court of the Russian Federation declares that it is not possible to consider the case, it shall be delayed. The presiding judge shall explain to the parties and their representatives their rights and obligations, and to other participants in the process–their rights, obligations and responsibility.

Procedure for Studying Issues

Study of the merits of a case being considered at a session of the Constitutional Court of the Russian Federation shall begin with the announcement by the reporting judge of the grounds and bases for its consideration, the merits of the issue, the content of the materials available and the measures adopted for the preparation of the case for consideration. Other judges of the Constitutional Court of the Russian Federation may ask questions of the reporting judge. At the end of the reporting judge's statement the Constitutional Court of the Russian Federation shall hear proposals by the parties and shall adopt a decision on the order for studying issues in the case. The order established by the decision of the Constitutional Court of the Russian Federation may be amended only by the Constitutional Court of the Russian Federation itself. Proposals of judges of the Constitutional Court of the Russian Federation concerning the order for the study of issues made during the course of the consideration of the case shall be reviewed by the Constitutional Court of the Russian Federation without delay.

The consideration of a case may be delayed in the event that the Constitutional Court of the Russian Federation finds an issue to be insufficiently prepared or requires additional study which cannot be conducted in that very session due to the failure to appear by a party, witness or expert, whose appearance was declared compulsory, as well as the failure to present necessary materials. In this case the Constitutional Court of the Russian Federation shall appoint a date on which the session is rescheduled. A session on a case whose consideration was delayed may begin from the beginning or from the time at which it was delayed.

Explanations of Parties

The presiding judge at the session shall propose that the parties give clarification of the merits of the issue being considered and set forth legal arguments to justify their positions. In the event that a position of a party is argued by several of its representatives, the sequence and time of their statements shall be determined by that party. The parties and their representatives shall not have the right to use their statements in the Constitutional Court of the Russian Federation for political statements and declarations and must not allow offensive statements against state bodies, public associations, participants in the process, officials and citizens. Explanations by parties shall be heard in full by the Constitutional Court of the Russian Federation. After an explanation by a party, it may be asked questions by the judges of the Constitutional Court of the Russian Federation and the other party, and also, with the consent of the Constitutional Court of the Russian Federation, by experts.

Expert Conclusions

A person possessing special knowledge on questions concerning the case being considered may be called as an expert to a session of the Constitutional Court of the Russian Federation. Questions on which an opinion should be given by an expert shall be determined by the reporting judge or the Constitutional Court of the Russian Federation. Before his/her statement, the expert shall take an oath and be warned of the liability for knowingly giving false opinions. An expert shall have the right, with the consent of the Constitutional Court of the Russian Federation, to review the materials of the case, pose questions to the parties and witnesses, and also make motions on the provision to him/her of additional materials. After the statement of an opinion the expert must respond to additional questions from judges of the Constitutional Court of the Russian Federation and the parties.

Testimony by Witnesses

Where studies of factual circumstances are classified under the jurisdiction of the Constitutional Court of the Russian Federation, persons holding information or materials on such circumstances may be summoned to the session as witnesses. Before the hearing of his/her testimony, a witness shall take an oath and be warned of the liability for knowingly giving false testimony. Witnesses must inform the Constitutional Court of the Russian Federation of circumstances concerning the merits of the case being considered which are known to him/her personally, and respond to additional questions of judges of the Constitutional Court of the Russian Federation and the parties. If necessary they may use written notes, as well as documents and other materials.

Concluding Statements of the Parties

Concluding statements of the parties shall be heard at the end of the court study. The Constitutional Court of the Russian Federation may allow the parties at their request time for the preparation of concluding statements. The parties, in their concluding statements, shall not have the right to refer to documents and circumstances not studied by the Constitutional Court of the Russian Federation.

Renewal of Examination of a Question

If after concluding statements by the parties, the Constitutional Court of the Russian Federation considers it necessary to clarify additional circumstances having material significance for the resolution of the case, or to study new evidence, it shall hand down a decision to renew consideration of the question. At the end of additional study the parties shall have the right to repeat concluding statements, but only in connection with the new circumstances or evidence.

End of Hearings of a Case

After the Constitutional Court of the Russian Federation declares the study of questions of the case as concluded, the presiding judge at the session shall announce the end of the hearing of the case.

- *Adoption of Decisions*

The final decision on a case under consideration shall be adopted by the Constitutional Court of the Russian Federation in a closed conference. Only judges of the Constitutional Court of the Russian Federation considering that case may participate in the conference. Employees of the Constitutional Court of the Russian Federation who keep protocols and support the normal functioning of the conference may be present in the conference room. During the course of a conference judges of the Constitutional Court of the Russian Federation shall have the right to freely set forth their positions on the disputed question and ask other judges to clarify their positions. The number and duration of statements at the conference may not be limited. In the protocol of the conference questions are put to a vote and the results of voting must be recorded. The protocol shall be signed by all judges present and shall not be subject to disclosure. Judges and other persons who were present at a closed conference shall not have the right to disclose the content of the discussion and the results of voting.

Decisions of the Constitutional Court of the Russian Federation shall be adopted through open voting by way of a survey of judges by name. In all events the presiding judge shall vote last. Decisions of the Constitutional Court of the Russian Federation shall be considered adopted provided that a majority of those judges participating in the voting voted for it, unless otherwise envisaged in this Federal Constitutional Law. In the event that during the adoption of a decision on a case testing the constitutionality of a legal act, agreement between bodies of state authority, or international agreement of the Russian Federation which has not entered into force, the votes are split equally, a decision shall be considered to have been adopted in favour of the constitutionality of the disputed act. In all cases decisions on disputes on competence shall be adopted by a majority of votes. Decisions on the interpretation of the Constitution of the Russian Federation shall be adopted by a majority of at least two-thirds of the total number of votes. Judges of the Constitutional Court of the Russian Federation shall not have the right to abstain from voting or evade voting.

Decisions of the Constitutional Court of the Russian Federation set forth in the form of a separate document shall contain, depending on the nature of the question being considered, the following information: 1) the name of the decision, date and place of its adoption; 2) the personal composition of the Constitutional Court of the Russian Federation, which adopted the decision; 3) necessary information on the parties; 4) the wording of the question being considered, bases and grounds for its consideration; 5) norms of the Constitution of the Russian Federation and this Federal Constitutional Law, according to which the Constitutional Court of the Russian Federation has the right to consider the issue in question; 6) demands contained in the petition; 7) factual and other circumstances established by the Constitutional Court of the Russian Federation; 8) norms of the Constitutional Court of the Russian Federation and this Federal Constitutional Law from which the Constitutional Court of the Russian Federation took guidance in adopting the decision; 9) agreements in favour of the decision adopted by the Constitutional Court of the Russian Federation, and, where necessary, arguments refuting the assertions of the parties; 10) the wording of the decision; 11) reference to the finality and binding nature of the decision; 12) the procedure for the entry of the decision into force, as well as the procedure, terms and special considerations for its implementation and publication. Final decisions of the Constitutional Court of the Russian Federation shall be signed by all judges who participated in voting.

Judges of the Constitutional Court of the Russian Federation who do not agree with a decision of the Constitutional Court of the Russian Federation shall have the right to issue a special opinion in writing. This opinion of the judge shall be included in the materials of the case and shall be subject to publication together with the decision of the Constitutional Court of the Russian Federation. A judge of the Constitutional Court of the Russian Federation who has voted for a decree adopted or opinion on the merits of a question considered by the Constitutional Court of the Russian Federation, but who was in the minority during voting on some other question or on the motivation of the decision adopted, shall have the right to set forth his/her opinion in writing on his/her non-agreement with the majority of judges. In such cases the written non-agreement of the judge shall also be attached to the materials of the case and shall be subject to publication in the Constitutional Court's official bulletin (*Vestnik Konstitutsionnogo Suda Rossiiskoi Federatsii)*.

- *Announcement, Publication, Legal Force of the Decisions*

Decisions of the Constitutional Court of the Russian Federation shall be disclosed in full in an open session of the Constitutional Court of the Russian Federation without delay after their signature. Decrees and conclusions of the Constitutional Court of the Russian Federation shall within two weeks from the date of signature be sent to: judges of the Constitutional Court of the Russian Federation: the parties; the President of the Russian Federation, Federation Council, State Duma, Government of the Russian Federation, Plenipotentiary for Human Rights; the Supreme Court of the Russian Federation, Prosecutor General of the Russian Federation and Minister of Justice of the Russian Federation. Decisions of the Constitutional Court of the Russian Federation may also be sent to other state bodies and organizations, public associations, officials and citizens.

Rulings and conclusions of the Constitutional Court of the Russian Federation shall be subject to publication without delay in official publications of bodies of state authority of the Russian Federation, and constituent entities of the Russian Federation which are affected by the decision adopted. Decisions of the Constitutional Court of the Russian Federation shall also be published in the Court's official bulletin (*Vestnik Konstitutsionnogo Suda Rossiiskoi Federatsii)*, and, where necessary, in other publications.

Decisions of the Constitutional Court of the Russian Federation shall be final, not subject to appeal and shall enter into force without delay after their announcement. Decisions of the Constitutional Court of the Russian Federation shall be directly effective and not require confirmation by other bodies or officials. The legal force of a decree of the Constitutional Court of the Russian Federation declaring an act unconstitutional may not be overcome by the repeat adoption of the same act. Acts or certain of their provisions declared unconstitutional shall lose force; international agreements of the Russian Federation which have not entered into force shall not be subject to introduction into force or application. Decisions of courts and other bodies based on acts declared unconstitutional shall not be enforced and must be reviewed where established by federal law. In the event that the declaration of a legal act as unconstitutional has created a gap in legal regulation, the Constitution of the Russian Federation shall be directly applied.

Decisions of the Constitutional Court shall be subject to execution without delay after publication or delivery of its official text, unless other terms are specially set forth in it.

Any failure to execute or improper execution or hindrance of the execution of the decision of the Constitutional Court shall give rise to the accountability established by the federal law.

4. Courts of General Jurisdiction in the Russian Federation

The System of Courts of General Jurisdiction in the Russian Federation

The system of Courts of general jurisdiction in the Russian Federation is described in the Federal Constitutional Law № 1-FKZ of February 7, 2011, "On Courts of General Jurisdiction of the Russian Federation". This Law defines the formation, composition and competence of general jurisdiction courts, from the Supreme Court of the Russian Federation to district courts, and defines the powers of federal court chairpersons and their deputies, the competence of court presidiums and judicial divisions, and the functions of general jurisdiction courts' administrations.

General jurisdiction courts are organized as an independent system of a number of courts with similar tasks and interrelated by administrating justice on civil, penal, administrative and other corresponding cases.

General jurisdiction courts consist of a three-level federal courts' system and a system of peace judges:

- *Justices of the Peace of the subjects of the Russian Federation* view cases in the first instance according to their jurisdiction as established by the procedural legislation;
- *Federal district courts* view cases in the first instance according to their jurisdiction as established by the procedural legislation as well as the appellation court for the cases viewed by the judges of peace;
- *Supreme Courts of the republics, of territorial, regional courts, courts of cities of federal importance (Moscow, St. Petersburg and Sevastopol city courts), courts of autonomous region and autonomous areas* view cases in the first instance according to their jurisdiction as established by the procedural legislation. At the same time they are considered to be the higher level courts for district courts and peace judges;
- *the Supreme Court of the Russian Federation* which is considered to be the supreme judicial body for civil, commercial, criminal, administrative and other cases under the jurisdiction of general courts.

Military courts form a part of the system of the court of general jurisdiction and execute judicial power in the Armed Forces of the Russian Federation, other troops, military formations and federal bodies of executive power in which military service is envisaged by the federal law. The powers, the order of organization and functioning of military courts is determined in details in the Federal Constitutional Law of June 23, 1999, "*On military Courts of the Russian Federation*", № 1-FKZ.

The following cases arewithin the competence of military courts:

1) Civil and administrative cases related to the infringed and/or questioned rights, freedoms and protected-by-law interests of military persons of the Armed Forces of the Russian Federation, other troops, military formations and bodies, citizens who are attending periodical military training, from actions (or inactions) of authorities of military office, military officials and results of the decisions taken by them;
2) Cases on crimes with which the following individuals are charged: military persons, citizens who are attending periodical military training and citizens who are discharged from military service and citizens who have passed periodical military training–on the condition that these crimes were committed by them during the time of military service or periodical military training;
3) Cases on administrative offences that were committed by military persons or citizens who are attending periodical military training;

4) Cases on compensation for the infringed right to fair court hearings within a reasonable time period or the right to the execution of court decision within a reasonable time period on cases which have been within the competence of military courts.

The following courts constitute *the system of military courts:*

- District (fleet) military courts are operating on the territory of one or several subjects of the Russian Federation on which military units and institutions of the Armed Forces of the Russian Federation, of other troops, military formations are located;
- *Garrison military courts* are operating on the territory on which one or more military garrisons are located.

In cases where a military unit, enterprise, institution or organization of the Armed Forces of the Russian Federation, other troops, military formations and bodies are located outside the territory of the Russian Federation, military courts may be formed in the place of their dislocation if it is envisaged according to an international treaty of the Russian Federation.

The Supreme Court of the Russian Federation

The Supreme Court of the Russian Federation is at the top of the system of the court of general jurisdiction.

Pursuant to Article 126 of the Constitution the Supreme Court of the Russian Federation shall be the supreme judicial body for civil, commercial, criminal, administrative, economic and other cases under the jurisdiction of general courts, shall carry out judicial supervision over their activities according to federal procedural forms envisaged in law and provide explanations on the issues of court proceedings. The Supreme Court was provided with the competence of the former High Arbitration Court in accordance with the amendments to the Constitution (Law of the Russian Federation dated February 5, 2014 № 2-FKZ "*On the Supreme Court of the Russian Federation and Prosecution Office of the Russian Federation*").

The Supreme Court of the Russian Federation shall carry out, in the procedural forms envisaged by federal law, judicial supervision of the activities of courts of general jurisdiction, including military and specialized federal courts.

Within the limits of its competence the Supreme Court of the Russian Federation shall examine cases as a court of second instance, in the order of supervision and for newly-discovered circumstances, and also, where envisaged by federal law, as a court of first instance.

The Supreme Court of the Russian Federation is the immediate superior judicial instance in relation to the supreme courts of republics, province (region) courts, and federal status city courts, courts of the autonomous regions and autonomous circuits, military courts of military circuits, fleets, types and groups of troops.

The Supreme Court of the Russian Federation shall give clarification on issues of judicial practice.

The Supreme Court of the Russian Federation views in the first instance civil, penal, administrative, and other cases under general jurisdiction courts' competence. Cases and files are viewed in the Supreme Court of the Russian Federation single-handedly or collectively according to the federal law.

The Supreme Court of the Russian Federation reinitiates case hearings on the already-viewed cases due to new circumstances discovered.

Decisions made by the Supreme Court of the Russian Federation cannot be reviewed by other courts and State bodies.

The Supreme Court of the Russian Federation exercises supervision by checking lawfulness and validity of lower courts decisions, verdicts, definitions and resolutions.

The Supreme Court of the Russian Federation is the immediate higher instance for the Supreme Courts of the Republics, region (province), cities with federal status, autonomous region, autonomous areas, district courts, military courts.

The role of the Supreme Court of the Russian Federation as the highest judicial body is reflected in its ability to clarify judicial practice. These clarifications are to unify interpretation and application when executing legal proceedings. Thus a unique legal practice and a unique legal environment are maintained all around the country.

The Supreme Court of the Russian Federation as the highest judiciary body has the right to propose legal initiatives inside its competence. On the basis of the legal practice analysis, summarizing the Supreme Court develops and introduces to the State Duma of the Federal Assembly law projects that are required by the judicial practice, by the need for judiciary improvement and the judges' status.

According to the legislation currently in force federal law projects on introducing changes and supplements into the Penal code of the Russian Federation can be introduced by other legal initiative subjects only upon conclusion of the Supreme Court of the Russian Federation.

Along with viewing cases and performing judicial supervision on the courts of general jurisdiction the Supreme Court of the Russian Federation performs the following *functions:*

- studies and summarizes judicial practice by requesting cases and information as well as learning directly in the courts about the federal law application practice;
- on the basis of generalizing judicial practice and analyzing judicial statistics clarifies different judicial practice issues.

The Supreme Court of the Russian Federation consists of *170 judges* and is headed by the Chairman of the Supreme Court (The Chief Justice).

- *The Chief Justice of the Russian Federation*

The Chief Justice of the Russian Federation is appointed for a *6 year* term by the Federation Council of the Federal Assembly of the Russian Federation upon introduction of the President of the Russian Federation based on the conclusion reached by the Highest Qualification Panel of judges of the Russian Federation.

The Chief Justice of the Russian Federation is a justice of the Supreme Court of the Russian Federation and exercises his or her authority according to the federal legislation by:

- Directly conducting the work of the Supreme Court of the Russian Federation. The Chief Justice of the Russian Federation exercises both organizational and procedural authorities;
- Convoking the Plenum and the Presidium of the Supreme Court of the Russian Federation and presiding over their meetings. The Chief Justice of the Russian Federation submits to Plenum and the Presidium meetings matters under their jurisdiction;
- Exercising the general direction of the Supreme Court of the Russian Federation agencies and departments, appointing and discharging the Supreme Court of the Russian Federation agencies and departments personnel;
- Distributing responsibilities between the deputies of the Chief Justice of the Russian Federation;
- Representing the Supreme Court of the Russian Federation in the relationships with the State, public and other bodies.

The Chief Justice of the Russian Federation has the right to participate in the meetings of the Federation Council and the State Duma, their committees and commissions as well as in the meeting of the Government of the Russian Federation.

In accordance with the procedural authorities the Chief Justice introduces, following the limit and order established in the federal law, supervision presentations on civil cases decisions as well as presentations on penal cases with renewal due to the newly-discovered circumstances; dismisses the decisions of the justices of the Supreme Court on refusal to fulfill the supervision claim and institutes a court decision review following the supervision order.

The Chief Justice organizes the work of studying and summarizing the judicial practice, analyzing judicial statistics, and introduces presentations to the State bodies, public organizations and State officials on eliminating law infringements, its causes and conditions.

- *Deputies of the Chief Justice of the Russian Federation*

The first Deputy and Deputies of the Chief Justice of the Russian Federation are appointed for a 6 year term by the Federation Council of the Federal Assembly of the Russian Federation upon introduction of the President of the Russian Federation based on the proposal of the Chief Justice of the Russian Federation, if there is a conclusion reached by the Highest Qualification Panel of judges of the Russian Federation.

Deputies of the Chief Justice:

- May take the chair at the meetings of the chambers of the Supreme Courts of the Russian Federation;
- May deliver protests on court decisions and sentences;
- May suspend execution of court decisions and sentences.

- *The Plenum of the Supreme Court of the Russian Federation*

The Plenum of the Supreme Court of the Russian Federation consists of the judges of the Supreme Court, the Chief Justice of the Russian Federation and his/her deputies. The Plenum deals with the most complicated matters regarding the functioning and justice administration of general jurisdiction courts. The Plenum views information on practice application studying and generalizing, thus clarifies it, views and decides legal initiative introduction matters as well as the requests to the Constitutional Court of the Russian Federation regarding constitutional laws and verification of other legal acts. The Plenum hears the reports on the Presidium of the Supreme Court of the Russian Federation work and reports of the Chairmen of the Cassation and Judicial Cambers as well as performs other functions granted by law.

The Plenum of the Supreme Court of the Russian Federation approves upon the Chief Justice of the Russian Federation introduction the composition of the judicial chambers, panels and the secretary of the Plenum, approves upon the Chief Justice of the Russian Federation introduction the composition of the Scientific and Consulting Council under the Supreme Court of the Russian Federation.

The Prosecutor General of the Russian Federation and the Minister of Justice of the Russian Federation participate in the Plenum sessions. They or their substitutes have the right to make correspondent introductions to be heard during the Plenum session. They have the right to express their opinion on the matters in discussion. Absence of the above-mentioned officials cannot stop the work of the Plenum session.

Upon the decision of the Chief Justice of the Russian Federation the following persons can be invited to take part in the Plenum session: the President of the Constitutional Court of the Russian Federation, the members of the Federation Council and the State Duma of the Federal Assembly, chairmen of the lower level courts, members of the Scientific and Consulting Council, other State bodies' representatives, scientific agencies, other organizations and citizens.

The resolutions of the Plenum of the Supreme Court of the Russian Federation are taken by the present Plenum members with an open majority voting under the condition that two-thirds of them are present. The resolutions of the Plenum of the Supreme Court of the Russian Federation are signed by the Chief Justice of the Russian Federation and the Plenum Secretary.

The resolutions of the Plenum of the Supreme Court of the Russian Federation are a form of execution of constitutional competence on clarifying general jurisdiction practice and are taken into consideration by the general jurisdiction courts when administrating justice.

Generally these judicial practice approaches are not only important from the point of view of law enforcement but in some cases play an important role for developing specific law sectors and are considered by the legislator while developing new legislation.

According to Article 93 part 1 of the Constitution of the Russian Federation the Plenum of the Supreme Court of the Russian Federation on the basis on the accusation made by the State Duma of the Federal Assembly of the Russian Federation against the President of the Russian Federation, makes conclusions on the existence or the non-existence of the signs of high treason or other grave crimes.

On the basis of Article 125 part 2 of the Constitution of the Russian Federation the Plenum of the Supreme Court of the Russian Federation addresses to the Constitutional Court of the Russian Federation a request regarding the correspondence of laws and other legal acts and agreements to the Constitution of the Russian Federation.

Upon presentation of the Chief Justice of the Russian Federation the Plenum approves the composition of the judicial chambers except for the Appellate Chamber of the Supreme Court of the Russian Federation from among judges of the Supreme Court of the Russian Federation.

- *The Presidium of the Supreme Court of the Russian Federation*

The Presidium of the Supreme Court of the Russian Federation is the highest and the last judicial instance for cases viewed under general jurisdiction. The Presidium consists of the Chief Justice of the Russian Federation and his/her Deputies. Among the members of the Presidium of the Supreme Court are some of the most respected justices of the Supreme Court of the Russian Federation. The composition of the Presidium of the Supreme Court of the Russian Federation is approved upon the introduction of the President of the Russian Federation based on the presentation of the Chief Justice of the Russian Federation and a positive resolution of the Highest Qualification Panel of Judges of the Russian Federation. The Presidium of the Supreme Court of the Russian Federation views cases when the majority of its members are present.

Following its supervision function the Presidium of the Supreme Court of the Russian Federation verifies entered into force court decisions made by the general jurisdiction courts and some of the judicial practice matters. In particular, the competence of the Presidium includes:

- ✓Viewing cases following the supervision function as well as due to new or newly-discovered circumstances;
- ✓Viewing the study information and judicial practice generalizations, analyzing the judicial statistics;
- ✓Viewing cases related to panels and the Supreme Courts' staff work organization, providing help to the lower courts in the correct law application matters, including giving answers to specific questions and executing other functions provided by the law.

The Presidium of the Supreme Court of the Russian Federation performs its functions during meetings conducted at least once a month and the decisions are valid if at least half of its members are present. The resolutions of the Presidium of the Supreme Court of the Russian Federation are taken by the present Presidium members by simple majority voting and signed by the Chief Justice of the Russian Federation.

- *The Appellate Chamber*

The Appellate Chamber consists of its chairman and members who are the judges of the Supreme Court of the Russian Federation. The members of the Appellate Chamber are appointed by the Federation Council upon the introduction of the President of the Russian Federation based on the presentation of the Chief Justice of the Russian Federation and a positive resolution of the Highest Qualification Panel of judges of the Russian Federation.

The Appellate Chamber:

- As the appellate court considers civil and administrative cases, decisions on which have been taken by the Judicial Chamber on civil cases, the Judicial Chamber on administrative cases and the Military Chamber of the Supreme Court of the Russian Federation;

- Considers the cases on new or newly-discovered circumstances.

- Judicial Chamber on civil cases, Judicial Chamber on criminal cases, Judicial Chamber on administrative cases and the Military Chamber

The members of these Judicial Chambers of the Supreme Court of the Russian Federation are appointed by the Plenum of the Supreme Court based on the presentation of the Chief Justice of the Russian Federation and consist of the chairmen of the chambers and ordinary members.

The Chambers of the Supreme Court are entitled to:

✓ Consider the cases as courts of first instance which may be considered by them in accordance with a federal law;
✓ Consider the cases as courts of cassation, appellate courts and on newly-discovered circumstances;
✓ Apply to the Constitutional Court of the Russian Federation pursuant to Article 125 §4 on the subject of correspondence to the Russian Constitution of the law which is to be applied in the concrete case;
✓ Summarize judicial practice, etc.

The panels of judges are to be formed in the Judicial Chambers of the Supreme Court. The members of the panels of judges of all Judicial Chambers of the Supreme Court are appointed by the Chairman of the Supreme Court. They are headed by their chairmen who are also appointed by the Chairman of the Supreme Court for a three-year period. One and the same judge may act as a chairman of the panel of judges several times.

5. The System of the Arbitration (Commercial) Courts in Russia

The System and Competence of the Arbitration (Commercial) courts

The system of the arbitration (commercial) courts is the following:

- 10 federal circuit (district) arbitration courts;
- 20 federal appellate arbitration courts;
- 85 arbitration courts of first instance in the subjects of the Russian Federation (arbitration courts of the subjects of the Russian Federation);
- Special arbitration courts (currently, there is only one special arbitration court in the country–*the Court on intellectual rights,* and itsformation was provided by the amendment to the Federal

Constitutional Law "On the arbitration courts in the Russian Federation" on December 6, 2011).

In 2014 the Supreme Court of the Russian Federation was provided with the functions of the High Arbitration Court.

The arbitration courts in Russia consider different commercial and other disputes which are in their competence in accordance with the Constitution, the Federal Constitutional Law "*On the arbitration courts in the Russian Federation*", the Arbitration Procedural Code and other federal laws.

The main tasks of the arbitration courts in the Russian Federation are the following:

1) Protection of violated or disputed rights and legitimate interests of persons engaged in business and other economic activities, as well as of the rights and legitimate interests of the Russian Federation, the subjects of the Russian Federation, municipal formations in the area of business and other economic activities, state power bodies of the Russian Federation, state power bodies of the subjects of the Russian Federation, bodies of local self-government, other bodies and officials in the said area;
2) Ensuring the accessibility of justice in the area of business and other economic activities;
3) A fair public hearing by an independent and impartial court within a reasonable time period;
4) Consolidation of law and prevention of offences in the area of business and other economic activities;
5) Forming respect for law and court;
6) Assistance in the establishment and development of a business partnership and the formation of the customs and ethics of business activity.

6. The Prosecution Service

Pursuant to Article 129 of the Constitution of the Russian Federation the prosecution service in the Russian Federation shall form a single centralized structure in which prosecutors are subordinate to superior prosecutors and the Prosecutor General of the Russian Federation.

The Prosecutor General of the Russian Federation is to be appointed and dismissed by the Federation Council upon the proposal of the President of the Russian Federation. The same rule is applied to the appointment of the Deputies of the Prosecutor General. The prosecutors of the subjects of the Russian Federation and other prosecutors (excluding the prosecutors of cities and districts) are to be appointed by the President of the Russian Federation.

The authority, organization and rules of the functioning of the public prosecutor's office of the Russian Federation are to be determined by federal law, namely the Federal Law of November 1995, "*On the Prosecution service of the Russian Federation*". Pursuant to Article 1 of this Law the prosecution service of the Russian Federation shall be a single, federal and centralized system of bodies exercising on behalf of the Russian Federation supervision over compliance with the Constitution of the Russian Federation and execution of the laws in force within the territory of the Russian Federation. As a result of legislative transformations, the Prosecution Service was finally formed as a structurally and functionally independent public authority outside any branch of authority.

The system of the Prosecution Service of the Russian Federation consists of:

- The Prosecutor General Office of the Russian Federation;
- The public prosecutor's offices of the subjects of the Russian Federation and military and other specialized public prosecutor's offices attributed to them;
- The municipal, regional, inter-district public prosecutor's offices and other specialized public prosecutor's offices attributed to them.

The structure of the Prosecutor General Office of the Russian Federation includes the Chief Military Prosecutor Office as one of divisions. It is headed by the Deputy Prosecutor General of the Russian Federation–the Chief Military Prosecutor. The Office of the Chief Military Prosecutor consists, in its turn, of departments and divisions. These ensure the performance of functions entrusted to military prosecutors in the supervision of the implementation of laws in the Russian Armed Forces and criminal prosecutions against military men.

The system of the Prosecution Service of the Russian Federation includes several scientific and educational institutions (The Research Advisory Council under the Prosecutor General of the Russian Federation, the Research Institute of the Problems of the Strengthening of Law and Order, the Institute of the Professional Development of Executive Staff).

The organization of territorial public prosecutor's offices corresponds to the federal form of the Russian Government. There are relevant public prosecutors' offices in every republic, territory, region, federal city, autonomous region, and autonomous territory of the Russian Federation.

Military public prosecutors' offices operate on the basis of public prosecutors' offices of the constituent elements of the Russian Federation: public prosecutors' offices of military districts, fleets, a public prosecutor's office of the Federal Border Service and other public prosecutors' offices subordinate to the Prosecutor General of the Russian Federation.

The functions of the Prosecution Service are the following:

- ✓ Supervision over the implementation of laws and the observance of human rights and freedoms by federal ministries, agencies, services and other relevant federal executive authorities, representative (legislative) and executive authorities of the constituent elements of the Russian Federation, local government authorities, military authorities, inspection authorities, their executives, regulatory authorities and heads of commercial organizations and NGOs, and also supervision over the conformity of legal acts issued by the laws to such laws;
- ✓ Supervision over the execution of laws by the operative and search authorities, inquiry and preliminary investigation authorities;
- ✓ Supervision over the execution of laws by administrations of penitentiary and enforcement authorities and institutions, administrations of prisons and other detention facilities;
- ✓ Supervision over the implementation of laws by bailiffs;
- ✓ Prosecution of crimes;
- ✓ Coordination of activities of the law enforcement authorities in combating crime.

In accordance with the procedural criminal legislation, public prosecutors participate in the consideration of cases by the courts of general jurisdiction and arbitration courts, and also appear for the prosecution in criminal proceedings.

The priority of supervision over the observance of human rights and freedoms has been established and is consistently put into practice. There have been essential changes made in the position of the public prosecutor in criminal and civil proceedings. The Prosecution Service has become one of the parties participating in judicial proceedings from the authority supervising over the legality of the consideration of cases in courts. The personnel of the prosecution authorities have been improved in a qualitative sense. There have been other changes made in the position of the prosecution authorities, their competence and terms of reference, content and forms of activity in the spirit of the times and in the context of new economic, political and social realities.

At present, a strong legal framework of comprehensive activities of the prosecution authorities has been basically set up as a tool maintaining the ideas of the legal state and ensuring the rule of law and legality. In accordance with the federal law, the Prosecution Service shall exercise authority independently from the public authorities (both federal and regional), local government authorities, public associations and in strict conformity with the effective legislation of the Russian Federation. In particular, the law envisaged the inadmissibility of interference in the activity of the Prosecution Service, any influence on a public prosecutor or inspector with the purpose of affecting their decisions or obstructing their activity. The orders of the public prosecutor falling within his/her powers prescribed by the law, are subject to unconditional execution in due time.

The law provides specific legal guarantees ensuring the independence of officers of the Prosecution Service. In particular, public prosecutors and investigators cannot be members of elective and other bodies formed by public authorities and local government authorities. Officers of the Prosecution Service cannot be members of public associations pursuing political objectives and take part in their activity. The formation and activity of such associations, their structures within the prosecution authorities and institutions of the Prosecution Service shall be prohibited. Public Prosecutors and investigators, performing their duties, shall not be bound by the decisions of public associations. Officers of the Prosecution Service do not have the right to combine their primary activity with any other activity, whether paid or not paid, except for teaching, scientific and creative activities.

The detention, reconduction or inspection of a public prosecutor or investigator (their personal belongings or vehicle) shall not be allowed, except in cases provided by federal law to ensure the safety of other persons, and also to detain for the commission of a crime. The prosecution authorities shall be solely responsible for the institution and investigation of a criminal case against them (except for cases when they are caught for a crime).

The centralization of the system of the prosecution authorities is shown in the subordination of low-level public prosecutors to higher public prosecutors and to the Prosecutor General of the Russian Federation.

In compliance with the Federal Law "*On the Prosecution Service of the Russian Federation*", the Prosecutor General of the Russian Federation shall issue orders, regulations, decrees, provisions and instructions for the obligatory execution by all officers of the prosecution authorities and institutions regulating the organization of the operation of the system of the Prosecution Service and a procedure of implementation of measures ensuring material and social welfare of the above officers.

CHAPTER TEN

LOCAL SELF-GOVERNMENT AND MUNICIPAL SERVICE

1. The Legal Basis, Constitutional Principles and Duties of Local Self-Government in the Russian Federation

Local government is considered to be an essential element of democracy. It is one of the fundamentals of the constitutional system of the Russian Federation and it is defined as an independent activity by the population, on its own responsibility, in settling directly or through bodies of local self-government of local affairs, proceeding from the interests of the population and its historical and other local traditions.

The Constitution lists self-government among the foundations of the constitutional order of the Russian Federation, along with the principles of a democratic federative secular organization of state and republican form of government.

Article 12 of the Constitution determines that the bodies of local self-government do not form a part of the system of state power. The Constitution has replaced the administrative subordination of local authorities to the regional ones with a legal regulation framework.

The legislative basis for local self-government in the Russian Federation includes:

- ✓ *The Constitution (chapter 8 "Local Self-Government");*
- ✓ *The Federal Law № 131-FZ of October, 2003, "On the General Principles and Organization of Local Government of the Russian Federation";*
- ✓ *Other federal laws, numerous acts of the President of the Russian Federation, Government of the Russian Federation, federal ministries;*
- ✓ *Constitutions (charters) of the subjects of the Russian Federation and other acts of the subjects of the Russian Federation;*
- ✓ *Charters of municipalities.*

Pursuant to Article 130 of the Constitution of the Russian Federation local self-government in Russia shall ensure the independent solution by the population of the issues of local importance, of possession, use and disposal of municipal property.

The provisions of chapter 8 of the Constitution stipulate the following guarantees:

- The independence of local communities in addressing issues of local importance;
- The diversity of local government organization models;
- When determining the boundaries of local self-government jurisdiction, regional authorities must take into account the preferences of local communities;
- Financial autonomy (albeit limited) of local governments is achieved via the discretional management of municipal property and implementation of budgetary rights with respect to local revenues and expenditures;
- The provision of adequate funding for performing state functions, if such functions were delegated to the local government by the decision of state (federal or regional) authorities;
- The reimbursement of local governments for the costs of implementing federal mandates.

The Federal Law № 131-FZ of October, 2003, "*On the General Principles and Organization of Local Government of the Russian Federation*" provides that local government is entitled to fulfill only those local affairs as well as powers, which are not in the competence of federal and regional authorities. All these powers are freely excised by local government.

The law defines the domain of local self-government, or the municipality, as any populated territory (city, town or township) to which the following four conditions apply:

1. It is self-governed;
2. It has municipal property;
3. It has its own budget;
4. It has elected bodies of local self-government.

In conformity with the Constitution, the law allows for the diversity of levels of territorial division at which local self-government can be instituted. It permits the setting up of local self-government both at the vicinity (*raion*) level and at the level of any towns or villages irrespective of the size of their populations.

The law has also established the main distinctive feature of the Russian model of self-government that consists in granting a uniform legal status to all local self-government entities. This means that all local governments enjoy the same institutional and administrative rights. The law does not allow subordination of one municipality to another.

Therefore, pursuant to the Federal Law "*On the General Principles and Organization of Local Government of the Russian Federation*" the entire territory of the Russian Federation should be divided into non-overlapping jurisdictions (territories) of municipalities or local self-government entities.

Most local responsibilities are stated in the form of obligations of local governments to maintain social infrastructure facilities that were transferred into municipal property in the course of segregation of property between the region and localities, rather than in terms of functions or public services that should be provided locally. Unlike many countries with strong institutes of local government, local governments in Russia are made responsible for the delivery of such public services as education and healthcare. However, the law allows local governments to limit service delivery to the capacity of the social infrastructure facilities that were transferred to the property of the municipality. Therefore, the assignment of expenditure responsibilities between the regional and local governments depends on the delineation of property between these two government levels.

Constitutional principles of local self-government:

From the perspective of the organization and principles of local self-government the following constitutional provisions are of high importance:

- Local self-government is independent, acting within the frameworks of its responsibilities;
- Bodies of local self-government are not part of the state power bodies;
- Local self-government ensures independent decisions by people of the issues of local importance, possession, usage and disposal of municipal property;
- Local self-government is realized by citizens by means of referendum, elections, other form of direct will declaration, by means of elected and other bodies of local self-government;
- The structure of the local self-government bodies is defined by the population independently;
- Changes in the borders of the territories of local self-government are possible with consideration of the opinion of the population of the relevant territories.

Current federal legislation assigns local governments with the following *responsibilities*:

1) Maintenance of municipal housing;
2) Setting up and maintenance of municipal schools and pre-school education institutions;
3) Setting up and maintenance of municipal health care and sanitary control institutions;
4) Setting up and maintenance of municipal law enforcement bodies;
5) Regulation of planning and development;
6) Organization, maintenance and development of municipal gas, heating and water supply and sewerage;
7) Organization of subsidized fuel deliveries to households and municipal institutions;
8) Construction and maintenance of local roads;
9) Land improvement and municipal parks;
10) Waste disposal;
11) Funeral services and graveyards;
12) Setting up and maintenance of municipal archives;
13) Public transport and communications;
14) Creation of appropriate conditions for providing the population with trade, catering and consumer services;
15) Creation of appropriate conditions for the operation of cultural institutions;
16) Conservation of cultural and historical monuments held in municipal ownership;
17) Organization and maintenance of the municipal information service;
18) Creation of appropriate conditions for municipal mass media;
19) Creation of appropriate conditions for municipal physical and sports institutions;
20) Social safety net and the promotion of employment;
21) Participation in environmental protection in the municipality;
22) Provision of fire safety in the municipality and the organization of the municipal fire service.

As can be seen, municipalities are assigned with the responsibility to finance and deliver a fairly wide range of public services. It should be stressed, however, that the above list of functions is not mandatory for each and every municipality, since the basket of public services offered by local governments in Russia traditionally depends on the availability of social infrastructure facilities needed for delivering such services.

2. Forms of Direct Participation of People in Exercise of Local Self-Government

According to the Constitution (Article 130) local self-government is exercised by citizens through local referendum, local elections, other forms of direct expression of the will of the people, and also through elected and other bodies of local self-government. The forms of direct participation of people in exercise of local self-government are stipulated in detail by the Federal Law "On the General Principles and Organization of Local Government of the Russian Federation" which provides the following forms:

1) *Local referendum*–voting by citizens on local affairs. A decision taken at a local referendum does not require confirmation by any bodies of state power, state officials or bodies of local government. Where its implementation requires the issue of a legal act, the appropriate body of local government is obliged to adopt such enactment;
2) *Municipal (local) elections*–the elections of deputies, members of other elective bodies of local government and elective officials of local government. They are carried out on the basis of universal direct and equal suffrage with a secret ballot, in compliance with the election legislation.
3) *Assembly of citizens*–are to be convened in small municipalities with a population of not more than 100 people for dealing with local affairs. They fulfill the functions of the representative organ of local government.
4) *People's law-making initiative*–is a right of people to initiate an adoption of a normative legal act on local affairs. The minimum number of an initiative group must be 3 percent of the total number of the population of the municipality. Draft legal acts on local affairs sent to the bodies of local government are subject to mandatory consideration for three months.
5) *Citizens' address to bodies of local government*–is a right to address individually or collectively the bodies of local government or local officials. The bodies of local government and local officials are obliged to respond to the citizens' addresses within one month.
6) *Voting on the recall of a deputy, a member of an elective body of local government, or an elective local official, voting on the change of borders of a municipality, transformation of a municipality* is to be carried out under the initiative of the population in the order established to local referendums.

7) *Public hearings* are carried out under the initiative of the population, representative body or head of a municipality. Public hearings must be carried out in the following cases concerning adoption of the following acts: the charter of a municipality and amendments to it, a local budget and a report on its execution, plans and programs of development of a municipality and rules of land tenure and building.
8) *Meetings of citizens* are used for discussion on subjects related to local affairs, and informing the population on the activity of bodies of local government and local officials and the implementation of territorial self-governments on a part of the territory of a municipality.
9) *Interrogation of citizens* is carried out in all the territory of a municipality or on a part of its territory for revealing public opinion and taking this into account in the process of decision-taking by local government.

3. Structure of Bodies of Local Self-Government

The definition of the constitutional term "*a body of local self-government*" was given in the Federal Law № 131-FZ of October, 2003, "On the General Principles and Organization of Local Government of the Russian Federation": "*Bodies of local self-government mean elected and other bodies empowered to solve issues of local significance and are not forming part of the system of bodies of state power*".

The above definition is based on the following constitutional provisions: (i) local self-government shall be exercised by the citizens through their direct will and through elective and other bodies of local self-government; (ii) bodies of local self-government shall have autonomy in managing municipal property and shall form, approve and execute their local budget, establish local taxes and fees and decide on other issues of local importance; (iii) bodies of local self-government are not incorporated into the system of bodies of state power.

Hence, the bodies of local self-government can be elective and non-elective. Elective bodies of local self-government include a representative body of local self-government (local council), the presence of which is a mandatory requirement for a settlement to be recognized as a municipal entity, or a territory within which local self-governance is exercised.

The charter of a municipal entity may provide for a position of Head of local administration–an elected official directing the implementation of local self-governance in the municipal entity. There is no federal legislation on non-elective (appointed) bodies of local self-government, in particular, laws to regulate issues on the internal organization of executive bodies of local self-government.

The Constitution assigns the establishment of general principles that will govern the organization of a system of bodies of state power and local self-government to joint jurisdiction of the Federation and its Subjects. The Russian Constitution (Article 131) provides that the structure of bodies of local self-government shall be determined at the discretion of the population. Thus, both federal and regional legislations set only general principles of organization of local self-government and not the structure of bodies thereof that may vary across the municipalities.

The Federal Law "*On the General Principles and Organization of Local Government of the Russian Federation*" stipulates the following types of local self-government in Russia:

- Local council–an elected mayor who is not a member of the local council;
- Local council–an elected mayor who is a member of the local council;
- Local council–the chairman of which is a mayor;
- Local council–an elected mayor who is not a member of the local council, and a manager of the municipality hired by the mayor with the consent of the local council;
- Local council and manager of the municipality hired by the council on a contractual basis;
- assemblies of citizens;
- Local council incorporating committees that oversee individual areas of executive activities, and no mayor.

Setting framework conditions for specifying the powers, procedure for establishment, term of office, organization of activities, names of bodies, officials and elected persons of local self-government is assigned in the Federal Law "*On the General Principles and Organization of Local Government of the Russian Federation*" to the competence of the Subjects of the Russian Federation. Hence, a list of alternative structures of bodies of local self-government may differ from region to region. However, there are not many forms of distribution of powers encountered in practice. Basically, all the regions tend to apply the "strong mayor–weak council" model, that in practice can take many forms. A classic version of this model is "an elected mayor who is simultaneously a chairman of the local council". And yet it can also be implemented in cases where the Head of the municipality is elected by and from among the deputies of the local council. Although elected by the local deputies he is "a strong mayor".

"Weak mayor–strong local council" is a less common model of local self-government in Russia, encountered mostly in rural areas. The "assemblies of citizens" model is also encountered in rural settlements with a small population size. The "hiring of managers on a contractual basis" is a rare occurrence and is rather the exception than the rule, whereas cases where mayors are to all intents and purposes appointed by regional governors are quite frequent.

- *Representative Body of Local Self-Government (Local Council)*

Representative bodies of local self-government may have different names in different municipalities. The Federal Law "On the General Principles and Organization of Local Government of the Russian Federation" provides that names of bodies of local self-government shall be established by municipal charters in accordance with the laws of a respective region, subject to ethnic, historical and local traditions. Common names of such bodies in the Russian Federation are *City (Vicinity) Duma, Council of Representatives and Council of Deputies* (hereinafter referred to as *local councils*). Local councils consist of deputies elected on the basis of universal equal and direct suffrage in accordance with federal and regional laws. The precise number of the deputies is specified in the charter of a municipality.

The following fall into the exclusive jurisdiction of local councils:

- ✓ Adoption of local legal acts;
- ✓ Approval of the local budget and report on its execution; adoption of plans and programs of local development and approval of reports on their execution;
- ✓ Establishment of local taxes and fees;
- ✓ Establishment of the procedure for management and disposal of local property;
- ✓ Auditing activities of local self-government.

- *Head of a Municipality*

The charter of a municipality may provide for a position of Head of a municipality–an elected official directing the implementation of local self-government. The Federal Law "*On the General Principles and Organization of Local Government of the Russian Federation*" stipulates that the Head of a municipality may be elected either by residents of the municipality or by the representative body of local self-government from among its members. In the former case the Head of a municipality may be elected from among the members of the local representative body and he/she presides over its meetings. The Head of a municipality may be referred to as a Mayor or Head of local administration.

The scope of issues of local importance that fall under the competence of the Head of a municipality is determined by the municipal charter, i.e. this may differ among localities as may the terms of office of the heads of different municipalities. The Head of a municipality is directly accountable to the municipal population and may also report to the representative body of local self-government if this is prescribed in the charter.

- *Local Administration*

The local administration is an appointed body of an executive branch of local self-government. These are formed by elected bodies of local self-government (a local council or a mayor) for the execution of issues of local self-government that fall within the competence provided by the municipal charter.

The federal legislation provides no guidelines on how the representative and executive powers should be delineated at the local level, and different regions address this problem in different ways (in most cases leaving it to municipalities' discretion). The most common arrangement is when an elected head is simultaneously a head of a local administration, although there are cases when managers of local administrations are hired on a contractual basis and when a representative body of local self-government combines both representative and executive functions through its committees and commissions, that is to say, when agencies of the executive branch are non-existent.

The design of the internal structure of local administrations is attributed by federal legislation to matters of local importance to be handled by local governments on their own. However, a list of departments (units, committees, etc.) in local administrations across the country is for the most part made up in accordance with a single list originating from the scope of local issues assigned nation-wide to the competence of local self-governments by the federal legislation. Since the list of local functions is primarily determined by the availability of objects of local infrastructure (such as schools and medical clinics) on the territory of municipality, the list of departments of local administrations essentially replicates the list of municipal property, but can also include departments that are responsible for non-mandatory functions that a municipality has assumed on its own initiative.

Accordingly, the structure of the executive branch of local administration normally includes one or several departments ensuring the operation of local self-government in general. It is usual for large municipalities to have *a budget department* to deal with the formulation of the local budget and the submission of the draft budget to the representative branch for consideration; *a legal department* responsible for the internal examination of all documents (draft resolutions) prepared by the local administration; *a department for capital investments* responsible for drafting and control over the execution of economic development programs. In addition to the general departments in many local administrations there are also departments responsible for the organization of work along the functional lines of business of local self-government: a *department of education, department of public transport*, etc., depending on the functions performed by a particular administration.

- *Control Board*

A control board in a municipality may be set up with the purpose of providing control over the execution of the local budget, the submission and consideration of the draft budget, and also over the following of rules concerning the order of operation and the disposal of municipal property.

It should be mentioned that a municipal charter may stipulate the setting up of *other bodies* of local self-government, providing them with their own competence.

4. Control Over Local Government Operations

There may be different types of control over local government operations in the Russian Federation:

(i) The administrative oversight of local governments on the part of a regional administration;

(ii) A financial audit of local governments;

(iii) The supervision of local governments by public prosecutors.

(i*) Administrative oversight of local governments on the part of a regional administration*

The Constitution of the Russian Federation introduced a fundamentally new type of relationship between different levels of government. A regulatory type of interaction replaced the administrative model of subordination. The direct subordination of municipalities to regions meant that any oversight was only possible within the framework of law.

Provisions of the Federal Law "*On the General Principles and Organization of Local Government of the Russian Federation*" whereby local self-government bodies are independent, i.e. accountable only to the law, still continue to apply in Russia. The Law entitles the federal government and regions to delegate certain federal and/or regional powers to local governments, provided that this delegation is accompanied by the transfer of necessary material and financial resources, and to monitor the execution of powers thus delegated.

(ii) Financial audit of local governments

The Russian Budget Code stipulates the right of local councils to exercise financial control at the stage of discussion, approval and execution of local budgets. It also grants local councils the right to set up auditing commissions for doing external audits of local budgets.

Sometimes local governments themselves initiate an external audit and hire independent auditing firms with a view to making their territories more attractive for foreign investors.

In accordance with the Budget Code regional authorities are entitled to monitor local spending only where local governments are grant recipients, and this right only applies to the funds that local governments receive from a regional budget.

(iii) Supervision of local governments by public prosecutors

The Public Prosecutor's Office of Russia is a single federal system of bodies of state power with territorial branches exercising control over correspondence of regulatory and legislative acts passed by the legislative bodies of state power of Russian regions and representative bodies of local self-government with the effective federal legislation. Should it reveal any infringements on the federal legislation, the Public Prosecutor's Office will lodge a protest with the infringer that specifies measures to be taken and time limits thereof. Should the prescribed measure fail to be taken, bodies of the Prosecutor's Office will apply to court.

Presently, the Public Prosecutor's Office plays a fairly active role in ensuring compliance with the legislation (federal, in the first place) of local governments. Many infringements relate to financial matters.

5. Municipal Service and Municipal Employees

Pursuant to Article 4 of the Federal Law "*On the General Principles and Organization of Local Government of the Russian Federation*" the regulation of the foundation of municipal service falls under the competence of bodies of state power in the field of local self-government. Citizens of the Russian Federation enjoy equal access to municipal service (Article 3 of the Constitution).

The terms and conditions of municipal service, the status of municipal employees are subject to regulation of the Federal Law № 25-FZ of March 2, 2007, "*On Municipal Service in the Russian Federation*" which replaced the previous Federal Law №8-FZ of January 8, 1998, "*On Foundations of Municipal Service in the Russian Federation*".

Pursuant to Article 2 of the Federal Law *"On Municipal Service in the Russian Federation"* municipal service means a professional activity of citizens constantly performed when occupying municipal offices by a labour contract.

The fundamental principles of municipal service which are provided by the Federal Law "*On Municipal Service in the Russian Federation*" are the following:

- ➢ The priority of citizens' rights and freedoms;
- ➢ Equal access to municipal service of all citizens who have a good command of the Russian language;
- ➢ The professionalism and competence of municipal employees;
- ➢ The stability of municipal services;
- ➢ Free access to information concerning the activity of municipal employees;
- ➢ Cooperation with public organizations and citizens;
- ➢ The unity of the main requirements which are submitted to municipal service, and also taking into account historical and other local traditions while performing municipal service;
- ➢ Legal and social care of municipal employees;
- ➢ The responsibility of municipal employees for non-performance or unduly poor performance of their professional duties;
- ➢ No party membership of municipal employees.

A municipal office is an office in a local authority, or the back office of the election committee of a municipal unit established according to the charter of a municipal entity. Such offices are provided with a fixed set of duties ensuring the performance of the functions of a local authority, election committee of a municipal entity or a person occupying a municipal office. The law provides that municipal offices are to be established by municipal legal acts according to the municipal office register in a respective subject of the Russian Federation approved by a law of the subject of the Russian Federation.

A municipal employee is considered to be a citizen performing municipal duties under the procedure specified by municipal legal acts pursuant to federal laws and laws of the subject of the Russian Federation for compensation paid from the local budget. Those employees whose duties are related to technical support of the activity of the bodies of local self-government and municipal electoral commissions (drivers, secretaries, cooks, etc.) do not occupy municipal offices and are not considered to be municipal employees.

Only those citizens, who have reached 18 years, having a good command of the Russian language and meeting the qualification requirements provided by the Federal Law "*On Municipal Service in the Russian Federation*", may work as municipal employees.

Municipal employees are obliged to pass certification once in every three years. However, the Federal Law provides a list of municipal employees who are not obliged to pass such certification (pregnant women, people older than 60 years, employees working as municipal servants for less than one year or working under a fixed-term labour contract).

The Federal Law "*On Municipal Service in the Russian Federation*" prescribes the qualification characteristics of a citizen in service, the procedure for the tender for occupation of municipal services, the qualification procedure for municipal officers, the grounds for the termination of a labour contract entered into with a municipal officer, the guarantees granted to a municipal officer, the pension conditions for a municipal officer and his/her family members and other issues related to municipal employees.

ABOUT THE AUTHORS

Dr. Elena A. Kremyanskaya

Education: Moscow State Institute (University) of International Relations (MGIMO-University). International Law Faculty. Postgraduate research at MGIMO-University.

Present position: Associate Professor of the Constitutional Law Department of the International Law Faculty of MGIMO-University, PhD. Alumni of the Hague International Law Academy and National School of Administration (ENA) in Paris (internship).

Lectures: Russian Constitutional Law, Theory of State and Law, Foreign Constitutional Law, Comparative Constitutional Law (in English).

Specific experience: A Member of the Advisory Board of the Federation Council Committee on Constitutional Legislation, Legal and Judicial Affairs and Civil Society Development.
A Member of the Editorial council of the law series "Constitutional Law of Foreign Countries" of MGIMO-University.

Scientific interests: issues of state development, human rights, legal aspects of decision-making by state bodies in Russia and foreign countries. Specializes on the Constitutional law of Russia and North America. Admitted for legal practice in Russia.

Contact email: elena.kremyanskaya@gmail.com

Dr. Tamara O. Kuznetsova

Education: Moscow State Institute (University) of International Relations (MGIMO-University). International Law Faculty. Postgraduate research at MGIMO-University.

Present position: Associate Professor of the Constitutional Law Department of the International Law Faculty of MGIMO.

Lectures: Russian Constitutional Law, Theory of State and Law, Foreign Constitutional Law.

Research interests: the legal status of the individual, the problems of the development of civil society, the institutions of direct democracy, electoral systems in Russia and abroad, elections in Japan, the legal status of the Emperor of Japan.

Contact email: tku22@mail.ru

Dr. Inna Rakitskaya

Education: Moscow State Institute (University) of International Relations (MGIMO-University). International Law Faculty. Graduated with honours. Postgraduate research at MGIMO-University.

Present position: Associate Professor of the Constitutional Law Department of the International Law Faculty of MGIMO-University, PhD.

Lectures*:* Russian Constitutional Law, Theory of State and Law, Foreign Constitutional Law, Labour Law.

Specific experience: A Member of editorial council of the law series "Constitutional Law of Foreign Countries" of MGIMO, has participated as an international observer (OSCE/ODIHR international observer) in the parliamentary elections in Ukraine (2007), presidential elections in Azerbaijhan (2008) and Ukraine (2010), in 2005-06 worked as a legal consultant in the governmental project related to the organization and realization of the round-the-world sailing of the Russian barque "Kruzenshtern"

Scientific interests : Constitutional Law of the Nordic Countries and the Electoral Law of the Nordic Countries, Constitutional law of Russia, human rights.

Contact email: inna_rakitskaya@hotmail.com